Puran, the Hindu religious tome, is an invaluable treasure of the world literature. Puran can be described as the mirror of human past, future and present. This book titled 'Message of the Purans' is a comprehensive compilation of the eighteen Purans. It is an earnest attempt to present the proverbial 'ocean in a bowl' before you. It is a compendium of the eighteen Purans, which are the tenets of Hindu religion:

- Shiv Puran
- Brahm Puran
- Padam Puran
- Skand Puran
- Shrimad Bhagwat Puran
- Koorm Puran
- Brahmvaivart Puran
- Bhavishya Puran
- Brahmand Puran
- Vishnu Puran
- Narad Puran
- Ling Puran
- Vaman Puran
- Matsya Puran
- Varah Puran
- Agni Puran
- Markandeya Puran
- Garud Puran

Religion and Spirituality

Goswami Tulsidas
- Sri Ramcharitmanasa (Doha- Chopai in Hindi, Roman Description in English) 1500.00

Ed. Acharya Bhagwan Dev
- Sanskar Vidhi 125.00

B.K. Chaturvedi
- Gods & Goddesses of India 150.00
- Shiv Purana 95.00
- Vishnu Purana 95.00
- Shrimad Bhagvat Purana 75.00
- Devi Bhagvat Purana 75.00
- Garud Purana 75.00
- Agni Purana 75.00
- Varah Purana 75.00
- Brahamvevart Purana 75.00
- The Hymns & Orisons of Lord Shiva (Roman) 30.00
- Sri Hanuman Chalisa (Roman) 30.00
- Pilgrimage Centres of India 95.00
- Chalisa Sangreh 40.00

S. K. Sharma
- The Brilliance of Hinduism 125.00
- Sanskar Vidhi (Arya Samaj) 125.00

Dr. B.R. Kishore
- Hinduism 95.00
- Rigveda 60.00
- Samveda 60.00
- Yajurveda 60.00
- Atharvveda 60.00
- Mahabharata 60.00
- Ramayana 60.00
- Supreme Mother Goddeses Durga (4 Colour Durga Chalisa) 95.00

Manish Verma
- Fast & Festivals of India 95.00

Prof. Gurpret Singh
- Soul of Sikhism 125.00

Shiv Sharma
- Soul of Jainism 125.00

Pt. Ramesh Tiwari
- Shrimad Bhagavad Gita (Krishna, the Charioteer) (Sanskrit, Hindi, English & Description in English) 400.00

Manan Sharma
- Buddhism (Teachings of Buddha) 150.00
- Universality of Buddha 150.00

Anurag Sharma
- Life Profile & Biography of Buddha 150.00
- Thus Spoke Buddha 150.00

Udit Sharma
- Teachings & Philosophy of Buddha 150.00

S.P. Ojha
- Sri-Ram-Charit Manas 95.00

Chakor Ajgaonkar
- Realm of Sadhana (What Saints & Masters Say) 30.00

K.H. Nagrani
- A Child from the Spirit World Speaks 10.00

F.S. Growse
- Mathura & Vrindavan, The Mystical Land of Lord Krishna (8 Colour photos) 495.00

Dr. Giriraj Shah
- Glory of Indian Culture 95.00

R.P. Hingorani
- Chalisa Sangreh (Roman) 60.00

Acharya Vipul Rao
- Srimad Bhagwat Geeta (Sanskrit & English) 75.00

Dr. Bhavansingh Rana
- 108 Upanishad (In press) 150.00

Eva Bell Barer
- Quiet Talks with the Master 60.00

Joseph J. Ghosh
- Adventures with Evil Spirits 80.00

Dr. S.P. Ruhela
- Fragrant Spiritual Memories of a Karma Yogi 100.00

Yogi M.K. Spencer
- Rishi Ram Ram 100.00
- Oneness with God 90.00

H. Seereeram
- Fundamentals of Hinduism 250.00

Books in Roman
- Bhajan, Lokgeet or Aartiyan (Roman English, Hindi) 95.00
- Hindu Vrat Kathayen (Including Saptvaar Vrat Kathayen) 40.00
- Chalisa Sangreh (Including Aarties in Roman) 60.00
- Shri Satya Narayana Vrat Katha (In English and Hindi) 25.00
- Sanatan Dharm Pooja 95.00
- Sudha Kalp 95.00
- Shiv Abhisek Poojan 25.00
- Daily Prayer (Hindi, English, French, Roman) 25.00
- Sanatan Daily Prayer 25.00
- Durga Chalisa 10.00
- Gaytari Chalisa 10.00
- Shiv Chalisa 10.00
- Hanuman Chalisa 10.00

Acharya Vipul Rao
- Daily Prayer 25.00

Books can be requisitioned by V.P.P. Postage charges will be Rs. 20/- per book. For orders of three books the postage will be free.

◊ DIAMOND POCKET BOOKS

X-30, Okhla Industrial Area, Phase-II, New Delhi-110020, Phone : 011-51611861, Fax : 011-51611866
E-mail : sales@diamondpublication.com, Website : www.fusionbooks.com

MESSAGE OF THE PURANS

Dr. B.B. Paliwal

DIAMOND BOOKS

ISBN : 81-288-1174-6

© **Publisher**

Publisher   : **Diamond Pocket Books (P) Ltd.**
               X-30, Okhla Industrial Area, Phase-II
               New Delhi-110020
Phone   : 011-51611861
Fax.   : 011-51611866
E-mail   : sales@diamondpublication.com
Website   : www.diamondpublication.com
Edition   : 2005
Price   : 150.00
Translated by : Sanjay Srivastva
Printer   : Aadarsh Printers,
                Navin Shahdara, Delhi- 32

Message of the Purans   Rs. 150/-
By - Dr. B.B. Paliwal

PREFACE

*P*uran, the Hindu religious scripture, is an invaluable treasure of the world literature. Delivery of topics, illustration of facts, the poise and naturalism of the explanatory style, the beauty and art of language etc. are such qualities pumped into the *Purans* which remind the adage of 'ocean in a bowl'.

Purans are such mirrors of our life and evolution which show us the image of each era. We can know about the emergence and characteristics of the gods and goddesses that we pray and worship. We can know about 'Manu', the first man of the universe, whose descendants we all are. *Purans* offer wide information on different *manvantars* (time periods) which is not only educative but is also interesting and exciting. The stories and episodes, linked with each other, draw the real picture of each era which can be seen and read by us like a motion picture.

We do not say that all the *Purans* or its contents are of high class, useful and flawless. Like other ancient texts the *Purans* too have been subjected to adulteration from time to time. As many of them were destroyed during foreign invasions and by the vagaries of time, they were reproduced by collecting the materials from here and there. They went through many alterations and additions. Some selfish people incorporated, out of context, the glory of pilgrimage, donation etc. with a view to benefit themselves. At some places the diverse and detailed methods of post-funeral rites have been unnecessarily inserted. Several unnecessary inept and unscrupulous topics have been incorporated but it would be unfair to reject these *Purans* due to these exceptions. As a matter of fact, the entire philosophy of our life, episodes from birth to death, the necessary activities of life – all are based on these ancient texts. We cannot imagine our smooth life in the absence of this knowledge. That is why it is said –

यान् यान् कामानभिप्रेत्य पठेत्प्रचतमानसः ।
तांस्तान् सर्वानवाप्नोति पुरुषो नात्र संशयः ।।

Which means that, whatever be the desire in mind, if the man reads the *Purans* with unwavering attention, he can get it without any doubt.

Therefore we have attempted to present just in one book the subject matter, teachings, religious beliefs, fasts and festivals, pilgrimage and its glory, incarnations etc. of the vast Purans so that readers could find all the contents of all the eighteen *Purans* in a nutshell.

Hopefully, this book would prove to be educative, interesting, and useful for readers. Do make aware with your inspiring comments and suggestions.

–Author

CONTENTS

Khand I
1. Puran : Introduction and Importance 9
2. Purans and Vedas : Distinctions 12
3. The Number of Purans 14
4. Distinctions of Purans 17

Khand II
1. Brahm Puran 25
2. Padm Puran 37
3. Vishnu Puran 49
4. Shiv Puran 58
5. Shrimad Bhagwat Puran 75
6. Narad Puran ... 112
7. Markandeya Puran ... 121
8. Agni Puran ... 130
9. Bhavishya Puran ... 135
10. Brahmvaivart Puran ... 148
11. Ling Puran ... 163
12. Varah Puran ... 170
13. Skand Puran ... 177

14. Vaman Puran ... 196
15. Koorm Puran ... 207
16. Matsya Puran ... 218
17. Garud Puran ... 226
18. Brahmand Puran ... 235

Khand III
1. Description of India *(Bharatvarsh)* in Purans ... 241
2. The Geographical Description of the Earth ... 244
3. Other Specialities of the Purans ... 250

Khand I

1

PURAN: INTRODUCTION AND IMPORTANCE

The Meaning

The word *Puran* is born out of the conjugation of two words *'Pura'* and *'Ana'* which literally means 'old' or 'ancient'. The word *'Pura'* means past. The word *'Ana'* means narration—or the one which presents the details of the facts of past or ancient period, principles, teachings, ethics, rules and occurrences. The oldest religious text first ever produced by Brahmaji, the creator of universe, is known as *Puran*. It was created earlier than *Vedas*, hence it is called *Puran* – old or ancient.

Puran came into existence since the beginning of the universe; therefore it commands the honour of being the first and oldest text of the universe. Like the sun is source of light so is the *Puran*, the source of knowledge. Whereas the sun brings daylight by spreading its rays and removing the darkness of night, similarly the *Purans*, through its rays of knowledge, remove the darkness of human minds and flood it with the light of truth. Though the *Purans* are the oldest texts yet its wisdom and teachings have not become old. Instead, in today's context, its relevance has increased. Since its inception, this world is based on the principles, teachings, and guidelines of *Purans*.

The Subject Matter

Since the ancient time, *Purans* are guiding the path of gods, *rishis, munis*, and human being. *Purans*, by imparting the knowledge of right and wrong, inspire the human being to lead their lives according to religion and ethics. *Purans* are the actual foundation of the human life. Without it the knowledge of human existence is impossible to understand. *Purans* help prevent man to commit forbidden acts by analyzing his good and bad deeds. It is eternal, true, and real religion.

Actually *Purans* are the extension of *Vedas*, which are written in a complex and dry language and style. Hence an elite section of readers only were interested in it. Probably, with this thought in mind, Vedvyasji might have created and recreated the *Purans*. It is said *'Poornati Poornaya'* which means complementary to *Vedas* are *Purans* (which are the analytical account of *Vedas*). What has been told in *Vedas* in a complex language has been explained in a simple language in the *Purans*.

The theory of incarnation has been established in the literature of *Purans*. Admitting the realm of non-characteristic (indistinct) and formless, the main subject of these texts is to establish devotion towards characteristic (distinct) and formful. Tales of sin and sacredness, duty and truancy, deeds and misdeeds have been told in *Purans* centring various gods and goddesses. No developed society can be contemplated bereft of such virtues as love, devotion, sacrifice, service, forbearance etc. Therefore one comes across a grand organization comprising various gods and goddesses in *Purans*. There is one more extraordinary aspect that is found in *Purans*. It is that the writer of Puran has never turned back from illustrating misdeeds and misdemeanours during the process of glorifying good deeds and also he has described in detail the evil tendencies of gods. Nevertheless his primary goal has been to establish goodwill and truth.

Divine Beacon

Being the oldest religious text, *Purans* are the divine beacon of knowledge, wisdom, and intelligence. We find in it the thorough analysis of the oldest religion, thought, history, politics, social science and numerous other subjects. Creation of universe (*sarg*), systematic destruction and re-creation (*pratisarg*), computation of various periods (*manvantar*) and its time limits, their lord Manu(s), complete mythological history of the sun dynasty (*surya vansh*) and the moon dynasty (*chandra vansh*), their hierarchy and character of various brilliant kings born in these dynasties find detailed description in it.

These *Purans* represent different stages and sides of life changing with time. These are such lighthouses which brighten the vedic culture and *Sanatan dharma* (eternal religion). It greatly influences our lifestyle and thought process. To fill ocean in a bowl is the mark of a good author. Some writer has expressed the gist of eighteen *Purans* in just one verse (*shloka*):

अष्टादश पुराणेषु व्यासस्य वचन द्वयम्।
परोपकारायः पुण्याय पापाय पर पीडनम्।।

That is, Sage Vyas has primarily said two important things in the eighteen *Purans* which are that the benevolence is the highest order of sacredness and to hurt someone is the worst of the sins in the world. Therefore man should lay his life on the path of benevolence instead of harming or hurting someone.

•••

2

PURANS AND VEDAS : DISTINCTIONS

"Though *Vedas* and *Purans* have been created by the same eternal being that is Brahmaji and the professed knowledge, discourses, facts, teachings, policies, and incidences are similar yet *Vedas* and *Purans* are totally different from each other."

The above mentioned statement can be easily understood by the following facts:

1. The creator of universe, Brahmaji, has created *Purans* before *Vedas*. *Purans* are the detailed and simpler form of *Vedas*. Which means that the knowledge expressed in brief in *Vedas* has been described in detail in *Purans*. In other words, "*Purans* are older, more detailed and more knowledge-enhancers than *Vedas*."

2. *Vedas* are supra-human effort and the clue to its coming into existence lies in infinity. Which is to say that these are not written by a human being, whereas the *Purans* are said to be created by both human and divine being. Meaning thereby that *Purans* are written by human in spite of being the creation of divinity. The readers would definitely be amazed on the above statement. They would be curious to know how can something be considered a human creation without actually being so? In fact the eighteen *Purans*, which we read, listen or mull over, are

actually eighteen sections of one *Puran*. In the beginning of universe, Brahmaji had created one *Puran* only. This *Puran* was divine. Originally, therein were about one billion verses (*shlokas*). But Maharshi Vedvyas presented it in easy and simple manner by dividing it into eighteen parts for the benefit and well-being of mankind. Maharshi Vedvyas limited the number of verses (*shlokas*) to four lacs in these *Purans*. Thus the divine *Puran* created by Brahmaji became a human creation after being divided into eighteen sections by Maharshi Vedvyas. Therefore *Purans* are said to be both divine and human.

3. The *Yogis*, observing *Ved Mantras*, religious rituals, and teachings written in *Vedas* by Brahmaji, were called *Rishis* whereas the *Yogis*, practising mythological knowledge, *mantras*, way of worship, fasting etc. as narrated in *Purans*, were called *Munis*. After acquiring the knowledge of '*Shruti*' from Bhrahmaji, *Rishis* lent meaning to it and expressed it in the word at proper time whereas the *Munis* expanded the knowledge on a grand scale oratorically. *Purans* are more subjected to change and easy to memorize than *Vedas*, hence have undergone several changes over the period of time. Due to being subjected to constant change, *Purans* have been considered the closest to the history.

All the *Purans* have been written in the narrative (dialogue) style; therefore, perhaps, its original form kept altering. But, undoubtedly, all these *Purans* are planted on the very soil of faith where the history, geography, and the logic of science are not as important as the human values stated in it. As a matter of fact, the importance of these *Purans* lies in the logic portrayed in it and that makes it significant.

•••

3

THE NUMBER OF PURANS

In the beginning of the universe, Brahmaji had created one *Puran* only. Comprising one billion verses (*shlokas*), this *Puran* was very voluminous and tough. Maharshi Vedvyas divided this huge *Puran* into eighteen sections with the sole idea of popularizing the knowledge and ancient discourse depicted in Puran by making it simple and easy for the common man. The total number of verses (*shlokas*) in these Purans is four lacs. All the eighteen *Purans* written by Maharshi Vedvyas and the number of *shlokas* in it are as hereunder:

PURAN	NUMBER OF VERSES (SHLOKAS)
1. Brahm Puran	Ten thousand
2. Padm Puran	Fifty-five thousand
3. Vishnu Puran	Twenty-three thousand
4. Shiv Puran	Twenty-four thousand
5. Shrimad Bhagwat Puran	Eighteen thousand
6. Narad Puran	Twenty-five thousand
7. Markandeya Puran	Nine thoudsand
8. Agni Puran	Fifteen thousand and four hundred
9. Bhavishya Puran	Fourteen thousand and five hundred
10. Brahmvaivart Puran	Eighteen thousand
11. Ling Puran	Eleven thousand
12. Varah Puran	Twenty-four thousand
13. Skand Puran	Eighty-one thousand and one hundred
14. Vaman Puran	Ten thousand
15. Koorm Puran	Seventeen thousand
16. Matsya Puran	Fourteen thousand
17. Garud Puran	Nineteen thousand
18. Brahmand Puran	Twelve thousand

According to one belief, Lord Vishnu appears in the form of Vyas in every *Dwapar* of all the *manvantars* and creates these eighteen *Purans* for the well-being of the mankind. By reading and listening to these eighteen *Purans*, even a sinful man becomes sinless and sacred.

Why are the *Purans* eighteen in number?

1. *Anima, Laghima, Praapti, Praakaamya, Mahima, Siddhi, Eishitva or Vashitva, Sarvakaamaavasaita, Sarvagyatva, Doorshravan, Shrishti, Parkaaypraveshan, Vaaksiddhi, Kalpvrikshatva, Sanhaarkaransamarthya, Bhavana, Amarta, Sarvanyaykatva* – these are said to be the eighteen achievements (*Siddhis*).

2. In the *Sankhya* philosophy—*Purush* (male), *Prakriti* (nature), mind, five original elements (earth, water, air, fire, and sky), five senses (ear, skin, eye, nose, and tongue), and five functional senses (*karmendriyan*) (*wak, Paani, Paad, Payu*, and *Upasth*) – these eighteen elements have been described.

3. Six *Vedangs*, four *Vedas, Meemansa, Nyayashashtra, Puran, Dharmashashtra* (Theology), *Arthshashtra* (Economics), *Ayurved, Dhanurved* (Archery), and *Gandharvaved* – these are the eighteen discipline of studies.

4. One year (*Sanvatsar*), five seasons, and twelve months – these constitute the eighteen distinctions of period.

5. The total number of chapters in *Shrimad Bhagwat Geeta* is eighteen.

6. There are a total of eighteen thousand verses (*shlokas*) in *Shrimad Bhagawat*.

7. Kali, Tara, Chhinnamasta, Shodashi, Tripur Bhairvi, Dhoomavati, Vagalamukhi, Matangi, Kooshmanda, Katyayani, Durga, Lakshmi, Saraswati, Gayatri, Parwati, Shriradha, Skandmata, Siddhidatri – these are the famous eighteen metamorphoses of Bhagwati Jagdamba.

Message of the Purans

8. Bhagwati Durga who appeared from the fraction of Shri Vishnu, Shiv, Bráhma, Indra and other gods is adorned with eighteen arms.

Up-Puran

Maharshi Vedvyas has also created some *sub-Purans* (*Up-Purans*) other than the eighteen *Purans*. *Up-Purans* are called the brief forms of *Purans*. These *Up-Purans* are listed hereunder:

Sanatkumar Puran	*Nrisingh Puran*
Durwasa Puran	*Manu Puran*
Kapil Puran	*Ushanah Puran*
Varun Puran	*Kalika Puran*
Saamb Puran	*Nandi Puran*
Saur Puran	*Parashar Puran*
Aditya Puran	*Maheshwar Puran*
Bhagwat Puran	*Vashishtha Puran*

•••

4

DISTINCTIONS OF PURANS

सर्गश्च प्रतिसर्गश्च वृती रक्षान्तराणि च।
वंशो वंशानुचरितं संस्था हेतुरयाश्रयः।।

According to the above *shloka*, *Purans* are said to have ten distinctions. Maharshi Vedvyas has also described the distinct ten marks of *Purans* as per *Vedas* and scriptures. The ten distinctions of *Purans* mean the ten topics discussed in *Purans*. These ten marks are said to be the identity of *Purans*. These ten distinct marks are as follows:

1. *Sarg*
2. *Visarg*
3. *Vritti*
4. *Raksha*
5. *Manvantar*
6. *Vansh*
7. *Vanshanucharit*
8. *Sanstha (annihilation)*
9. *Hetu (Uti)*
10. *Apashraya*

After coming to know of these ten marks, the readers would certainly be curious to know its meaning. How do they present the identity of *Purans*? In fact we can easily understand the knowledge, discourses, facts, teachings and policies narrated in *Purans* by studying these distinctions in detail. These distinctions can be said to be the soul of *Purans* along with its identity. As a matter of fact, the study of these distinctions only offers the detailed knowledge about *Purans*.

1. Sarg

How did the cosmos emerge? How and when did the universe emerge and develop? How did *satwik* (holy), *rajoguni* (princely), and *tamsik* (unholy) tendencies develop? How did sun, moon, and other planets and stars emerge? How did *lok*s create? In what manner did directions, senses, functional senses, and the five elements come into being? How did *yug*, *manvantar*s, *siddhi*s, and *maya* (illusion) surface? These are some of the important questions which always keep rising in the minds of curious people. These questions have been answered through the distinct mark of *Puran* named *Sarg*. "From the emergence of cosmos to the systematic progression of *maithuni* (organic) universe is the description known as sarg."

Nine types of *Sargs* have been described in *Purans*:

1. *Mahatatva sarg*   4. *Mukhya sarg*   7. *Manushya sarg*
2. *Bhoot sarg*   5. *Tiryak sarg*   8. *Anugrah sarg*
3. *Vaikarik sarg*   6. *Dev sarg*   9. *Kaumar sarg*

The *Mahatatva sarg, Bhoot sarg*, and *Vaikarik sarg* have been termed as *Prakrat sarg*. *Mukhya sarg, Tiryak sarg, Dev sarg, Manushya sarg,* and *Anugrah sarg* – these five have been said to be *Vikari sarg*. It is only the *Kaumar sarg* which is of both types– that is *Prakrat* as well as *Vikari*.

2. Visarg

The moveable and immoveable universes created by Brahmaji who emerged from a fraction of the infinite person (Shri Vishnu) are called *Visarg*. In other words, the creation of living beings is called *visarg*. Therein Brahmaji, the creator of universe, offers the living beings (*jeev*) different *yonis* according to their good and bad deeds of past lives. For example fish, mouse, elephant, horse, human and bird *yonis* are awarded as per one's deeds.

3. Vritti

Vritti means the necessary material for the livelihood of moveable and immoveable species. In other words, the necessary and useful objects created by Brahmaji and meant for sustenance of species are called *vritti* of living beings (*jeev*). For example – fruit, grains etc. For all the moveable and immoveable living beings (*jeev*), their sustenance depends only on a few regular objects made of five basic elements. But the situation of human being is totally different among all the living beings. For sustenance they have found some tips from scriptures and have developed some according to their need. Actually according to *Purans*, " immoveable objects are the *vritti* of moveable and immoveable living beings." Meaning thereby that the substances which are non-living like wheat, fruit etc. are the only foods for living beings (*jeev*).

4. Raksha

1. When the demon named Hiranyaksh had carried off the earth by force and the humble cry of the earth spread through the three *loks* then lord incarnated as Varah and executed demon Hiranyaksh to save the earth.
2. Hiranyaksh's brother demon Hiranyakashipu had seized the three *loks* with the power obtained from rigorous *tapasya*. A wild pandemonium was created throughout the three *loks* due to his tortures. Gods, *gandharvas*, snakes (*nags*), demigods (*yakshas*), *rishis*, *munis*, and men all had threat on their lives. Then, for the well-being of universe, incarnated as Nrisingh, lord had executed Hiranyakashipu.
3. While during the sea-churning the lord had facilitated and simplified the process with his incarnation as *kacchap* (tortoise), during that time when the demons had defeated the gods and had secured the nectar emerged from the churning of sea leading to a great crisis, then the lord incarnated in Mohini *avatar* to save the universe.

The above-mentioned three examples clarify that *Parbrahm Paramatma* (The Supreme Soul) incarnate in each *yug* (period) as animal, bird, human, *rishi* etc. and perform multitude of histrionics (*lila*). Therefore his *avatars* are called *lilavatar*. In his *lilavatars* he protects his devotees by executing anti-religion, sinful and evil persons. Since the lord incarnate for the well-being and protection of universe therefore his histrionics (*lilas*) have been named as '*Raksha*' in *Purans*.

5. *Manvantar*

Manu, god, Manuputra (sons of Manu), Indra, Saptarshi, and the fractional incarnations of God – the period constituting these six characteristics is called *Manvantar*. One thousand four *yugs* (*chaturyug*) make one day of Brahmaji. One *chaturyug* is made of four *yugs* namely *Satyug*, *Tretayug*, *Dwaparyug*, and *Kaliyug*. In his one day Brahmaji creates fourteen Manus. It means that there are fourteen *Manvantar* in one thousand *chaturyug*. The lord of each *Manvantar* is one Manu. Thus the time period of one *Manvantar* is approximately seventy-one (71) *chaturyug*. Each Manu enjoys his rights during this period of time only. According to human calendar, the aggregate time of the four *yugs* is 43,20,000 years; this time is called one *Manvantar*. Two thousand *Manvantar* make a *Kalp* i.e. 43,20,000 x 2000 = 8,64,0000000 years make one day and night of Brahmaji.

Which are the fourteen *Manvantars* and its respective lords Manu? Who have been the Indras during *Manvantars*? Which incarnations did Lord Vishnu take during these *manvantars*? The answers of these four important questions have been explained in the following table:

Manvantar	Manu	Indra	Lord's Incarnate
First	Swayambhu	Yagya-Purush	Yagya-Purush
Second	Swarochish	Vipashchit	Vibhu
Third	Auttam	Sushanti	Satyasen
Fourth	Tamas	Shibi	Hari
Fifth	Raiwat	Vibhu	Vaikunth
Sixth	Chakshush	Manojav	Ajit
Seventh	Vaivswat	Urjaswi	Vaman
Eighth	Savarnik	Daityaraj Bali	Sarvabhaum
Ninth	Dakshsavarni	Kartikeya	Rishabhdev
Tenth	Brahmsavarni	Shanti	Vishwaksen
Eleventh	Dharmasavarni	Vrish	Dharmsetu
Twelfth	Rudrasavarni	Ritdhama	Swadhama
Thirteen	Rauchya	Devspati	Yogeshwar
Fourteen	Bhautya	Shuchi	Brihbhdanu

6. Vansh

The past, present, and future generation of all the kings created by Brahmaji, the creator of universe, is called *Vansh*.

Vansh also means the generations of gods, *rishi*s, *muni*s and demons etc. along with that of kings. This means that, in addition to kings, the past, present and future of the progenies of gods, *rishi*s, *muni*s and demons etc. are also described in it.

Suryavansh and *Chandravansh* mainly have been described in *Purans*. *Suryavansh* is said to have begun with Vaivswat Manu, the son of Sun (*Surya*). Lord Sun procreated Vaivswat Manu from the womb of Sangya, the daughter of Vishwakarma. Vaivswat Manu had nine sons named Ikshwaku, Nabhag, Dhrisht, Sharyati, Narishyant, Pranshu, Arisht, Karush and Prishadhra. Ikshwaku was born from the sneeze of Vaivswat Manu. King Sagar, Anshuman, Dilip, Bhagirath (who had brought river Ganga on the earth after rigorous *tapasya*), Raghu, Aj etc. were the kings in Ikshwaku dynasty. In *tretayug,* it was the Ikshwaku dynasty where Lord Shri Ram was born and became famous as *Suryavanshi*.

The Chandravansh is said to have begun on the earth with Budh (Mercury), the son of Moon. Chandradev (Moon) procreated Budh (Mercury) from the womb of Tara, the wife of *Devguru* Brihaspati (Jupiter). Budh married with Vaivswat Manu's daughter Ila (according to *Purans*: due to a boon of Shivji; she (Ila) was capable of metamorphosing herself into both male and female. She was called Ila in the female form and Sudyumn in the male form.). Ila gave birth to Pururva who was married to a court dancer (*apsara*) named Urvashi. In the Pururva's succession were born many such brilliant kings as Jahnu Muni (who drank Ganga after becoming furious over her misdemeanour and later Ganga became famous as his daughter Janhvi), Kushik (in whose house *Devraj* Indra was born as his son), Gaadhi, and Vishwamitra etc. King Gaadhi's daughter Satyawati was married to Richeek Muni. His son was Maharshi Jamdagni and grandson Parashuram. In the succession of Ayu, the elder son of Pururva, were born kings like Nahush (who sat on the seat of Indra after terminating Vritrasur), Yayati, Puru, Yadu, etc. In the succession of King Yadu was incarnated lord Shri Krishna who was called Chandravanshi.

Thus there is detailed description of dynasties of various kings in the *Purans*. We can acquire relevant information about emergence of various dynasties through this in an easy and simple manner.

7. *Vanshanucharit*

Whereas there is description of succession of kings, gods, *rishi*s etc. in the *Vansh*, the detailed description, at the same place, is available of their acts in the *Vanshanucharit*. The acts of gods, extremely bright kings, and highly *tapaswi rishi-muni*s are depicted in *Vanshanucharit*.

Due to *Vedas* and *Purans* being contemporary, depiction of the *Vanshanucharit* of various kings is also found in *Vedas*, but, owing to brevity and subtlety in *Vadas*, many questions remain unanswered in the mind of common man. On the other hand *Purans* undertake detailed description of it delving into the chronology, discourses and stories. Therefore, perhaps, the *Purans* have turned out to be so voluminous and special in comparison to *Vedas*.

8. *Sanstha*

Annihilation *(pralaya or deluge)* is called *Sanstha* by the learned scholars. Annihilation means the end of universe. On completion of one day, Brahmaji winds up his creation before retiring to bed. This means that the entire universe is destroyed by annihilation after one thousand *chaturyug*. Since the night of Brahmaji, like day, is also one thousand *chaturyug* long, therefore the sight of annihilation remains present for so long. Annihilations *(pralaya)* are of four types according to *Purans*:

1. *Naimittik Pralaya*
2. *Prakritik Pralaya*
3. *Aatyantik Pralaya*
4. *Nitya Pralaya*

The submergence of three *lok*s is called *Naimittik Pralaya*.

In this annihilation (*pralaya*), rescinding the world in himself, Brahmaji goes to sleep.

When Brahmaji submerges the universe in himself then *mahtatva, ahankar*, and *panchtanmatrayen* – these seven natures merge into the original nature. This is called *'Prakritik Pralaya'*. When time for this type of annihilation arrives, then the cosmos made of five elements (*panchbhoot*) deserts its physical form and disappear into its spiritual form (*kaaran swaroop*).

The form of *moksha* (emancipation) has been perceived through the *Aatyantik Pralaya*. When, on awakening of wisdom, the false pride of a man dissolves and he faces his true self then he rests in the company of soul after being free from the bonds of illusion (*maya*). This true state of illusion-free soul is called *Aatyantik Pralaya*. According to enlightened scholars, all the species and objects in the universe take birth and die every second. That is to say that creation and destruction go on regularly. This is called *Nitya Pralaya*. This type of continuous annihilation (*pralaya*) carries on undetected as the time goes on.

9. *Hetu*

The meaning of the word *Hetu* is means or reason. *'Uti'* is the word that is also used for *Hetu* at certain places. *Jeev*, the living soul, has been described as *Hetu* in the distinct marks of *Purans*. *Jeev* is the *Hetu* (means) of *Sarg, Visarg*, and *Pralaya* (annihilation). Actually *Hetu* are those desires of *jeev* which render them in the bondage of deeds.

10. *Apashraya*

Wakefulness, dreaming, and sleeping – these are the three states (*vritti*) of *jeev*. He, who is present in all these three states in the illusory form of *vishwa, taijus*, and *pragya* respectively and who also exists independently in the form of *turiyatatva* beyond these three states, is Brahm. It is for the same *Parbrahm* that the word *Apashraya* has been used in *Purans*. If we give a thought to living beings and objects, especially with name and form, we would find that Brahm is present in them himself. When the living and non-living substances are destroyed on the completion of their time cycle, Brahm remains present in this universe even then. In the same manner, Brahm appears to be existing in all the states from the beginning of cosmos to the end of *mahapralaya* (annihilation). Though present in it, yet he has an isolated existence out of it. The indestructible Brahm is the root element of *Purans*. The description from *Sarg* to *Hetu* is aimed at clarifying this tenth mark of *Puran*.

Although the above-mentioned ten marks have been attributed as identifying marks of *Purans*, yet some scholars recognize only five marks namely *Sarg*, *Vansh*, *Vanshanucharit*, *Manvantar*, and *Pralaya* (annihilation) as the identifying marks of *Purans*. This often creates a doubt among the minds of curious people about the exact number of the distinct marks of *Purans*. But, matter of factly, both the statements mentioned above are correct because *Maha-Purans* have ten distinct marks due to being expansive and smaller *Purans* have five due to being brief in description.

•••

Khand II

1

BRAHM PURAN

Introduction

First of all, Brahmaji created *Puran* at the beginning of universe. Maharshi Vedvyas had divided this *Puran* into eighteen parts because the original *Puran* was very detailed and difficult-to-understand for common man. Thus the oldest and detailed Puran created by Brahmaji was divided into eighteen parts by Maharshi Vedvyas. Among the count of eighteen *Purans* written by Vedvyas, the *Brahm Puran* is placed first. This *Puran* is also called as *'Adi Puran'* for being the first *Puran*. This *Puran* has been called *'Brahm Puran'* due to being created and narrated by Brahmaji. Although, first of all Brahmaji, narrating the original story of *Puran* to Daksh, Mareechi, Kashyap and other *prajapatis*, had established the *parbrahm* (the Supreme God) stature of Lord Shri Krishna, yet the story of *Brahm Puran* begins with the dialogues between Maharshi Lomharshan Sootji and Shaunak and other *rishis*.

Number of Verses (*shloka*s) and Sections

Brahm Puran comprises ten thousand verses (*shloka*s). Some scholars say the number of *shloka*s to be fourteen thousand in this *Puran*. *Brahm Puran* has been divided into 246 chapters instead of being divided into sections or *skand*.

The Gist of Brahm Puran

Born from the lotus navel of Lord Vishnu, Brahmaji has been said to be the creator of the universe. His glory knows no bound. First of all, his glorious creation that is universe has been described in detail in this *Puran*. According to *Brahm Puran*, Lord Narayan who resides in water is the eternal man (*adi purush*). Lord Narayan had produced a huge golden egg with the purpose of creating the universe. Brahmaji had appeared from this egg only. Dividing this egg in two parts, Brahmaji had created *Dyulok* from one part and *Bhoolok* from the other. After placing the sky between the two *loks* (worlds), he installed the earth floating on the water. Thereafter he created the moveable and immoveable world.

The character of King Prithu has been described in this *Puran* following the description of the creation of the universe. Angered with the tortures of King Ven, *rishi*s had assassinated him. After that they churned the right arm of Ven in order to protect the subject. Extremely brilliant King Prithu was born as a result of this arm churning. It was he who, in order to protect his subject, had milked the earth disguised in the form of a cow and produced jewels, vegetations, medicines, trees, and grains hidden in its depth. This globe became famous by the name of Prithvi after being adopted as daughter by King Prithu.

After this the fourteen *manvantar*s, its lords, Manus and Vaiswat Manu's descendents have been described. In this series the wedding of King Raivat's daughter Raivati and Vasudev's son Balram, execution of the demon Dhundhu by King Kuvlashva to earn fame as Dhundhumar, transportation of King Satyavrat in person to the heaven (*swarg*) by Maharshi Vishwamitra, birth of King Sagar and turning the sixty-thousand sons of King Sagar into ashes by Maharshi Kapil, the fractional incarnate of Lord Vishnu – these religious tales beginning with the narration of the character of *Suryavanshi* kings make *Purans* very interesting and educative.

After the depiction of some of the important characters of the *Suryavanshi* kings, there is detail of the birth of Moon

(*Chandradev*) from the radiance of Maharshi Atri, the *manas putra* of Brahmaji, and further the dynasty of Moon is described. Why Maharshi Vishwamitra, a *Brahmin* by nature, was born in the house of *Chandravanshi* king Gaadhi, and Parshuram, a *Ksatriya* by nature, was born at house of Maharshi Jamdagni – this question can be easily answered with the help of the story narrated in *Puran*. During the narration of Moon dynasty, the supernatural histrionics of *Chandravanshi* lord Shri Krishna have been narrated.

After the details of *Chandravansh* there is detailed description of seven islands including Jumbo island, the glory of India (*Bharatvarsh*), subterranean zone (*patal*) and hells, position of planets in the sky, and the importance of hymns devoted to God.

The wondrous glory of Lord Sun, description of his one hundred and eight (108) names, procedure of worship, fasting, his emergence from the womb of mother of god (*devmata*), Aditi, and the description of pilgrim of Lord Sun named Konaditya (Konark) situated in Orissa are the educative, extraordinary and important aspect of this *Puran*.

In addition to this, the combined discourse on the special characterization of Bhagwati Parwati and her determination to duty is another uniqueness of this *Puran*. Whereas, the description of securing the desired boon from Brahmaji by undertaking arduous *tapasya* expresses the *tapomayi* (inclination for disciplined hardship) aspect of her personality, at the same time giving away her entire power earned through *tapa* to the alligator in order to save life of a boy illustrates her dimension of compassion. There are even more discourses related with Bhagwati Parwati and Lord Shiv which are narrated in serial.

The extraordinary importance of God's name and the glory of Lord Jagannath are the other distinctions of this *Puran*. The disappearance of Indraneelmayi idol of Lord Vishnu, reconstruction of the idols of gods, its reinstallation by King Indradyumn, the procedure of visiting and worshipping

Lord Jagannath, the bathing festival of Shri Krishna, Balram, and Subhadra on the full moon of the month of *Jyestha*, the importance of their sight and worship and the journey to Gundicha, and the procedure to set off for twelfth journey are exhaustively described in this.

Glorification of pilgrimages is the third and the most important feature of *Brahm Puran*. Descriptions on various pilgrimages, the holy blessings earned by worship and donation made at those places are covered in more than half of the chapters of this *Puran*. Before narrating the greatness of pilgrims in this *Puran*, there is the description made by Maharshi Gautam of river Ganga descending on earth. The glory of Gautami Ganga (Godavari), description of her two forms, the importance of bathing in Godavari, fasting, functions, donations, and execution of post-funeral rites are described in detail in this *Puran*.

Who had brought King Bhagirath or Maharshi Gautam river Ganga on the earth? The curiosity to know the truth in this matter has always been propping in the minds of people. This *Puran* quells the confusion by addressing in detail the mythological details of the two forms of holy Ganga and their descent on the earth.

According to one fable, since king Bhagirath of Ikshwaku dynasty had brought Ganga on earth therefore the Ganga is famous in the north by the name of Bhagirathi. But the honour of taking Ganga in the south goes to Maharshi Gautam. It is after his name that the Ganga is called Gautami (Godavari) Ganga in the south.

Extremely delightful, spectacular, and poetic description has been made in the *Puran* about most of the pilgrim spots situated at the bank of Gautami (Godavari) Ganga. Some of the main pilgrim spots (*teerth*) narrated in this *Puran* are Varah teerth, Bhanu teerth, confluence of Aruna-Varuna, Kapot-Kapoti teerth, Garud teerth, Govardhan teerth, Shwet teerth, Shukra teerth, Indra teerth, Agni teerth, Ila teerth, confluence of Suparna, Panch teerth, Shami teerth, Pururava teerth,

Chakra teerth, Pippal teerth, Naag teerth, Matra teerth, Avighna teerth, Shesh teerth, Shanaishchar teerth, Som teerth, Dhanya teerth, Govind teerth, Shri Ram teerth, Putra teerth, Tapas teerth, Lakshmi teerth, Saraswat teerth, Bhadra teerth, Vyas teerth, Chakshu teerth, Vipra teerth, Narsingh teerth, Paishachnashan teerth, Kushtarpan teerth, Purushottam teerth, Shri Vishnu teerth etc. The related mythological stories are educative and introductory to the history of pilgrim spots.

There is elaborate narration on the result of good and bad deeds, heaven-hell and Vaikunth etc. in the *Brahm Puran*. Numerous educative, useful, and interesting stories have been presented in this *Puran* which are very helpful and useful in improving the human lives. The detailed description of extremely sacred and mellifluent theatricals *(Brij-lila)* in relation to Lord Shri Krishna has found delightful and special citation in it.

Along with the perceptive discussions on *Yog* and *Sankhya*, the proper family etiquettes and duties etc. have been established in it.

Thus this holy *Puran* is absolutely useful for reading, narrating, and thinking for family men, the unmarried (*brahmchari*), saints, seers and seekers of knowledge.

Brahm Puran is an extremely sacred *Puran*. Those, who reverentially study, read and listen to this *Puran*, earn place in *Vaikunthlok*, the ultimate abode of Lord Vishnu. This *Puran* delivers affluence, fame, prolonged life, pleasure, esteem, strength, health, and wealth to people and ends their misfortunes. People, who reverentially read this holy Puran with dedication, get all the desired things and powers effortlessly. The devotees, who respectfully listen to this wish-fulfilling holy text by concentrating in the lotus-feet of lord Vishnu, cleared of all the sins secure their place in *moksha*. Dedicated reading, listening and understanding *Brahm Puran* provides people with knowledge, affluence, opulence, superior intelligence, patience, dutifulness, wealth, pleasure, and *moksha*.

It is said :

यान् यान् कामानभिप्रेत्य पठेत्प्रयतामानसः ।
तांस्तान् सर्वानवाप्नोति पुरुषो नात्र संशयः ।।

Meaning that, there is no doubt in the fact that reading this *Puran* with unwavering concentration of mind fulfils all the cherished desires of people.

Story from *Brahm Puran:*
Story of King Indradyumn

It was *Satyug*. A famous king Indradyumn ruled over Avanti (Ujjain). He was very courageous, truthful, benevolent, dutiful, devoted to Brahmins, and a great scholar. There was none other to match him in generosity, performing *yajna*, and *tapa*. Thus, rich with all kinds of affluence, opulence and superior virtues, King Indradyumn was enjoying his kingship rightfully.

Once a thought of worshipping Lord Narayan emerged in the heart of King Indradyumn. He said to his family-teacher (*kulguru*), "*Gurudev!* This universe comes into being at the wish of Shri Vishnu and annuls itself by the end of *kalp* at his wish. Fulfilment of the desires of people is his nature. He, the Supreme God (*Parbrahm Parmeshwar*), is the fosterer of universe. The living being becomes free from the cycle of life and death merely by his compassionate sight. *Gurudev!* I have enjoyed all the pleasures of the earth by the blessings of Lord Vishnu and now I want freedom from this world, made of illusion, by pleasing him. But I have no idea how I can pray him. *Gurudev!* You are very learned. You know very well how a family man can earn the right to find place in the ultimate abode of Shri Vishnu. You kindly guide me."

Kulguru said, "King! The human life has been divided into four stages according to *Vedas*. Man should always lead his life according to these four phases (*ashrams*). Man should study during *brahmcharya ashram* (unmarried phase) accompanying his teacher. He should enjoy affluence and material pleasure during *grihasth ashram* (domestic phase) after marrying. He should depart for jungle for prayer and worship of God during *vanprastha ashram* after relinquishing material pleasures. Finally, in the *sanyas ashram*, he should dedicate his attention solely to the holy feet (*Shri Charan*) of Lord Vishnu and should give up infatuation for his mortal body. King! You have come up with a supreme idea. Only fortuitous men have the luck to pray and worship Lord Vishnu. But King! You still have some years left to enter into the phase of *vanprasth*. Therefore according to the rule for *grihasth* (family man) you should have fortune of praying the lord by going to the land called Purshottam *(Purshottam kshetra)*."

Then, with the intent to pray Lord Purshottam, King Indradyumn marched towards *Purshottam kshetra* with his queens, *kulguru*, councillors, commanders, and many *rishi-muni*s. The citizens of the kingdom also followed their king when they heard about it. Thus, travelling like this, they arrived at the shores of southern sea in a few days.

On reaching there, King Indradyumn paid a visit to the sea, which was full of divine gems. It was vast, horrifying, and of blue hue. The abode of Lord Vishnu, the sea is extremely sacred, which washes away all the sins and fulfils all the desires. Besides, Indradyumn visited several soothing places and rivers.

On seeing a banyan tree at the *Purshottam kshetra*, Indradyumn began to think, "I will pray *Parbrahm Parmeshwar* Lord Vishnu here only. I have understood well that this place is the *Purshottam kshetra*, the core pilgrim spot of God, because there is standing a banyan tree like the *Kalp* tree. His idol made of *Indraneel mani* (precious stone) used to be here only, which has been put out of sight by the lord himself. Now I will engage in such efforts as would enable me to see Lord Narayan in person. I will dutifully observe the resolve (*vrat*) through dedicating my heart in the lotus-feet of God in devotional spirit by way of *yajna*, donation, *hawan*, worship and fast, but before this I must seek the advice about it from the *kulguru*." Having thought this, he told the *kulguru* about his sacred wish.

Message of the Purans

The *Kulguru* said, "King! Your idea is excellent. *Yajna, hawan*, worship, donation, *tapa*, fast etc. are the great methods to discover Shri Vishnu. Great kings and emperors, *rishi-muni*s etc. have discovered God through these means only. Therefore King! You, according to my advice, should arrange an *Ashwamedh yajna* after building a temple here. This *yajna* is the easiest and the simplest way of approaching Lord Vishnu. That would most certainly fulfil your wish."

Then Indradyumn invited all the kings on the earth and said to them, "Respectful Sirs, this place is a beneficent region which offers pleasure and emancipation. Therefore, for the benefit of mankind, I want to organize an *Ashwamedh yajna* after building a temple here. But this job is impossible without your support. Therefore kindly help me in accomplishing this task."

Having come to know the intent of Indradyumn, all the kings gladly offered him money, gems, gold and such other substances and thus extended support.

After that construction of the temple started off. Skilled craftsmen were called and put in charge of the job. Cut rocks of mount Vindhyachal began to be brought there. Subsequently, inviting *rishi-munis*, king Indradyumn initiated the *yajna*.

After completion of the *yajna*, Indradyumn became worried about the idol of Lord Purushottam. Which substance—stone or wood—is better for the idol of Lord Vishnu? This worried him day and night.

One day he worshipped Lord Vishnu and said during the prayer, "Lord! I bow to your holy feet again and again. God! How can an insignificant man like me understand your illusion (*maya*), which is beyond apprehension of even deities? In this world made of illusion, I, infected with different ailments, am suffering from numerous griefs. Tied in the noose of my deeds, I have become drained of wisdom. Lord! This world, like ocean, is replete with sensory whirlpools. The waves of desire and grief are there in it. This is listless and ever changing.

Lord! Charmed by your illusion, I am wondering in it since eternity. I have taken birth a many times. I have studied *Vedas*, scriptures, *Purans* etc. I have witnessed meeting and separation of wives, sons, friends and foes etc. I have had the opportunity to experience several kinds of happiness and sorrow. But I see no end to this vicious cycle of life and death. My consciousness is fading. Experiencing deep agony, I seek your shelter. Lord! You are extremely kind and affectionate for devotees. Kindly salvage me. I have no well-wisher except you. People who take refuge in you become free from all fears. Deities, demons, and *rishi-munis* have achieved extreme capabilities (*siddhi*) by worshipping and praying you. Merely your remembrance destroys all the sins and the person becomes entitled for emancipation (*moksha*). Abode of kindness! Be pleased on my trifle self and bless me."

Praying like this, Indradyumn folded his hands before lord Vishnu and, spreading a cloth there, fell asleep thinking about the lord.

Lord Vishnu appeared in his sleep. Conch (*shankh*), wheel (*chakra*), lotus, club (*gada*), and bow-arrow were gracing his arms. Attired in yellow, Shri Hari's face was shining with divine radiance. He was riding his designated transport, Garud.

He spoke to Indradyumn in sweet voice, "Son! Put off your worthless worries. I am extremely happy with your *yajna*, donations, reverence, and devotion. I am going to tell you find the way for the idol to be installed here. Son! There is a big tree on the seashore, a little away from this place. A part of it is rooted in the earth and a part in water. You go there alone with an axe tomorrow at dawn and, upon recognizing, tear it off without hesitation. Two Brahmin deities will come there as soon as the tree will fall." Lord Vishnu disappeared after saying this.

King Indradyumn was awestruck on seeing this dream. In the morning he took bath reminiscing God and offered donation to Brahmins and then arrived at the place as told by Lord Vishnu. After searching the tree, he tore it off. He was about to break it in two parts when he saw two Brahmins approaching him. Actually they were Lord Vishnu and the god of architecture, Vishwakarma, who had come there in disguise of Brahmins. They ignorantly asked King Indradyumn the purpose behind cutting the tree. Gladly, Indradyumn told them everything.

Then Lord Vishnu in the disguise of Brahmin said, "King! The thought which has come to your heart is great in spite of living in this illusory world. King! My colleague is a great architect. His adroitness in architecture is similar to Vishwakarma's. He will make the idol, as per my instruction. Meanwhile let us take some rest under the shadow of that tree." Hearing him, Indradyumn went to sit under the cool cover of the tree. Vishwakarma created the idols of Shri Krishna, Balram, and Subhadra in a few moments in accordance to the direction of Lord Vishnu.

Indradyumn's surprise had no bounds when he saw this. He said respectfully, "God! Both of you do not appear some ordinary Brahmin. Your deeds are extraordinary. You actions are like that of gods. It seems as if God has come before me in human form. God! Are you God or human? Are you *yaksh* or *vidyadhar*? Are you not Brahma and Lord Vishnu? Please oblige me by introducing yourself."

The God offered his actual introduction and said, "Son! My arduously faithful devotees get a chance to see me and you have found me before you due to your determined devotion. I bless you that you will get my ultimate abode (*paramdham*) after enjoying the earth happily for many years. This pilgrim spot will become famous by the name of Indradyumn theertha. The person who will take a holy bath here just once will be entitled to a place in paradise. Twenty-one generations of that person would be salvaged who executes post-funeral rites here. Nearby, there is a beautiful enclosure covered with trees. Devotees would keep these idols inside the enclosure for seven days in *Mahanakshatra* on fifth of *shukla paksh* of the month of *Ashar*. King! Here the parade of my procession would take place for seven days. That procession (*yatra*), which will fulfil the wishes of devotees, would be famous by the name of *Gundicha yatra*. All the wishes would be fulfilled by my blessings of those people who would reverentially worship and pray Balramji, Subhadraji, and myself." Lord Vishnu along with Vishwakarma went out of sight after saying this.

After this, Indradyumn installed those idols arranging a large function. Indradyumn secured God's ultimate abode after enjoying all the affluence according to the dictate of the blessing of God.

The famous temple named Gundicha is situated at the bank of Indradyumn lake. The cherished affluence is achieved by paying visit to Lord Vishnu there. Devotees earn their right to Vaikunth by visiting Shri Krishna, Balram, and Subhadra through undertaking a methodical journey in Vishuyog on the full moon of *Falgun* month on the eleventh day of *Prabodhini*. The devotees, who pay twelve visits to the temple in the month of Jyeshtha according to the procedure narrated in texts and pay their homage, get at the end the emancipation after enjoying all the affluence existing on the earth.

It is called *Dwadash yatra* on the completion of these twelve journeys. It should be methodically completed at the end of *Dwadash yatra*. Taste the water of some holy pond on the eleventh day of full moon of *Jyeshtha* month and take full bath while remembering Narayan.

Later, after bathing, perform the act of offering water to gods and forefathers in accordance with the texts. After that, repeat *Gayatri mantra* in mind for one hundred and eight times having dressed up in clean clothes. After that, chant *mantra* related with sun and circumambulate sun god (*suryadev*) thrice. After that go home in silence and chant the great *mantra* ॐ नमो पुरुषोत्तम 108 times doing the worship and prayer of Lord Purushottam methodically.

Message of the Purans

Then reverentially pray to God:

> नमस्ते सर्वलोकेश भक्तानामभयप्रद ।
> संसार सागरे मग्नं त्राहि मां पुरुषोत्तम ।।
> यास्ते मया कृता यात्रा द्वादशैव जगत्पते ।
> प्रसादात्तव गोविन्द सम्पूर्णास्ता भवन्तु मे ।।

"O Purushottam! Who makes devotees fearless, I fold my hands before you. I am drowning in this worldly ocean. Save me. O lord of this universe! Govind! May all the twelve journeys that I have undertaken for realizing you be fruitful for me!"

After paying respect to God, worship your teacher (*guru*). Then, out of devotional dedication, spend the night awake. Invite twelve Brahmins next day morning of *dwadashi* (twelfth day of the month). Pray the Brahmins after praying the God. After that, offer cows, cloths, gold, umbrellas, shoes, and bronze utensils to the Brahmins and the *guru*. Next to feasting them, offer twelve pitchers of water, *laddoo* (sweet), and alimony. Then circumambulate them thrice. Then see them off with folded hands. After this, feast your close ones, beggars, and relatives and then take your meal.

Thus, people, who accomplish the *Dwadash yatra* methodically, succeed to secure place in *Vaikunth lok*.

•••

2

PADM PURAN

Introduction

'Padm' means 'lotus flower'. Since the creator of universe, Brahmaji, having emerged from the lotus navel of Lord Narayan, has expanded the knowledge related with the creation of universe: therefore this *Puran* has been termed as *Padm Puran*. *'Padm Puran'* is placed at the second spot among all the eighteen *Purans* written by Maharshi Vedvyas. It can be placed at the second position by the count of verses (*shlokas*) too. The first place is held by *Skand Puran*.

Padm Puran consists of the five important distinctions namely *Sarg, Pratisarg, Vansh, Manvantar,* and *Vanshanucharit*. This *Puran* is also said to be *Vaishnav Puran* due to propounding worship, prayer and various forms of Lord Vishnu. Various mythological discourses and messages have been described in this *Puran*, by way of which the devotional scripts related with Lord Vishnu has been presented in more detail than the other *Purans*.

Number of Verses *(Shlokas)* and Sections

The number of verses in this *Puran* is fifty-five thousand (55,000). *Padm Puran* has been divided into five sections on the basis of discourses, messages, facts, and lessons. These five sections are as follow:

1. *Srishti Khand* 3. *Swarg Khand* 5. *Uttar Khand*
2. *Bhumi Khand* 4. *Patal Khand*

Message of the Purans

The Gist of *Padm Puran*

The son and pupil of Maharshi Lomharshan, Ugrashrava Muni, had read *Padm Puran* on the request of Shaunak and other *rishi-muni*s at a place named Naimisharanya in the ancient time.

1. *Srishti Khand*

Srishti Khand is the first section of this *Puran*. The *Padm Puran* is said to begin from this section only. Consisting thirty-two chapters, this section is divided into five sub-sections. These five sub-sections are – *Paushkar parva, Teerth parva, Triteeya parva, Vanshanukeertan parva,* and *Moksha parva.*

Several intriguing mysteries related with the universe have been clarified in this section. Maharshi Pulatsya has given detailed description from the birth of cosmos to its systematic development on being asked the questions related with the emergence of universe by Bhishm at the beginning of this section. Deities, forefathers, *munis*, and the seven kinds of universe for human beings have been described in the context of the birth of moveable and immoveable world. Describing the bounden duty towards forefathers in accordance to scriptures, the proper place and its importance for *tarpan*, post-funeral rites (*shraadh*), and *pind-daan* have been established. What rules should be followed during *shraadh*? Which donations please the forefathers (*pitra*)? The detailed solution to all these important questions has been presented.

The birth of Pushkar teerth (pilgrim spot) and its glory has been narrated in this section. The lore goes like this that a lotus flower had slipped away from the hands of Brahmaji and fell at this pilgrim spot while he was performing a large *yajna;* therefore this place got the name Pushkar. This pilgrim spot is very dear to Brahmaji.

It has been said in narrating the glory of Pushkar teerth that a man gets pleasure of woman, progeny, and wealth by observing fast on the twelfth day of the month of Magh at this pilgrim spot. The entire grief of the men ends who spend the eleventh day of the month of Ashwin without a morsel of food and then observe twelfth day as *vrat* (fast) at this pilgrim spot. There, in this section, is description of *pind-daan* performed by Lord Shri Ram for his father at the Pushkar teerth.

The story of incarnation of Lord Vaman, ocean-guzzling by Agastya muni, execution of demon Mahishasur by goddess Kshemamkari, demon Tarak by Kartikeya, and demon Hiranyakashipu by Lord Nrisingh are the important mythological discourses and messages of this section.

In addition to this, the emergence of Rudraksh, its importance, sight of Lord Narayan by Markandeya rishi at the time of annihilation, and the story of the incarnation of Lord Nrisingh have been tastefully illustrated.

In this section the educative and mythological dimensions of the story of faithful Shaivya in the context of devotion towards husband, story of a *shudra* in the context of renouncing greed, and the story of Tuladhar in the context of truthfulness have been presented.

Finally, the *Srishti Khand* has been concluded narrating the importance of *amla, tulsi,* and Goddess Ganga.

2. *Bhumi Khand*

Many discourses related with the glory of devotion towards Vaishnav have been described in the Bhumi Khand. In the beginning of this section, there is reference of explaining the original form of soul by *Maharshi* Kashyap to Daitya demon's mother Diti. The oneness of soul (*atma*) and supreme soul (*parmatma*) has been explained by Maharshi Kashyap while narrating about four types of human beings – *Udibhaj, Swedaj, Andaj, Jarayuj.*

After this, there are deep deliberations between the Brahmin named Somsharma and Vashishtha rishi. The prayer and worship of Lord Narayan has been preached about in this discourse after explaining the eleven forms of duties along with good manners and deeds of previous lives. In this context there is reference of Somsharma undertaking worship of Lord Vishnu at the Kapil Sangam teerth and the moving episode of blessing him with desired fulfilment of wishes by Lord Vishnu.

Message of the Purans

After the above-mentioned episode, the life of King Ven of Ikshwaku dynasty has been described. Subsequently there are stories of earning desired boon from Lord Vishnu by Ang, the son of Atri rishi, invoking curse on Sunita, the daughter of Yam (the death god) by a *gandharva* (demigod) named Shankh and marriage of Sunitha with Ang rishi. There is description of conversion of *tapaswi* king Ven into an evil man due to influence of unqualified preaching of an unscrupulous saint, King Ven's execution by Saptrishi, and evolution of Prithu.

After this a beautiful and educative description has been made of the preaching by Lord Narayan to King Ven about donation and pilgrimage, story of faithful Sukala, dialogue between he-pig and she-pig, a speech on her previous birth by she-pig and her salvation by queen Sudeva. The glory of lord Shiv and the favourite *stotra* of Lord Vishnu have been mentioned in this. In the context of *Pitru teerth* there is story of the Brahmin named Pippal turning egoist after receiving boon from Trinity (*tridev*) and sending Pippal to Sukarma, a great devotee of his father, by Lord Vishnu in the guise of stork. The famous mythological story of Puru offering his youthfulness to king Yayati has been described in this context. Finally this section has been concluded with the story of Maharshi Chyavan and deliberation on knowledge, *vrat* and *strota* given to son Ujjwal by the bird named Kunjal.

3. Swarg Khand

The third section of *Padm Puran*, which is *Swarg Khand*, has a total of sixty-two chapters. In the beginning of this section, evolution of universe along with moveable and immoveable world and planets and *Nakshatras* has been described in detail. After this, the Indian mountains named Malay, Mahendra, Vindhyachal, Rikshvan etc; holy rivers named Narmada, Saryu, Ganga, Saraswati, Shipra, Godavari (Gautami), Yamuna etc.; districts named Panchal, Shoorsen, Matsya, Kaushal, Awanti, Magadh, Sindhu etc. and several kings have been detailed. Furthermore the age of four *yug* dividing the period, respective situation of religion and activities in it, and the corresponding characteristics and nature of people born in it have been described.

In this section, along with the famous mythological story of Shakuntala and Dushyant, characters of brilliant kings like Divodas, Harishchandra, and Mandhata have been looked into subtly. Presenting the glory of various pilgrims along the banks of Narmada including Pushkar is an important feature of this *Puran*. Explaining the greatness of Pushkar, it is said in this section:

"Pushkar is equal to visiting ten thousand pilgrim spots. As Lord Vishnu shines above all the deities, so does Pushkar among all the pilgrim spots. Indra, Sun god, Vasu, Shiv, Brahmaji and such deities along with Lord Vishnu are present in this pilgrim spots. The men who perform *tapasya* here, or those who spend their time in this pilgrim spot, easily get the reward of visiting all the pilgrim spots and, enjoying affluence, they achieve emancipation at the end."

Among various pilgrims, the glory of Vitata teerth of Kashmir (birthplace of the snake named Takshak), *teerth* at the confluence of Sindhu and Samriddh, Kapal Mochan teerth, Arbudshem teerth, Pundarik teerth, and Sannihita teerth etc. has been illustrated.

Within *Karmyog*, the four phases of life (*ashram*) namely *brahmcharya, grihasth, vaanprasth, sanyas* have been explained along with its rules.

The description of fasts (*vrat*), being extremely beneficial and provider of affluence and emancipation, is the special feature of this section. In this, the glory of Janmashtami and Ekadashi (eleventh day of a month) fast has been explained by Lord Shiv on being asked by Devarshi Narad and Devi Parwati.

The procedure for the fast of Janmashtami according to *Padm Puran* is as follows:

"The fast for Janmashtami is observed on the eighth day of Krishna paksh of the month Bhadrapad. In this the devotees should take a bath in the morning with the water consisting of black sesame. Then put five gems in a pitcher and clean the pitcher with milk etc. then apply sandalwood paste on it and make Moon and Rohini of the size of a thumb on it. After that worship Lord Shri Krishna. Light incense and earthen lamp after adorning God with white cloths. Then break your fast."

Thus methodically executed fast for Janmashtami provides both affluence and emancipation to the devotee.

It has been clarified in this section with help of the story of the salvation of a female-demon by a Brahmin named Dharmadatt that the sins of previous birth are destroyed and the persons get the cherished rewards by worshipping Lord Vishnu in the month of Kartik.

Explaining the importance of *Tulsi*-worship in the *vrat* during the month of Kartik, it is said that *Tulsi* is very dear to Lord Vishnu and all the deities and *rishi-munis* reside in *Tulsi* during the Kartik month because of his blessings. Therefore there is special importance to worship and pray *Tulsi* in the Kartik month.

"All the *Purans* are analogue to the body of Lord Vishnu." At the end of *Swarg Khand*, the above-mentioned statement has been explained through personifying *Puran* as Lord Vishnu. Imbibing intriguing mystery, the personified form of *Puran* as Lord Vishnu is as follows:

Sr. No.	Puran	Personified Form of *Puran* as Lord Vishnu
1.	Brahm Puran	Forehead
2.	Padm Puran	Heart
3.	Vishnu Puran	Right Arm
4.	Shiv Puran	Left Arm
5.	Shrimad Bhagwat Puran	Both Eyes
6.	Narad Puran	Navel
7.	Markandeya Puran	Right Leg
8.	Agni Puran	Left Leg
9.	Bhavishya Puran	Right Knee
10.	Brahmvaivart Puran	Left Knee
11.	Ling Puran	Right Ankle
12.	Varah Puran	Left Ankle
13.	Skand Puran	Hair
14.	Vaman Puran	Skin
15.	Koorm Puran	Back
16.	Matsya Puran	Abdomen
17.	Garud Puran	Fat
18.	Brahmand Puran	Bones

Ending this section, it is said that there is no superior worship than that of Lord Vishnu. Devotees should keep praying and worshipping Lord Vishnu by offering donations, worshipping and fasting etc. As a result, all their wishes are fulfilled and they become entitled to the ultimate abode of Lord Vishnu, enjoying all kinds of affluence.

4. *Patal Khand*

Shri Ram and Shri Krishna *avatars* of lord Vishnu are the topics of discussion in the *Patal Khand*. Their noble characters along with all the histrionics have been included in it. Mythological details of Shri Ram, succeeding victory over Ravan during Shri Ram *avatar* have been presented. This section begins with the return of Shri Ram to Ayodhya from Lanka along with Sita and Lakshman. Delightful description of the meeting of Shri Ram with Bharat has been made in this narration.

Then there is a wonderful description of coronation of Lord Shri Ram and his kingdom famously known as *Ramrajya*. Resurrecting the dead son of the Brahmin and placing Lord Vaman in Kanyakubj by Shri Ram are such episodes which present the religious dimension of his character. After this there are episodes of organizing *Ashwamedh yajna* by Shri Ram, execution of demon Vidyunmali by Shatrughna, detaining the *yajna-horse* by Angad, the son of King Veermani, and assassination of Shatrughna and Pushkal, the son of Bharat, by Lord Shiv battling for Veermani.

In this context, the episodes of fight between Lord Shiv and Hanumanji, resurrection of Shatrughna and Pushkal by Hanumanji with the help of medicine named Sanjivani, and disappearance of Lord Shiv after making a visit to Shri Ram have been beautifully illustrated.

After this the episodes of holding the *yajna*-horse by Lav and Kush at Valimiki's ashram, rendering of Shatrughna unconscious, and releasing of the *yajna*-horse in the wake of mother's reward have been described. Then there is episode of the return of Lord Ram to Ayodhya with Lav, Kush, and Sita and concluding the *yajna*. The story of the wedding of Chyavan Muni and the greatness of Shaligram and river Gandak have also been described under this episode.

The greatness of Shri Krishna has been described in this section after narrating the greatness of Shri Ram. Emancipation of the inhabitants of Braj and Dwarka out of the blessings of Shri Krishna has been described in the narration of the glory of Shri Krishna. Further there is description of eight cronies of Shri Radha – Padma, Vishakha, Lalita, Shyamala, Shaivya, Dhanya, Bhadra, and Haripriya. After this, various forms of Lord Narayan with his four arms, characteristics of each form, five types of prayers and worships, and procedure for purification of heart have been described.

After this, worship of Shri Madhav, *pap prashnam stotra*, glory of *tulsi* and the month of *Vaishakh*, and meditation on Shri Krishna have been established.

Although different histrionics of Shri Ram and Shri Krishna *avatars* of Lord Vishnu is detailed in this section, yet the episode of Naradji in guise of a maid, geographical material, and glory of all the important festivals throughout the year have been detailed.

5. *Uttar Khand*

First of all, the dialogue between Devarshi Narad and Lord Shiv has been described in this section. The glory of Badrikashram and Lord Narayan has been described through this. After this, there is famous mythological episode of Jalandhar, the demon king, and Tulsi Vrinda. Subsequently, there is detailed description of descend of holy Ganga on the earth and glory of Haridwar, Prayag, Varanasi (Kashi), and Gaya etc. and many more pilgrim spots.

After that, the glory and procedure of Sanvatsardeep *vrat* and Janmashtami *vrat* have been described. After that, narrating the story of King Dashrath and Shanidev, the Shani stotra, which pleases Shanidev, has been described.

The evolution of *ekadashi* by lord Mahadev and the detailed description of the *ekadashi*s of Krishna and Shukla *paksh* (phase) of all the twelve months are found in this section. There after procedure of Chaturmas *vrat,* worship of Yamraj, glory of Gopichandan and twelfth day of Shravan month, and Vishnu *Sahastranam* (a thousand names) *stotra* have been described.

After the above-mentioned episodes, the story of execution of demon Shankhasur and salvation of *Vedas*, and glory of the months of Kartik and Magh and the Shookar region have been beautifully analyzed. After this, brief introduction has been made of Matsya, Koorm, Varah, Nrisingh and other *avatars* of Lord Vishnu.

Extremely complex and meaningful analysis of each chapter of *Shrimad Bhagwat Gita* has been made at the end of *Uttar Khand*. Personifying the eighteen chapters of *Gita* with his self, Shri Vishnu says, "The first five chapters of *Gita* are my face. The next ten chapters are my arms, then one chapter is my abdomen, and the last two chapters are my feet. Thus the eighteen chapters depicted in *Gita* are my form only."

Thereafter, this *Puran* has been concluded with the procedure for weekly schedule for delivery of *Shrimad Bhagwat*, the story of Lord Shri Ram and his one hundred and eight names.

A Story from *Padm Puran* : Story of the Faithful Shaivya

In old times, there lived a Brahmin named Kaushik in a city named Pratishthanpur. He was suffering from leprosy due to the sins committed in the previous birth. His relatives deserted him. But, in spite of the dreadful disease, his wife Shaivya worshipped him as if he was a god. She used to massage his legs regularly, bathe, dress and feed him. Thus, leaving her comforts aside, she had dedicated herself into the service of her husband. Kaushik was very wrathful by nature. He used to scold Shaivya frequently. But Shaivya tolerated

Message of the Purans

everything nonchalantly. Kaushik Brahmin was unable to move around.

He said to Shaivya one day, "Dear! I had seen a beautiful prostitute passing by our house. She has descended into my heart. I have begun to like her but I do not have the strength to reach her. So you take me to her and arrange a meeting."

Saintly Shaivya did not feel anger despite listening such words from her husband. She decided to take her husband to the prostitute and went to her house. She told the entire story on being asked by the prostitute about the purpose of her visit. Then the prostitute advised her to bring her husband after midnight. Listening to this, Shiavya returned home happily.

Shaivya raised her husband on her shoulders that night and slowly started for the prostitute's house. It was midnight. There were clouds in the sky. The road was visible by occasional lightning. Raising her husband on shoulders, Shaivya was going through the main road in such a pitch darkness. There was a cruciform on the way, on which a *rishi* named Mandav was crucified in suspicion of a thief. Though Mandav could use his *mantra* power to save himself from this punishment but he was aware of the sin he used to commit as a child by piercing ants with pricks. As a result of the sin he was crucified. Therefore he had embraced this punishment for his past misdemeanour.

Shaivya could not see the cross in the darkness and, inadvertently, Kaushik's leg shook the cross. Infuriated with this Mandav rishi said, "The sinful soul, who has aggrieved me by shaking the cross, will lose his life by the dawn. He will be doomed by seeing the sun."

Listening the curse of Mandav rishi, Shaivya said, "Brahmin dev! This deed was committed by my husband unaware. You are an extremely bright *rishi*. You have earned the knowledge of *Vedas* and scriptures. It does not match your honourable stature to deliver curse on being disturbed like this. Kindly take your curse back."

Mandav rishi said in rage, "Wretched woman! My curse cannot be retracted. Your husband has given me deep pain and he has to bear the brunt of his mistake."

Then Shaivya said, "*Munivar*! Kindly withdraw your curse or there will be no sunrise tomorrow. I will stop the sun with the strength of my *satitva*, if I have served my husband with true dedication." Saying this, she went away with her husband.

Even the sun was helpless before the *satitva* of faithful Saivya and did not rise for many days. The universe became a place of acrimony. The Indra along with all the gods went to Shaivya and beseeched her to withdraw her vow for the good of people. But the faithful Shaivya refused their request.

Finally the deities went to the refuge of Brahmaji and said praying, "*Pitamah* (grandfather)! Save us. Saint Shaivya has held *Surya dev*. *Rishi-muni*s used to provide us food through *yajna* and *hawan* etc; but these sacred deeds are impossible without a morning. God! Please help us."

Seeing the distress of gods, Brahmaji said, "Sons! Sun is not rising because of the greatness of Shaivya. All the forces of universe turn powerless before the power of sacredness. Therefore the return of morning is possible only through placating Shaivya. All of you return to your respective *lok*s. I myself would device some solution so that the system of day and night goes on and the life of the husband of the faithful lady could also be saved." After departing from the gods, Brahmaji appeared before Shaivya.

Seeing Brahmaji, Shaivya devotedly prayed him and asked politely the purpose of his arrival.

Glad with the prayer of Shaivya, Brahmaji said, "Daughter Shaivya! The order of day and night has broken due to stopping of *Surya dev*. Such sacred deeds as *yajna* and *hawan* have stopped to take place, deities are not getting their food and the universe has become a place of acrimony. That is why I have come to you. Be kind on deities, and free *Surya dev* from your bondage."

Folding her hands, Shaivya said, "God! Mandav muni has imprecated my husband that he will die with the sunrise. How can I let the misfortume befall on my husband? Now only you can guide me, lord."

Brahmaji promised to cure and resurrect Kaushik. Then Shaivya freed *Surya dev* and sunrise took place. Kaushik died at the sunrise but Kaushik became healthy and came to life due to the boon of Brahmaji. Acknowledging Shaivya's faithfulness (*pativrat*) towards her husband, the deities hailed her sounding conch, *mridang*, and *dhol*. Subsequently both the husband and wife went to heaven (*swarglok*) riding the divine plane.

•••

3

VISHNU PURAN

Introduction

Although the size of *Vishnu Puran* is very brief among all the eighteen *Purans*, yet it is placed superior and important in comparison to the other *Purans* owing to the description of the knowledge which removes illusion, substances, morals, and discourses narrated in it. That is why, the place of *Vishnu Puran* is highly important and appropriate in the ranking of eighteen *Purans*. Created by Maharshi Vedvyas, this divine text introduces devotees with the true form of Lord Vishnu by annulling their darkness resulting from attachment.

Actually the *Vishnu Puran* can be said to be an easy means by which devotees can get Lord Vishnu easily. This *Vishnu Puran* can be said to be such a divine bridge between Shri Vishnu and his devotees as connects them in the bond of mutual love and devotion. If said in nutshell, *Vishnu Puran* is a complete and extraordinary text of devotion, knowledge, and god-worship.

Number of Verses (*Shlokas*) and Sections

Vishnu Puran consists of a total of twenty-three thousand (23,000) verses. That means it is said to be the gist of twenty-three thousand verses. The entire *Vishnu Puran* is divided into six fractions (*ansh*) [*ansh* is the word which has been used in this *Puran* instead of *khand* (section) or *skandh*] and there are 126 chapters in these 6 *ansh*.

The Gist of *Vishnu Puran*
1. *Pratham Ansh* (First Fraction)

There are twenty-two (22) chapters in the *Pratham ansh* of the *Puran*. This *ansh* begins with the beautiful situation where Maharshi Parashar has detailed the twenty-four substances, emergence of moveable and immoveable universe, and glory of Lord Vishnu for answering the universe-related questions of Maitreya rishi. According to the *Puran, pradhan, purush, vyakt* and *kaal* – all of these four are a form of Lord Vishnu and these forms of him are separately the cause of birth, fostering, and destruction of the universe, nevertheless Lord Visnu has an isolated existence despite being present in the four forms. Merely due to his histrionics he is situated in the form of *vyakt, avyakt, purush*, and *kaal*. Made of twenty-four substances, the entire cosmos, universe, moveable and immoveable world have emerged from the fraction (*ansh*) of Lord Shri Vishnu. From the birth of universe to various *sarg*s have been described delightfully in this *Puran*.

The story of Dhruva, the greatest devotee of Lord Vishnu, has been beautifully illustrated in this *ansh*. Six-year-old Dhruva, devoid of fatherly love, having gone through arduous *tapa* to get supreme father Lord Vishnu and, pleased with his *tapa*, offering him a place in his lap by God is the gist of this mythological story. Whereas this mythological discourse perpetrates devotion for Lord Vishnu in the hearts of devotees, there it shows up the benign dimension of the Lord as well.

After the story of Dhruv, the characters of extremely bright King Prithu, Prachinbahir, and *Praacheta*s born in the hierarchy of Dhruv have been described. The birth of Daksh Prajapati, the *manas-putra* of Brahmaji, and the description of his descend presents the detail of the beginning of the organic universe. Risking his life for devotion of lord Vishnu by *bhakt* (devotee) Prahlad and protection of his devotee through Nrisingh *avatar* are such mythological discourses which demonstrate the selfless love between God and devotee.

Maharshi Kashyap and his descend has been described by at the end of *Pratham ansh*.

2. *Dwiteeya Ansh* (Second Fraction)

The Dwiteeya *ansh* of *Vishnu Puran* comprises sixteen (16) chapters. This *ansh* begins with the description of descend of Priyavrat, the son of self-styled Manu. After this, the oldest appearance of the earth has been described by presenting the geographical details of seven islands including Jumbu. The system of sun, *Nakshatra*, and signs (*rashi*), and description of seven firmaments (*urdhvalok*), *pataal*s, and *Gangavirbhav* is an important side of *Puran*. In addition to this, different hells and glory of God's name as described in *Puran* is capable of opening the eyes of wisdom of people wandering in the darkness of ignorance.

The message of wisdom of *adwait* has been given at the end of *Dwiteeya ansh* through the dialogue between King Sauveer and King Jadbharat, a Vishnu devotee of first *manvantar* and son of King Rishabhdev. At one place, on a question raised by King Sauveer, Jadbaharat says describing the oneness of Brahm, "King! The soul is one, vast, moderate, pure, formless, and isolated from nature. It is beyond birth and growth, omnipresent, and absolute. It is supremely knowledgeable. This Omnipotent neither had any assotiation with name and class nor has or will ever have. It is one despite being present in various species."

3. *Triteeya Ansh* (Third Fraction)

Comprising eighteen (18) chapters of *Vishnu Puran*, the *Triteeya ansh* begins with detailed description of the fourteen *manvantar*s, their rulers fourteen Manus, Indra, deities, *Saptarshis*, and the sons of Manus. Whereas, on the one hand, there are various names of Vyas according to *chaturyug* and description of glory of *brahm-gyan* (the knowledge of *Brahm*), on the other hand, there is detailed description of of *Rigved, Shukla Yajurved, Saamved*, and the expansion of the branches of *Taittireeya Yajurved*. *Brahmcharya* and such *ashrams*, the household etiquettes, nomenclature, methods of wedding rituals, and post-funeral rites have been presented according to scriptures in this *ansh* of *Puran* like the ocean in a bowl.

4. *Chaturtha Ansh* (Fourth Fraction)

The fourth fraction of *Vishnu Puran* is adorned with twenty-four (24) chapters. In the beginning of this *ansh*, the detail of Vaivswat Manu's dynasty within *Suryavansh* (Sun dynasty), birth of King Ikshwaku, and the character of kings in his descend namely Maandhaata, Trishanku, Sagar, Saudas, and Lord Ram have been described. Thereafter *Chandravansh* (Moon dynasty) has been described having described the character of kings namely Budh, Pururava, Raji, Yayati etc. Besides, in this *ansh*, Yadu, Turvasu, Anu, Puru, Kroshtu, Andhak, Kuru etc. and other famous royal dynasties are described.

5. *Pancham Ansh* (Fifth Fraction)

In all of the thirty-eight chapters of the fifth fraction of *Vishnu Puran*, sequence of Shri Krishna *avatar* of Lord Vishnu to the destruction of Yadu dynasty, and Pandava's ascendance to heaven have been described. Within this, a very delightful and poetic description has been made of the histrionics of Lord Shri Krishna.

6. *Shasht Ansh* (Sixth Fraction)

The sixth and the last fraction of *Vishnu Puran* comprises just eight (8) chapters. In this *ansh*, the evils and virtues of *Kaliyug-dharma* have been analyzed. The detailed description of three kinds of annihilation namely *naimittik*, *prakritik*, and *aatyantik* is another uniqueness of this *Puran*. In addition to this, describing spiritual activities as well as three kinds of penance and the Supreme Truthful form of God, *Brahmyog* has been established.

Concluding the text, Maharshi Parashar says at the end, "The sin created by all the evils is easily destroyed by merely listening to this sacred *Puran*. The great reward that one gets from *awabhooth* bathing at the end of *Ashwamedh yajna*, the same can be earned by merely listening to this *Puran*. This *Puran* is a great protector of people frightened from the world, very listenable, and holier than the holiest. This removes all the evils and nightmares of people, auspicious among the most auspicious, and provides progeny and wealth.

A Story from *Vishnu Puran* : The Story of King Prithu

Once upon a time, a king named Ang was born in the dynasty of Dhruv, the devotee of Vishnu. He was very religious and affectionate towards his subjects. Leaving his kingship and kingdom, he went to forest in his old age to do *tapasya*. When Bhrigu and other *muni*s noticed that there was no one left to protect the earth after him, then they crowned his son Ven. No sooner than Ven became the king, he turned outrageous in the ego of his power and affluence. He announced in his kingdom that *rishi-muni*s should not perform any type of *yajna* and *hawan*. Those guilty of violating the king's order were punished. All the religious activities came to a stop due to his fear.

In spite of persistent disturbance in carrying out religious activities, all the *rishi-muni*s collectively went to King Ven and submitted to him humbly, "King! Kindly listen to us carefully. This would augment your life, power, and prestige. King! A man gets heaven and such *loks* if he observes *dharma* by mind, speech, body, and intellect and he becomes entitled for *moksha* (emancipation) if he observes *dharma* by doing work without expectations of reward. Therefore you should not become party to the idea of destroying the *dharma* of your subject. King! The *yajna* and *hawan*, which would take place in your kingdom, would please the deities who, in turn, will give you the desired boon. Therefore you should not allow to discontine the *yajna* and such rituals causing disregard to the deities."

The wicked Ven said haughtily, "*Munis*! You people are very foolish. Having deserted all the wisdom, you have drowned your intellect in non-religious activities. That is why you want to pray and worship some imaginary god ignoring the real God, that is I, who fosters you. The people who disregard their king, the true God, get solace neither in this *lok* (the world) nor in the *parlok* (ethereal world). Deities reside in the body of the king. Therefore you worship me alone and offer the part of *yajna* to me only."

The intellect of Ven had debased completely due to ego. He had become very cruel, oppressive, non-religious, and misguided; therefore he paid no heed to the prayer of *rishi-munis*.

Listening to his sinful words, *munis* said in anger, "Ven! You are very non-religious and sinful. You will destroy this universe if you survived a few more days. You are being disrespectful to the *Parbrahm* Lord Shri Vishnu by whose kindness you have got this kingdom of earth. Your death is justified for the benefit of the world."

Thus resolved to kill the evil Ven, they launched attack on him. Then they soon killed him and returned to their respective *ashrams*. Ven's mother, obsessed with affection, began to protect the dead body of her son. The terror of thieves and dacoits grew in the kingdom after the death of Ven.

One day some *munigana* were having discussion on the subject of religion at the bank of river Saraswati. A group of dacoits passed by the place at that time. Seeing them, the *munigana* began to ponder over it. Just one thought kept rising in their heart, "Lawlessness has spread in the kingdom soon after the death of Ven. Thieves and dacoits have grown in great number in the kingdom and they are robbing the poor subjects. Although *rishi-muni*s are of peaceful nature, yet their *tapa* weakens in no time by ignoring the plight of poor. The dynasty of king Ang should not be destroyed because it has produced several brave and religious kings in the past. Therefore we must produce their inheritor who could protect the subject with his capability."

Then, having consulted among themselves for the inheritor of the kingdom, they churned Ven's thigh with great force wherefrom a dwarf emerged. He was dark coloured and all parts of his body were zigzag. As soon as he took birth, he accepted upon himself all the dreadful sins of King Ven. He and his descent were called 'Nishad' who lived in forests and mountains.

After that, *muni*s churned Ven's arms. A male-female couple with divine visage appeared from it. Seeing the palm line of the man's right hand resembling with that of Lord Vishnu and the symbol of lotus in feet, they considered him a fraction of Lord Vishnu.

Munigana said gladly, "This man has appeared with the power of Lord Narayan and this woman is real incarnation of Laxmi. This divine man will be famous by the name of Prithu for expanding his fame. Embellished with beautiful clothes and ornaments, this extremely beautiful woman will be his wife named Archi. Lord Vishnu himself has incarnated in the form of Prithu and Laxmi as Archi in order to protect the world."

Soon after his birth, the able sage-like son Prithu released the sinful Ven from the hell through his noble deeds. Thereafter, *rishi-muni*s organized Prithu's coronation. All the deities were present on this auspicious occasion: Lord Vishnu gifted his *Sudarshan Chakra* to Prithu, Brahmaji gifted *Vedmayi* armour, lord Shiv gifted the divine sword with ten cyclic symbols, two fans by *Vayudev* (the god of air), prestigious necklace by *Dharmaraj* (the god of *Dharma*), suave crown by *Devraj* Indra, *Kaaldand* by *Yamraj* (the god of death), divine bow by *Agnidev* (the god of fire), and a royal throne made of gold was gifted by *Kuber*.

When *munigana* started praying Prithu, then Prithu said, "Respected sirs! Which virtue of mine should you pray for when I have shown none so far in this *lok*? Pray *Parbrahm Parmatma* (supreme soul) alone. Pray me only when my virtues come to light. In any case, noble men do not pray insignificant men when there exists Lord Vishnu. Like learned persons feel bad for talking about their knowledge, similarly persons, famous around the world, hate themselves to be prayed. Therefore please do not pray me." All the *rishi-munis* were touched by the statement of Prithu. Then Prithu consoled them by offering their desired objects. They all showered their blessings on King Prithu.

The earth had become devoid of grain during the same time when *rishi-munis* had crowned Prithu. The subjects had physically turned emaciated in the absence of grain. They entreated King Prithu for help.

Listening to the pathetic request of his subjects, Prithu's heart melted with compassion. He could know with a little contemplation the reason for loss of grain from the earth. He came to know that the earth had concealed all types of grains and medicines within her. Then he raised his bow out of rage and was ready to shoot arrow at the earth. Seeing him stretching the arrow on the bow, the earth began to escape changing herself into a cow.

Seeing the earth running away in the form of a cow, the furious Prithu began following her. Whichever place she would go to save her life, King Prithu was visible at every place with bow and arrow.

When she did not get refuge anywhere, she returned scared to Prithu and said, "Great King! Why do you want to kill a weak and trifle like me, when you are always ready to protect all the livings? Will your *Kshatriya dharma* permit to assassinate a female? Even ordinary people do not raise their hand upon women for doing some misdemeanour. How, then, a compassionate and kind can do so? Further, kindly think, where would you inhabit your subjects after executing me?

Then Prithu said, "Earth! You have not given grain to my subject despite taking your share from *yajna*, therefore I will finish you. Your intellect has corrupted. You have concealed the grain and such seeds, created by Brahmaji, in your womb.

By not producing it, you are killing many lives. Execution of the person is justified according to scriptures who fosters only himself and is cruel towards other living beings. Now I will turn your womb into smithereens with my arrows and will have all the grains with the power of *yog* after quelling the hunger of my subject."

King Prithu appeared as real *Kaal* (the death) due to the intensity of rage. Seeing his dreadful appearance, the earth said praying him in humble voice, "King! Only the evil people were eating the grain created by Brahmaji. Several kings had stopped giving respect to me; therefore I had concealed the grains in my womb. Arrange an able calf, a pail, and someone to milk me, if you want to get the grain. I will offer you those substances in the form of milk. One thing more, O king! You turn me plane so that the water rained by Indra could remain on me throughout the year. This would be beneficial for all of you."

Then making the self-styled Manu into a calf, Prithu milked the earth completely with his own hands. Then he turned the earth's surface into plane by breaking the mountains with the help of the point of his arrows. Then he adopted the earth as his daughter. Earlier the earth was called *Medini* due to being made of *med* (white blood) of the demon named Madhu-Kaitabh but she became famous by the name of Prithvi after becoming the daughter of King Prithu. Thus, fulfilling the wish of the earth, Prithu rescued his subjects.

4

SHIV PURAN

Introduction

Shiv Puran is an important and well-known *Puran*, which describes in detail the core analysis, mystery, glory, and prayer of *'Shiv'* (well-being), the manifestation of a form of *Parbrahm Parmeshwar*. Lord Shiv is said to be the principal among the five gods. Establishing Lord Shiv as *avyakya* (inexplicable), *ajanma* (eternal), the main source of the creation of universe, fosterer and destroyer, Maharshi Vedvyas has introduced his formless and real existence in this holy *Puran*.

Along with detailed description of the original element of Shiv, *Shiv-avatar*, his glory and educative, interesting, delightful, and inspiring stories of his histrionics have been compiled beautifully in this *Puran*. Besides, the procedure of Lord Shiv's worship and several educative episodes are included in it.

Number of Verses (*Shlokas*) and Sections

The number of verses described in the Vishnu Puran is twenty-four thousand. Further, the entire *Shiv Puran* is divided into seven sections (*samhita*). These sections and the respective number of verses therein are as follows:

Sr. No.	Section (Samhita)	Number of Verses
1.	Vidyeshwar Samhita	2,000
2.	Rudra Samhita	10,500
3.	Shatrudra Samhita	2,180
4.	Kotirudra Samhita	2,240
5.	Uma Samhita	1,840
6.	Kailash Samhita	1,240
7.	Vaayveeya Samhita	4,000

The Gist of *Shiv Puran*

The *Shiv Puran* begins with the questions raised by Shaunak *muni* about the gist of *Puran*. Asking question with Lomharshan Sootji, the disciple of Maharshi Vyas, they ask, "O great among all the *munis*! You are aware of all the principles. Hence you quell our curiosity by telling in detail about the gist of *Puran*. *Munivar*! How does the wisdom, obtained from knowledge, detachment, and devotion, expand? How can a common man remedy such mental evils as *kaam* (lust), anger, attachment, greed, and ego? Since all the living beings are of *tamsik* (epicure) nature in *kaliyug*, therefore how and by which means is it possible to cleanse their minds? Kindly benefit all the living beings by answering to these meaningful questions." *Maharshi* offered the knowledge of this supremely sacred *Shiv Puran* in reply to these questions of Shaunak *muni*.

1. *Vidyeshwar Samhita*

The superiority of three means namely listening, hymning, and thinking have been endorsed in *Vidyeshwar Samhita* after explaining about the goal and the means. Thereafter the importance of the worship of *ling* (the idol form of Lord Shiv) has been told introducing the formless and real existence of Lord Shiv. In addition to this, the installation of *Shivling*, its sign, method of worship and the holy deeds enabling to reach the abode of Shiv are described in detail in this *Puran*.

Whereas the elaborate description of the glory of five deeds, evening worship, *Pranav, Gayatri, Agnihotra, Agniyajna, Devyajna, Brahmyajna,* and *Panchakshar mantras* are like divine nectar for seekers, at the same time, the narration of the highest order of reward achieved through bathing in various rivers at specific periods and sacred places is supremely beneficial and educative for common people.

The narration of Lord Shiv's creation of seven days and the rewards from their ruling deities and planets are detailed beautifully. Lord Shiv had contemplated of days for the benefit of people. First of all he contemplated his own day, Monday, which gives health. After that he made the day of *mayashakti* (the power of illusion), Tuesday, which provides wealth. He conceived Wednesday to protect the diseased progeny during his infancy. Thereafter Lord Shiv created Thursday (the day of Lord Vishnu, protector of the world) to eliminate lethargy and sin in order to benefit all the worlds (*lok*s). After that he conceived Brahmaji's day, Friday, to foster and protect the world. After that Lord Shiv created Saturday and Sunday, the respective days of Indra and Yamraj, in order to give the reward for the holy deeds of living beings. It respectively renders affluence to them and removes fear of death. Thereafter Lord Shiv designated sun and seven planets as the ruler of the seven days.

The procedure for worship of the idols of deities, and the description of special rewards achieved though various methods of worship during special dates and arrangement of constellation (*nakshatra*) are the other peculiarities of this *Puran*. The importance of courtesy extended to the devotees of Shiv has been exhibited by presenting the details of the glory of *pranav* in the form of *khadling*, analysis of his subtle form, *Onkar*, and the physical form, *Panchakshar mantra*, its method of chanting, description of the grandeur of *Shivlok* (abode of Shiv) along with different other *lok*s.

Other than Shivling, the glory of Rudraksh along with its various distinctions has been described in the *Puran*. Rudraksh is very dear to Lord Shiv. These are called Rudraksh for being born out of the tears flown from the eyes of Lord Rudra (Shiv). Man's all sins are destroyed by seeing, and touching Rudraksh and by chanting with it. He becomes exactly like Lord Neelkanth, who wears thirty-two Rudraksh around his throat, forty on the head, six on each ear, twelve on each hand, sixteen on each arm, one in terse at the centre of head, and one hundred and eight on the chest. He experiences happiness and peace in his life. Wearing of Rudraksh is the means to attain the divine wisdom of Lord Shiv. All class of men can wear Rudraksh. Devotees wearing Rudraksh earn name and fame in the society.

Infinite rewards are achieved through worship while wearing the necklace made of fifty or twenty-seven beads of Rudraksh. Do wear Rudraksh necessarily on the auspicious days and festivals of eclipse, *sankranti*, *amavasya*, and *purnamasi* (full moon day). Use of non-vegetarian food and wine is prohibited for people wearing Rudraksh.

Some Important Rudraksh

One-faced Rudraksh: One-faced Rudraksh is part of the real Lord Mahadev. The divine wisdom rises in the mind due to wearing it.

Two-faced Rudraksh: Two-faced Rudraksh is the symbol of the *Ardhnareeshwar* form of Lord Shiv. The blessing of Lord *Ardhnareeshwar* is always maintained on devotee by wearing it.

Three-faced Rudraksh: Three-faced Rudraksh represents fire. Such severe sins as *brahm-hatya* (killing a Brahmin) are annulled immediately by wearing it and the blessing of *agnidev* (the lord of fire) continues forever.

Four-faced Rudraksh: Four-faced Rudraksh is considered synonymous of Brahmaji. Man becomes rich and healthy by wearing it. He attains divine wisdom.

Five-faced Rudraksh: Five-faced Rudraksh is the real form of *Panchbrahm*. The satisfied Lord Shiv provides desired fruits to the devotees who wear it.

Message of the Purans

Six-faced Rudraksh: Kartikeya is the lord of six-faced Rudraksh. Ganeshji is also considered its deity. It provides infinite power and desired results to the people.

Seven-faced Rudraksh: The lord of seven-faced Rudraksh are seven *matrikayen*, seven horses, and *Saptarshi*. Man becomes healthy and respectable by wearing it.

Eight-faced Rudraksh: Eight *matrikayen* reside in eight-faced Rudraksh. These Rudraksh satisfy eight Vasu and Ganga. Deities are pleased on them who wear it.

Nine-faced Rudraksh: Dharmraj is the lord of nine-faced Rudraksh. Fear of death of any kind vanishes by wearing it.

Ten-faced Rudraksh: The ten *Dikpal* (lord of direction) are the lord of ten-faced Rudraksh. Man becomes darling of all the ten directions by wearing it.

Eleven-faced Rudraksh: Rudra is the god of eleven-faced Rudraksh. Devraj Indra is also said to be its main deity. Happiness increases by wearing it.

Twelve-faced Rudraksh: Twelve-faced Rudraksh is a form of Lord Vishnu. People who wear it become dear to Lord Vishnu.

Thirteen-faced Rudraksh: These Rudraksh are a form of *Kaamdev* (the lord of passion). These fulfil all the desires of the wearers and bless them. *Kaamdev* is pleased upon them who wear it.

Fouteen-faced Rudraksh: Fourteen-faced Rudraksh have appeared from the eyes of Lord Shiv himself. All the ailments are relieved by its influence and the man becomes healthy in every respect. People who wear the above-mentioned Rudraksh do not fear from ghost, spirit, *pishach, shakini, dakini* etc. Pleased deities fulfil all the desires of the person wearing Rudraksh.

2. Rudra Samhita

The second *samhita* that is *Rudra Samhita* is divided in five parts namely *Shrishti, Sati, Parwati, Kumar,* and *Yuddh.* A serialized and sectionwise study has been presented in this *Samhita* with the description of the life of Lord Shiv and his histrionics.

The First *(Shrishti) Khand*

The first part of *Rudra Samhita* is called *Shrishti Khand*. In the beginning of this *khand* there is episode of ego of *Devarshi* Narad under the spell of attraction and breaking of that spell by the compassionate Lord Shiv. Seriously engaged in *tapa*, *Devarshi* Narad had won the *kaam* (passion) by the blessing of Lord Shiv. This gave rise to the undue ego in his heart. He lost touch with truth due to being attracted into the illusion created by Lord Shiv. Overwhelmed with his ego, he became smug in self-praise. Seeing his devotee under influence of attachment, Lord Shiv broke the spell of *Devarshi* Narad with the help of Shri Vishnu and obliged him with his blessings. This episode makes clear that Lord Shiv always protects his devotees who fall into the whirlpool of illusion.

In this context *Devarshi* Narad had urged Brahmaji to explain various characters of Lord Shiv, his elemental form, appearance in the physical form, and marriage etc. To quell his curiosity, Brahmaji, after establishing the realm of the *parbrahm* during annihilation, has described in detail the emergence of the Sadashiv from the *nirgun* and formless, Sadashiv transforming his own power into the formation of Ambika, and emergence of the substance of nature in a systematic way by a fraction of Shiv. The discourse on the elemental Shiv narrated by Brahmaji is the representative of superiority and importance of *Shiv Puran*.

In the episode where Lord Shiv designate the task of creation of universe to Brahmaji and the task of protection to Shri Vishnu, the oneness of the three gods namely Shiv, Vishnu, and Brahma has been established. In the context of creation of universe, the detailed description of Daksh, Marichi, and such *prajapatis*, and the progenies of the daughter of Daksh have been made. The episode of attainment of the Kuber's designation by Prince Yajnadatt owing to the blessings of Lord Shiv has been described at the end of this *khand*. "Lord Shiv offers blessings to devotees, pleased with their normal worship." This idea has been beautifully illustrated in the Kuber's episode.

The Second *(Sati) Khand*

Sati Khand is the second part of *Rudra Samhita*. In this *khand*, replying the queries of *Devarshi* Narad, Brahmaji has described creation of Trinity (*Tridev*) by Sadashiv, creation of gods preceding creation of *Kaamdev* (god of passion) and Daksh's daughter Rati and their marriage. After that, there is episode of the emergence of Devi Sandhya and offering of the desired boon to her by Lord Shiv pleased with her arduous *tapa*. Lord Shiv freed the childhood completely from the *Kaambhav* (sensuality) on demand of such a boon by Devi Sandhya. After securing the boon, Sandhya consigned herself to the flames of *yajna* at Maharshi Meghatithi and again took birth as his daughter named Arundhati. She was married to Maharshi Vashishtha during this birth.

After this episode, there is very beautiful description of securing boon from Devi Jagdamba through prayer and worship by Daksh Prajapati, the beginning of organic universe, and invoking curse upon *Devarshi* Narad by Daksh.

Thereafter, descent of Bhagwati Jagdamba in the house of Daksh by the name of Sati, and arduous *tapa* undergone by her to marry Lord Shiv is described. After that, a poetic, and charming episode of Lord Shiv agreeing to the marriage on the request of gods, and taking a procession to the house of Daksh Prajapati has been presented.

The concept of knowledge and devotion has been analysed by Lord Shiv in this *khand* on the query of Goddess Sati. Seeing Lord Shiv folding hands before Shri Ram, Sati takes Shri Ram's test under the influence of illusion, mental desertion of Goddess Sati by Lord Shiv, and omission of Lord Shiv by Daksh – these famous episodes are important constituents of this *khand*. The background of the sacred story of Goddess Sati leaving her life has been clarified by this means. The episode of Goddess Sati leaving her life in the honour of her husband at the *yajna* organized by Daksh Prajapati delineates her *pativrat dharma*. Angered by the death of Goddess Sati, Lord Shiv produces Veerbhadra to destroy Daksh's *yajna* and subsequent resurrection of dead Daksh are the episodes which establish the 'destroyer and simple' (*Bhole Bhandari*) form of Lord Shiv.

At the end, Brahmaji says clarifying the glory of *Sati khand*, "Equipped with extraordinary characters of Lord Shiv and Goddess Sati, this *khand* is extremely benevolent and fulfils all the wishes. The devotees attain emancipation (*moksha*) after enjoying all the affluence merely by listening to it reverentially. This is provider of paradise, fame, longevity, and rewards like children and grandchildren.

The Third (*Parvati*) Khand

This is said to be *Parvati Khand* due to detailed description of the character of Bhagwati Parvati in the third part of *Rudra Samhita*. At the beginning of this *khand*, *Parampita* (the Supreme Father) Brahmaji has described about the divinity of Himalaya after establishing its two forms namely *sthavar* (static or inanimated) and *jangam* (dynamic or animated).

The detailed description of Parvati *avatar*, through the womb of Mena, wife of Himalaya, as a result of the boon of Goddess Jagdamba has been made in this *khand*. After this, the interesting and delightful description of Lord Shiv turning *Kaamdev* (the god of passion) into ashes, and test of Bhagwati Parvati by *Saptrishis* on the direction of Lord Shiv has been given. The main description of this *khand* is the wedding of Shiv and Parvati. All the gods who are striving for the marriage of Shiv-Parvati have been detailed in this *khand*. There has been the effort through this *khand* to highlight all the aspects of the extraordinary character of Shiv and Parvati. Actually this *khand* presents the *Ardhanareeshwar* form of Lord Vishnu.

The Fourth *(Kumar) Khand*

The characters of the sons of Shiv have been described in this *khand* of *Rudra Samhita*. First of all the descriptin of the birth of Shiv's son, Kumar Kartikeya, and execution of Tarkasur by him has been made in this *khand*. After this, the story of Bhagwati Parwati giving birth to Ganesh, beheading of Ganesh by Lord Shiv, and his resurrection by adding elephant's head on him have been described beautifully. Therafter designating Ganeshji as chieftain of all gods by Lord Shiv, the description of *Ganesh Chaturthi vrat* has been made. Further, the narration of Lord Ganesh's wedding and inhabitance of Kumar Kartikeya in the Kraunch mountain is very educative.

The fifth *(Yuddh) Khand*

The fifth part of *Rudra Samhita* has been called *Yuddh khand*. Numerous histrionics of Lord Shiv as executioner have been illustrated in it. Transforming into executioner mode, Lord Shiv executes all the evils for the benefit of the three worlds *(lok)*. This notion has been clarified tastefully by the means of *Yuddh khand*.

In this *khand*, first of all, there is story of receipt of three divine towns by sons of demon Tarkasur named Tarkaksh, Vidyunmali, and Kamalaksh as a result of the boon of Brahmaji and the execution of those demons by Lord Shiv pleased with the prayer of gods. In this episode, an extremely poetic and elaborate description has been made of the divine chariot of Lord Shiv made of subtle and bulk materials. For example:

"The divine chariot of Lord Shiv is made of gold. There are placed Sun in its right wheel, and moon in the left wheel. There are fitted twelve spokes in the right wheel of the chariot, where twelve suns are seated. The left wheel pertains sixteen spokes, which are adorned by the sixteen stages of moon. The six seasons are the suspensions of those wheels. The front part of the chariot is space, and its seating place is Mandarachal. The sunrise and the sunset are the humps of the chariot. The mountains Mahameru and Shakhaparwat are its shelters. *Sanvatsar* is the speed of the chariot, *Uttarayan* and *Dakshinayan* both are iron support, *muhurt* its rope, and *kala* are its nails. *Kashthayen* are its nose-typed front part and *kshana, akshadanda,* and *nimesh* are its wood in the lower side. *Dwilok* is the upper canopy of this chariot and heaven, and emancipation (*moksha*) are the flags. Abhrum, the wife of Airawat, and Kaamdhenu are placed at the end of *jueyn*. Nature is its *ishadanda*, intelligence *nagwal*, ego is corner, and five *mahabhoot* have been said to be its strength. Senses adorn it from all the sides. Faith is the gait of the chariot. *Ved, Puran, Nyaya, Meemansa,* and religious scriptures are the ornaments of the chariot. Imbibing the propitious characteristics, the *mantras* are adoring the place of the gong. Ganga and other holy rivers are seated in the form of beautiful women. The four auspicious forms of *Vedas* are the four horses of the chariot and Brahmaji is its charioteer."

In fact, the *Parbrahm* form of Lord Shiv and his lordship on the entire cosmos has been established by the above-mentioned description. Lord Shiv is creator, fosterer, and destroyer of this universe. Adorning this chariot, Lord Shiv became famous by the name of Tripurari by destroying the sons of Tarak and their divine towns. *Devagana* (gods) acted as the animals of Lord Shiv in this battle. Due to being the lord of animals, Lord Shiv was called as Pashupati.

The execution of Shankhachud, and the glory of Tulsi and the rock of Shaligram have been described by Lord Shiv in this *khand*. Besides the detailed description of emergence of demon Andhakasur from the radiance of Lord Shiv, attracted to the beauty of Devi Parwati, attack by Andhakasur on the Shivlok, Andhak being punished by Lord Shiv have been made. In the context of this story, Lord Shiv accepting Shukracharya, the *guru* of demons, as his son and the glory of *mahamrityunjaya mantra* have been explained.

At the end, *Rudra Samhita* along with *Yuddha khand* has been concluded with the detailed description of the emergence of *Shivling* named Kritivaseshwar, and Kandukeshwar, its method of worship and glory.

3. *Shatrudra Samhita*

The birth of various *avatars* and histrionics of Lord Shiv have been described in *Rudra Samhita*. Five *avatars* of Lord Mahadev have been described in the beginning of this *Samhita*. These *avatars* are – *Sadyojaat, Vaamdev, Tatpurush, Aghor*, and *Ishan*. Taking the above-mentioned *avatars*, Lord Shiv inspires Brahmaji to create the universe in various *kalpas*.

Subsequently the eight idols of Lord Shiv (Sharva, Bhav, Ugra, Bheem, Pashupati, Rudra, Ishan, and Mahadev) and their *Ardhnareeshwar* (half male and half female) form have been established. Earth, water, fire, space, *kshetragya*, sun and moon are placed through these eight idols of Lord Shiv. Inclusive of the twenty-eight histrionic *avatars* of Lord Shiv, his other *avatars* namely Nandishwar, Grihpati, Hanuman, Durvasa, Pipplad, Dwijeshwar, Yatinath, Hans, Krishnadarshan, Awadhooteshwar, Bhikshuvarya, Sureshvar, and Kirat etc. have been described succinctly. Describing ten *avatars* of Lord Shiv like Mahakaal etc. and eleven Rudra *avatars*, various dimensions of his *avatars* have been observed in this *khand*. A brief description of twelve *Jyotirlings* has been presented at the end of this *Samhita*.

4. *Kotirudra Samhita*

The twelve *Jyotirlings* that have been introduced in brief in the *Shatrudra Samhita*, the same have been explained in detail, from its inception to the importance of its vision and worship, in *Kotirudra Samhita*. Establishing the glory of twelve *Jyotirlings* in this *Samhita*, the related mythological and educative descriptions have been serially mentioned.

The twelve *Jyotirlings* described in this *Puran* are as follows:

Jyotirling	The place of emergence	Present location	State
Somnath	Verawal	50 Km. from Junagarh	Gujarat
Mahakaaleshwar	Awantika	Ujjain	Madhya Pradesh
Kedarnath	Rudraprayag	Rudraprayag	Uttaranchal
Bhimshankar	Dakini	160 Km. from Pune	Maharashtra
Vishveshwar	Kashi	Varanasi	Uttar Pradesh
Rameshwaram	Setubandh	Rameshwaram	Tamil Nadu
Ghumeshwar	Verul	27 Km. from Aurangabad	Maharashtra
Naageshwar	Darukavan	210 Km. from Aurangabad	Maharashtra
Trayambkeshwar	Brahmgiri	39 Km. from Nasik	Maharashtra
Baidyanath	Santhal Pargana	Jasideeh	Jharkhand
Parmeshwar	Bank of Narmada	80 Km. from Indore	Madhya Pradesh
Mallikarjun	Shrishail	250 Km. from Hyderabad	Andhra Pradesh

Clarifying the religious importance of the above-mentioned twelve *Jyotirlings*, it is said that the symbol of undefined form of Lord Shiv, these twelve *Jyotirlings* fulfil all the wishes and provide emancipation to devotees. Men become sinless and claim their right on *Shivlok* by its vision and worship. People meet the emancipation after enjoying all the affluence by reverentially reading, listening, and understanding the story of twelve *Jyotirlings*. At the end, this *Samhita* has been concluded with describing Shiv *sahastranam stotra* (thousand-name verses), procedure and glory of *Shivratri vrat*, and other fundamental knowledge about Shiv.

5. *Uma Samhita*

The extraordinary character of Goddess Parwati and the histrionics related with her have been illustrated in the *Uma*

Samhita. Since Parwati has emerged out of the half part of Lord Shiv, and is the fractional form of Lord Shiv therefore, by describing the glory of Uma, the *Ardhnareeshwar* (half male and half female) form of Lord Shiv has been glorified indirectly. In its beginning, there is the story of offering the desired boon to Shri Krishna by Shiv-Shiva. Subsequently journey to *Yamlok*, one hundred and forty hells, the sins which dump in hell and description of resultant tortutre in those hells, and the complicated secrets of post-death scenario have been established.

The subtle and fundamental core knowledge of this *Puran* is reflected in the description of self-study of *Ved* and *Puran*, glory of various kinds of donations, symptoms of death, methods to win over the *Kaal* (death), and the glory of various spiritual powers and dedication to God.

Besides the fundamental core knowledge, there is mention of the mysterious *avatars* of Bhagwati Uma namely Kalika, Mahalakshmi, Saraswati, Durga, Shatakshi, Shakambhari, Bhramari, etc. and execution by them of dreadful and great warrior demons namely Mahishasur, Madhu, Kaitabh, Shumbh, Nishumbh, Raktbeej, etc.

In addition to this, the glory of *kriyayog* of Bhagwati, different holy *vrat*s (fasts), different festivals, procedures for worship, and listening, reading, and contemplating of *Uma Samhita* have been illustrated.

6. Kailash Samhita

The original seminal form of Lord Shiv is illustrated in this *Samhita*. Besides this the *dwait* and *adwait* philosophy and such subjects from the perspective of *rishi-muni*s have been discussed in detail.

Explaining *Pravanarth*, analysis of the meanings of *Pranav* and meditation of the form of Sadashiv verbally, importance of observing the *varnashram dharma*, worship with wisdom, description of *Brahm yajna* and *Nandi shraadh* etc. performed before leaving for ascetic life (*sanyas*), the classical method of *sanyas*, integrity of life and world with Lord Shiv – these are the fundamental bases of *Kailash Samhita*. The above-mentioned topics have been described in detail in this *Samhita*.

7. *Vaayveeya Samhita*

In the beginning of this *Samhita*, Maharshi Sootji has introduced with the places of education and eighteen *Purans*. Subsequently, establishing the glory of Lord Shiv in the form of supreme element (*Paramtatva*), the substantial analysis of *pashu* (life), *paash* (nature), and *pashupati* (God) has been made by *Vayudev* (the god of air). Living (*jeev*), non-living (*prakriti* or nature) and God (*niyanta* or supreme god)– these three have been termed respectively as *pashu*, *paash*, and *pashupati* by the god of air (*Vayudev*). The learned people call it as *kshar* (nature), *akshar* (animal), and the supreme element (*pashupati*).

After the above-mentioned description, there is description of Shiv's *Rudra avatar* and his glorious appearance. Establishing the appearance of fire and *som*, the entropy of universe, the awareness of God, and importance of *pashupatvrat* are mentioned as the distinct features of this *Samhita*.

Besides there is gistful description of five types of *Shiv-dharmas*, their four legs, *gyanyog*, method of worshipping Shiv, *varnashram-dharma*, the glory of five-letter *mantra*, the process of *shivling-mahavrat*, three kinds of education, the method of *khadvashodhan*, and the method of the installation of the flame of Shiv have been analysed in detail.

Story from *Shiv Puran* : Disillusionment of Narad

Once upon a time, Narad Muni, the head of all *muni*s, underwent *tapasya* for a long time in a beautiful cave of Himalaya mountain. Indra got worried due to the intense *tapa* of Naradji. The king of gods, Indra, became apprehensive lest Narad begin to demand his throne after the success of the *tapa*.

With this thought, Indra decided to disturb the *tapa* of Naradji. He called up Kaamdev (the god of passion) and asked him to disrupt Naradji's *tapasya*. In no time, Kaamdev applied all of his illusory tricks where Naradji was doing *tapasya*. Spring, too, delightfully expressed its influence there in myriad forms.

But the place where Naradji was performing *tapasya* was the same place where Lord Shiv had turned Kaamdev into ashes and, as a result, the entire region was declared free from the influence of Kaamdev. Therefore, owing to the blessings of Lord Shiv, neither Kaamdev nor the spring, despite their best efforts, could create any vice in the heart of Naradji. The ego of both of them had shattered due to the blessings of Mahadev. Seeing Kaamdev failing in his job, Indra went there himself and began lauding Narad's patience and *tapa*.

On hearing his praise from the mouth of Indra, Naradji was filled with pride. He misunderstood himself as conquerer of lust (*kaama*). He failed to acknowledge out of ignorance that the influence of Lord Shiv was the main reason behind Kaamdev's defeat. As a matter of fact, he had fallen into the God's illusion.

Full of pride, Narad *Muni* arrived at Kailash at the very moment and began boasting about his tale of win over Kaam. Seeing Narad in a state of delusion, Lord Shiv advised him to exercise restrain from egoistic and self-praise talk but Naradji did not comprehend his advice. Assuming that Lord Shiv was envious of his growing influence, he went to *Brahmlok*, quite pleased in his heart, and repeated his tale of win over Kaam there also. Next he repeated the same in *Vishnulok* too.

Although Lord Vishnu was aware of the truth, yet he lauded Naradji's wisdom and detachment. Thus the ego of being the conquerer of Kaam overpowered Naradji's mind. At last, by Shivji's wish, Lord Vishnu decided to end the false pride of Naradji. In a moment, he created a beautiful city on the route of Naradji. This city was full of all the affluence like paradise.

When, drowned in self-praise, Naradji was going through

the sky-route, his sight fell on this beautiful city. He descended in that city out of curiosity, on seeing its beauty and opulence. The city was ruled by King Sheelnidhi. Seeing Naradji as guest, he gave him deserving reception. After this, Sheelnidhi called in his daughter whose name was Shrimati. By the illusion of Lord Shiv, Naradji's heart filled with vice and he fell to the influence of Kaam (lust) on seeing the extraordinary beauty of Shrimati. Listening to Sheelnidhi planning for the *swayamvar* (marriage) of Shrimati, Naradji began contemplating to marry her: 'Women are attracted to the physical beauty and it is Lord Vishnu alone in the universe who is the source of beauty for the entire world. Therefore, I should borrow his beauty from him for one day.' The very moment he arrived at the *Vaikunth lok* and disclosed his intent to Shri Vishnu.

According to the direction of Lord Shiv, Shri Vishnu transferred his getup in the body of Naradji but made up his face like that of a monkey. However, Naradji did not get wind of it.

'Shrimati would certainly choose me as her husband, seeing me as handsome as Shri Vishnu.' With this thought he went happily to sit in the *swayamvar* gathering. People who were present there could not recognize Naradji due to the illusion (*maya*) of Lord Shiv. But two *Shivgana* (followers of Shiv), sitting in that gathering in the disguise of Brahmin, knew the entire plan. They began mocking and jeering at Naradji, seeing him under the influence of lust (*kaam*).

The marriage ritual (*swayamvar*) started. Lord Vishnu was also present in the gathering in the guise of a king. Shrimati put the garland around his neck. Along with Shrimati, Shri Vishnu disappeared from the place. Since lust had excited Naradji, he became enraged due to his dejection. At that time the *Shivgana* in the disguise of Brahmin ridiculed him and asked him to look at his monkey face. Naradji was greatly surprised listening to them. When he saw his monkey face in the mirror, he became inflamed with anger and dejection.

Message of the Purans ──────────────── •• 73

Under the spell of Lord Shiv's illusion, he cursed the *Shivgana* the very moment to take birth in *daitya-yoni*. The *Shivgana* left the place silently acknowledging the curse as the wish of Lord Shiv.

After that, burning with anger, Naradji arrived at Vaikunth. His intelligence and wisdom had vanished due to the illusion of Lord Shiv and therefore he invoked curse on Shri Vishnu to suffer from the seperation with his better half. Shri Vishnu accepted the curse with the understanding that it was the histrionics of Lord Shiv. It was then that Lord Shiv withdrew the illusion (*maya*) spread by him and Naradji returned to his normal condition. He started feeling guilty for his conduct.

Then Shri Vishnu said, "*Munivar*! You had ignored the advice of Lord Shiv out of your ego. Shivji has recompensed you for the same offence because he only is the one who grants retribution for every deed. The master of all, Lord Shiv helps let go the ego. One gets wisdom through realizing his *Sachhidanand* form. All the gods perform their duties by his directions. Actually, he is situated in every atom of this universe. Therefore hey *munivar*! Leave your all the doubts aside, and sing the praise of Lord Shiv and read Shiv's *Shatnam stotra* with unwavering dedication. Lord Shiv will certainly be kind to you."

The doubt of Naradji vanished by listening to Shri Vishnu and he set off praying and worshipping *Shivlings* situated at various places singing the *Shatnam stotra* of Lord Shiv. Thus his mind became free of malice by the blessings of Shivji and he got the honour of becoming *Devarshi*, i.e., *rishi* of gods.

•••

5

SHRIMAD BHAGWAT PURAN

Introduction

Infinite meaning, knowledge, science, and philosophical substance are brimming in every verse, sentense, word, letter, *dhatu*, consonant, vowel, *upsarg*, and *pratyaya* of Sanskrit language. Further, the big tomes of Sanskrit are the encyclopaedia of various subjects. There are many such texts which are combination of infinite, varied, and different subjects and are beautifully written and worded. Our *Purans*, too, are such treasures. Among them, *Shrimad Bhagwat* is a world-revered epic and its substance-secret, and range of topics are not only looked up to by scholars but are also the touchstone to judging one's learnings. In fact, Bhagwat was the best means to examine the scholarship of learned ones in the ancient times. That is the reason why *Shrimad Bhagwat* holds unique place in the Sanskrit literature especially *Puran* literature.

This *Puran* is an extraordinary combination of knowledge, action (*karma*), and prayer (*upasana*). This is an open secret of *Vedic* literature and deep subjects of Sanskrit literature. Not only this but its depth of knowledge is infinite. There is interesting detail of geography, astronomy, history, philosophy, science, law, arts, and other countless subjects in it. Along with, this is the best ladder to the divine knowledge – the key to *Vedas*, exposure of nature's secrets, and emancipation. There is extremely interesting detail of spiritual, divine and physical scientific system in it. The ultimate uniqueness of this *Puran* is that deep mysteries of *Vedas* have been unfolded in the pretext of narrating the history of *Bharat* (India).

Maharshi Vedvyasji, the author of *Shrimad Bhagwat*, has also offered the highest place to this great religious text among his eighteen *Purans*. It is his own statement that when he did not get peace in spite of creating *Purans*, he created *Shrimad Bhagwat* and then he experienced the ultimate bliss.

The word *'Bhagwat'* means "what belongs to God." *Bhagwat* has been used in place of *bhakt* (devotee) in various context of *Shrimad Bhagwat*. The God resides in the heart, eyes, in every pore of the devotee; the devotee is meant for God only. His goal, means, and life everything is dedicated at the holy feet of God. Similarly, whatever is there in the *Shrimad Bhagwat*, and whatever is there in oneself, all belongs to God; everything is God.

Shri Krishna in *Bhagwat* and *Bhagwat* in Shri Krishna – this is the mutual relation. After coming to know about this secret, one clearly observes God in *Bhagwat* and Bhagwat in God. It is doubtful if there exists an equivalent divine expression of spiritualism in verse in the entire world literature.

This is a supernatural *Puran*. There is vivid description of *varnashram dharma*, human *dharma*, *karma yog*, *astang yog*, *gyan yog*, *bhakti yog* etc., the means to realize God. The easy way to realize God has been explained in it through means-based and goal-based devotion.

Explaining the importance of devotion, Lord Shri Krishna has said himself –

"न साधयति मां योगो न सांख्यं धर्म उद्धव।
न स्वाध्याय स्तपस्त्यागो यथा भक्तिर्ममोर्जिता।।"

Which means "Hey Uddhav! Complete devotion is the way by which one can realize me easily; neither *yog*, nor knowledge, nor *dharma*, nor study of *Ved*, nor *tapa*, nor donations can be as successful as devotion. Only revered devotion can facilitate my realization."

Spirituality, psychology, social sciences, birth of universe, *kaaltatva*, and the history of the race of Aryan has been described in such a beautiful, simple, and decent language that it perpetrates the holy ideas quite naturally in the hearts of readers. According to a renowned scholar, "if a story, while reading *Puran*, appears improbable or is difficult to perceive by simple mind, you must know that there is deep substance in it. *Puran* should be studied and contemplated keeping this rule in mind."

What can a man not do with perseverance and devotion? Divine affluence descends on man with pure devotion and love to God. He who understands that God is the supreme authority can make possible even the impossible deeds. A little child like Dhruv develops dedicated devotion to God sitting in the dense and frightening forest. The three *lok*s started trembling due to his perseverance and devotion. This is the might of devotion to God!

Educative and discourse-based examples, worth emulating, have been presented one episode after another in this text. Lord Shri Krishna is the real God and supreme soul (*parbrahm parmatma*). He is devoid of all evils and is always complete with all the noble virtues. Becoming supremely sacred, a man can realize the otherwise unattainable level merely by listening, contemplating, chanting and thinking about his name, virtues, and histrionics etc.; how then one can even imagine of any vices in him! Therefore, if there is any such context in the God's histrionics, it should be taken in a sacred sense and never in a maligned sense.

The episodes of nonvegetarian food, wine, debauchery, violence, stealing, untruthful speeches, lust (*kaam*), anger, greed, attachment, ego, cunningness, envy etc. have appeared in *Shrimad Bhagwat* at various places due to context. It should neither be considered a principle nor worth emulating. Considering it unworthy, it should be rejected only. In fact the direction given in *Shrimad Bhagwat* from place to place to leave these vices, shortcomings, and bad manners should be followed

Message of the Purans

honestly. If there appears a notion of defect in some noble person – for example lust, anger, attachment in Brahmaji – it should then be understood that by showing the intensity of lust, anger, and attachment, it is being carefully advised to reject these vices and that is the sole purpose of the script.

God reveals himself in Bhagwat, "If someone, even though the lowest order of evil-doer, prays me continuously becoming my devotee in all earnest, he deserves to be called a saint because he is a real resolute person. Soon he becomes a holy man and realizes the ultimate peace staying with him perennially."

The means of realizing God are very easy in *Kaliyug* – merely by chanting the hymns of God's name can fulfil the objective. What to say if one gets the opportunity to attend *satsang* (discussion with saintly persons)! It is said in the *Shrimad Bhagwat* –

"तुलयाम लेवनापि न स्वर्ग नापुनर्भवम्।
भगवत्संगिसंगस्य मर्त्यानां किमुताशिष:।।"

Which means, "A little proximity with the devotee of *Bhagwat* is of greater value than the cherished emancipation which destroys the vicious cycle of life and death let alone a place in heaven; who then counts the wealth and kingdom on this earth!"

"कलेदोषनिधे राजन्नस्ति ह्योको महान गुण:।
कीर्तनादेव कृष्णस्य मुक्तसंग: परं व्रजेत्।।
कृते यद्ध्यायतो विष्णुं प्रेतायां यजतोमरवै:।
द्वापरे परिचर्यायां कलौ तद्धरिकीर्तनात्।।"

'*Kaliyug* is a vault of faults; but there is a great merit to it. It is that all the addictions go away in *Kaliyug* merely by chanting the hymns of Shri Krishna and the supreme soul is realized. The reward, which one gets by meditation and *dhyan-yog* in *Satyug*, organizing grand *yajnas* in *Tretayug*, and methodical prayer and worship of God in *Dwaparyug*,

Message of the Purans

can easily be achieved just by chanting the name or hymns of Shri Hari.'

Innumerable holy gains are received by listening and reading *Shrimad Bhagwat* and the devotee achieves freedom from the cycle of life and death. Lord Shri Krishna says himself–

"यः पठते प्रयतो नित्यं श्लोकं भागवतं सुत।
अष्टादशपुराणानां फलमाप्नोति मानव।।"

Which means, "He, who reads one verse a day with holy dedication, gets reward of reading eighteen *Purans*."

"नित्यं मम कथा यत्र तत्र तिष्ठन्ति वैष्णवः।
कलिबाह्या नरास्ते वै येदर्चयन्ति सदा ममहः।।"

"Vishnu's councillors like Prahlad etc. remain present where everyday my deliberations go on. The persons are protected from the curse of *kali* who always pray and worship my treatise named *Bhagwat*. *Kali* cannot influence them adversely."

"यत्र तत्र भवेत् पुण्यं शास्त्रं भागवतं कलौ।
तत्र तत्र सदैवाहं भवामि त्रिदशैः सह।।"

"I remain present with all the deities wherever the holy *Shrimad Bhagwat Puran* is kept in *Kaliyug*. Not only this but all the famous pilgrims reside there in the form of river and lake; all the *yajna*s, seven towns, and all the sacred mountains perpetually reside there."

This sacred text called *Shrimad Bhagwat* provides life, health, and satisfaction; a man becomes free from all the sins by reading or listening to it. Journey to all the sacred places and holy dip in all the pilgrim spots collectively are not holier than listening to *Shrimad Bhagwat*. Mainly nine kinds of devotion have been described in *Shrimad Bhagwat* – *shrawan* (listening), *kirtan* (chanting of hymns), *smaran* (remembrance), *vandan* (prayer), *archan* (offerings), *paadsevan* (service at the feet), *dasya* (surrender), *sakhya* (friendship), *atmanivedan* (self-entreaty). *Premlakshana* (sign of love) is eleventh, and *parabhakti* (supreme devotion) is the twelfth devotion.

Paadsevan (service at the feet), *archan* (offerings), *vandan* (prayer), *dasya* (surrender), *sankhya* (friendship) – are the external means of the route to devotion. *Atmanivedan* (self-entreaty), *smaran* (remembrance) are internal means. *Shrawan* (listening), and *kirtan* (chanting of hymns) are both internal as well as external means. These external traits have to be internalized. The main symptom of devotion is that the devotee's external traits shift from materialistic substances and internalize on the image of deity.

There are twelve *skandh* in *Shrimad Bhagwat Puran*. From foot to thigh is the first *skandh*, from thigh to waist is the second *skandh*, navel is the third *skandh*, abdomen is the fourth *skandh*, heart is the fifth *skandh*, arms including throat is sixth *skandh*, mouth is seventh *skandh*, eyes are the eighth *skandh*, cheeks and eyebrows are ninth *skandh*, *brahmarandhra* is the tenth *skandh*, and soul has been said to be the twelfth *skandh*. Thus our whole body is embodiment of *Bhagwat*.

In fact *Shrimad Bhagwat*, like four *Vedas*, is extremely important in its all the four forms namely occurrence, preaching, prayer, and hymns. It is another form of the scriptures of *Vedas* and is like a juicy fruit: one can probably acknowledge its glory by tasting it only. In fact its glory is inexplicable.

Its weekly recitation method has been described in the *Shrimad Bhagwat*. Moreover, Lord Shri Krishna has said himself that he becomes pleased with a devotee if he merely looks upon *Bhagwat* or utters its name. Therefore common man can get its full benefit by reading, listening, and contemplating *Bhagwat* with reverance at their convenience.

Number of Verses *(Shlokas)* and Sections

Shrimad Bhagwat Puran is rich by eighteen thousand (18,000) verses. The entire *Puran* is divided into twelve skandha (sections). The number of chapters detailed in these 12 sections is as follows:

Skandh	Chapters	Skandh	Chapters
First	19	Seventh	15
Second	10	Eighth	24
Third	33	Ninth	24
Fourth	31	Tenth	90
Fifth	26	Eleventh	31
Sixth	19	Twelfth	13

The Gist of *Bhagwat Puran*

First of all, establishing the glory of *Shrimad Bhagwat*, its weekly recitation method has been described. A man achieves emancipation (*moksha*) wiping out his sins in seven days by reading and listening *Shrimad Bhagwat* in the prescribed way. Besides the stories of absolving the plight of the devotee by *Devarshi* Narad, the influence of God, and salvation of the ghost named Dhundhukari have also been described.

1. The First *Skandh*

The first *skandh* of *Shrimad Bhagwat* begins with the prayer of God's form of *parbrahm*. In the second chapter, on being asked questions about Shri Krishna by Shaunak etc. *rishi-muni*s, Maharshi Sootji has described in detail the glory of devotion to God, and discourse about God. After this, the brief introduction of God's *avatars* has been made. From the fourth to sixth chapter, an extraordinary description of the glory of hymns depicting God's fame, and the character of the previous birth of *Devarshi* Narad has been made.

In the seventh chapter, in the context of stories related with Shri Krishna, Sootji has described the story of beheading of Draupdi's sons while in sleep by Ashwathama, defeat and capture of Ashwathama by Arjun, and, on the suggestion of Draupdi and Shri Krishna, leaving Ashwathama alive after removing the *mani* (gem) from his forehead. In the eighth chapter, the episode of use of *brahmashtra* on the womb of Uttara by Ashwathama and inactivation of the *brahmashtra* by Lord Shri Krishna has been narrated.

In the ninth chapter, an extremely emotional description has been made of the visit of Shri Krishna and Yudhisthir to grandfather Bhishm, and prayer of Shri Krishna by Bhishm before leaving his life. In the tenth chapter departure of Shri Krishna to Dwarika and in the eleventh chapter a beautiful depiction of his welcome in Dwarika has been made. There is the description of the birth of Abhimanyu's son Parikshit in the twelfth chapter, and departure of Dhritrashtra, Gandhari, and Vidurji to the forest in the thirteenth chapter. In the fourteenth and fifteenth chapters, return of Arjun from Dwarika, and Pandava's departure to Himalaya have been described.

In the sixteenth chapter, Parikshit's conquering of world is described, and the form of *Kaliyug* has been established by the dialogue between the Earth and the Dharma. Then, in the seventeenth chapter, is the description of the suppression of *Kaliyug* by King Parikshit and, for this, the five vices namely gambling, liquor, attachment to women, violence, and gold have been identified.

In the eighteenth chapter, there are episodes of inflicting disrespect to Shameek rishi by Parikshit under the influence of Kali and subsequently invoking curse on Parikshit by Shringi muni, the son of Shameek rishi. King Parikshit had died due to this curse after seven days with the bite of a snake named Takshak. Having come to know about the curse invoked upon King Parikshit at the end of the story, Maharshi Shameek feels remorse about his son's deed; this episode expresses the very face of *rishi-muni*s where they deject lust, anger, ego, and attachment and accept forgiveness, compassion, and selflessness as the true *dharma*. In the final chapter King Parikshit goes to live at the bank of river Ganga where with the description of the arrival of Maharshi Shukdev this *skandh* ends.

2. The Second *Skandh*

Comprising ten chapters, this *skandh* in its first two chapters after establishing the hugely expanded form of

Lord Narayan and his bulk and subtle forms has described method of meditation and *krammukti* and *sadyomukti*. The description of prayer and worship of different deities for the fulfilment of desired wishes has been made in the third chapter. Supremacy of devotion to God has been established in this chapter only. In the fourth and fifth chapters there is the detail of questions asked by King Parikshit in regard to universe, and furthr, detailing the emergence of universe from the hugely expanded form (*virat roop*) of God, the beginning of the discourse by Shukdev muni has been described. The different adornments of the huge form of Shri Vishnu have been described in the sixth chapter.

The seventh chapter presents a brief introduction of different *avatars* of God. In this, contextual mythological stories of God's *avatar* namely Hari, Dattatreya, Hans, Sanakadi (Sanak, Sanandan, Sanatan, and Sanatkumar), Nar-Narayan, Dhruv, Prithu, Hayagreev, Rishabhdev, Varah, Nrisingh, Shri Ram, Dhanvantari, Parshuram etc. have been described.

What are the number, form, and sign of substance (*tatva*)? What is the ultimate reward of the practitioners of yog (*yogishwars*)? What is the spiritual procedure for worship of God? What is the shape of soul's bond and emancipation and how does it exist in its form? How does the species emerge after being lost in the nature during annihilation? The eighth chapter is full of these meaningful and spiritual questions raised by Parikshit.

The vision of God's abode by Brahmaji and the *chatushloki* (forty verses) preaching by God offered to Brahmaji have been described in the ninth chapter. The series of *prakrit sarg* along with ten distinction namely *sarg, visarg, sthan, poshan, uti, manvantar, ishanukatha, nirodh, mukti,* and *ashraya* have been described in the tenth chapter.

3. The Third *Skandh*

The third *skandh* begins with the meeting of saints Vidu and Uddhavji. Thereafter different histrionics of God have been narrated by Uddhavji in the second and third chapters. Episodes of departure of Uddhavji to Badrikashram and Vidurji to Maharshi Maitreya are presented in the fourth chapter. After that, the sequence of creation, expaded body of God and emergence of Brahmaji, God's prayer by Brahmaji, ten kinds of creations, *manvantar* etc., division of time, and expansion of universe have been explained from the fifth to twelfth chapters. The story of God's Varah avatar is described in the thirteenth chapter.

In the fourteenth chapter the horny Diti engaging into coupulation at an improper time with her husband Kashyap muni and as a result birth of demon Hiranyaksh and Hiranyakashipu is described in the seventeenth chapter. In the context of this story, due to the curse of Sanakadi munigana, the two councils of Shri Vishnu named Jai and Vijay fell from Vaikunth and took birth in the name of Hiranyaksh and Hiranyakashipu from the womb of Diti. The war between lord Varah and Hiranyaksh in the eighteenth chapter and the episode of execution of Hiranyaksh is described in the nineteenth chapter. Brahmaji has once again described the different types of creation in the twentieth chapter.

From the twenty-first to twenty-fourth chapters the story of Lord Vishnu offering boon to Kardam muni and, as a result of the boon, taking Kapil avatar from the womb of Kardam's wife Devhuti has been described. Lord Vishnu had created *Sankhya shashtra* (philosophy) in this avatar only. The deep mysteries of *Sankhya shashtra* have been explained by Kapil muni between twenty-fifth to thirty-third chapters and thus he has removed the doubts of his mother Devhuti. Thus this *skandh* ends right here.

4. The Fourth *Skandh*

The fourth *skandh* of *Shrimad Bhagwat* begins with the family details of the self-styled Manu's daughters. The mythological details of dishonour to Lord Shiv by Daksh Prajapati, Devi Sati leaving her life in Daksh's *yajna*, emergence of Virbhadra, defiling of Daksh's *yajna*, and completion of Daksh's *yajna* by Lord Shiv have been described from the second to seventh chapters. The stories related with Dhruv, the Vishnu devout, have been narrated from the eighth to thirteenth chapters. The child Dhruv's departure to jungle, realizing boon from Lord Vishnu through *tapasya*, the war between Dhruv and Yaksh (demigod), boon bestowed on Dhruv by Kuber, Dhruv's departure to *Vishnulok*, and Dhruv's ascent along with the story of King Ang have been described in it.

There is the episode of the character of King Ven in the fourteenth chapter. From the fifteenth to twenty-third chapters there is the description of the episodes of emergence of King Prithu, his crowning ceremony, prayer of Prithu by the earth, milking of the earth, *Ashwamedh yajna* organized by King Prithu, appearance of Lord Vishnu at the sanctum of King Prithu's *yajna*, arduous *tapasya* of Prithu, and his departure to the other world. The dynasty of Prithu and Lord Rudra's preaching to *pracheta*s have been described in the twenty-fourth chapter.

The reality of human life, spiritual philosophy, and the basic knowledge have been presented in this *skandh* with the help of the story of King Puranjan. Devarshi Narad had introduced this story while preaching King Prachinbahir.

The educative tale of King Puranjan is like this:

A renowned king named Puranjan lived in the ancient times. He had a friend named Avigyat. His deeds were mysterious. Still the two friends were affectionate to each other. King Puranjan was a pleasure-seeking person.

Looking for a suitable place for his abode, Puranjan sighted a town with nine gates at the southern region of the Himalaya. The town was full of prosperity with all kinds of objects of pleasure. His eyes fell on a beautiful maiden in the town, who was accompanied by ten assistants and infinite number of friends. A fierce snake which had five hoods was the protector of the town. On seeing the beautiful maiden, Puranjan swept into lust and he proposed to her for marriage. Accepting Puranjan's proposal, the maiden married him. After the wedding, Puranjan spent many years in the town and enjoyed all the materialistic pleasures.

One day, riding his five-horsed-chariot, Puranjan went on hunting with his eleventh commander-in-chief. On his return, he found that the queen was furious and was sitting in a closed room known as *kopbhawan*. He succeeded to please the queen by adopting several means and again drowned into his routine of materialistic pleasure. Thus Puranjan's youth went by.

Seeing Puranjan engaged in materialistic and sensuous pleasures, his enemies – Gandharva Chandveg and Yavanraj Bhaya – attacked his township with three hundred and sixty soldiers. The five-hooded-snake fought bravely. But at the end he was defeated. After that, all the affluence of Puranjan vanished. He lost his sanity. His pleasure and affluence depleted. Soldiers captured him by the order of Yavanraj Bhaya. Prajwar, the elder brother of Yavanraj Bhaya, consigned Puranjanpuri to flames. Subsequently Yavanraj Bhaya gave capital punishment to Puranjan.

Explaining the meaning of Puranjan's story, Devarshi Narad says in the nineteenth chapter, "Hey King! The *jeev* with body in this story is Puranjan, the *jeev's* body with nine holes has been said to be the town with nine gates, ignorance and illiteracy is the maiden inhabiting the town, ten senses are her assistants and the desires of these senses have been said to be her friends. Taking shelter into ignorance, *jeev* enjoys various materialistic pleasures through senses. *Pran, apaan, udaan, vyaan,* and *samaan* – these five life-air (*pranvayu*) are the protectors of the body like the five-hooded snake of the town. The knowledge-senses (*gyanendriyan*) are five horses of Puranjan's chariot, sin and sacrament are the two wheels, mind is rein, intelligence is charioteer, heart is the place to sit, senses are armoury, and mind is the eleventh commander-in-chief. Accepting materialism through senses is hunting. Riding this chariot-like body, *jeev* runs after insignificant materialism. The enemy Gandharva Chandveg is the speed of time, and the three hundred and sixty soldiers symbolize the three hundred and sixty days of a year which deplete one's age. Battling with them everyday, the *panch-pran jeev* embraces defeat. Prajwar, the brother of Yavanraj Bhaya, is the one who inflicts suffering through hot and cold fever and pushes man into the jaws of death."

After Puranjan's story, there is description of offering boon to *Prachetas* by Lord Narayan. After that, this *skandh* ends with the preaching of Devarshi Narad to *Prachetas*.

5. The Fifth *Skandh*

The history of such renowned kings as Priyavrat, Agneedhra, Naabhi, Rishabhdev and Bharat has been described in this *skandh*. In the context of depicting the story of Bharat, his birth in the *yoni* of a deer, then his birth in the Brahmin's *yoni* by the glorious sacredness of river Gandak, and resolving of the doubts of King Rahugan followed by offering him spiritual discourse have been described. After that, introduction of Bharat dynasty and *bhuvankosh* have been described. Descend of holy Ganga and prayer of Lord Sankarshan created by Rudradev have been described in the seventeenth chapter.

The mythological geographical position of Bharatvarsh (India), six islands, and mountains of all the *loks* have been described from the eighteenth to twentieth chapters. The chariot of Sun and its speed is in the twenty-first chapter, and position of various planets and their speed have been described in the twenty-second chapter. After this, the *Shishumar* cycle has been established.

Describing about the *Shishumar* cycle (solar system) it has been said in the *Puran* that *Shishumar* (marine creatures specifically) are coiled up with their face pointing downwards. The pole is situated at the end of its tail. Prajapati, *Agni* (the god of fire), Indra, and *Dharma* are present in the middle region of the tail. *Dhata* and *Vidhata* are seated in the root of the tail. It has *Saptrishi* around its waist. This *Shishumar* is shrinked and coiled up in the right side. The fourteen *Nakshatra* (from Abhijit to Punarvasu) of *Uttarayan* at its right side and the fourteen *Nakshatra* (from Pushya to Uttarashara) of *Dakshinayan* are situated at its left side. Agastya at its upper chin, *Yam* (the god of death) at lower chin, *Mangal* (Mars) in the mouth, *Shani* (Saturn) at the loin, Sun at the chest, Jupitar at the Aquarius, Vishnu in the heart, Moon in the mind, Venus in the navel, Ashwini Kumar in the breasts, Mercury in the *pran* and *apan*, Rahu in the throat, Ketu all over the body, and the entire constellation are situated in the pores. The *Shishumar* cycle has been said to be Lord Vishnu's embodiment of Ved. It is considered very important from the Astrology's point of view. Finally, describing about different hells this *skandh* has been concluded.

6. The Sixth *Skandh*

This *skandh* begins with the story of Ajamil. In this, there is story of an unscrupulous Brahmin living in Kanyakubj (Kannauj) named Ajamil, who despite committing sin throughout his life proves his right over Vaikunth because of calling Narayan, his son at the time of his death. The glory of the name of God has been established with this episode. After that, the story of God offering boon to Daksh, and Daksh invoking curse on Devarshi Narad is described. Subsequently descent of Daksh's daughters have been described. Devguru Brihaspati repudiating the gods and gods appointing Vishwaroop as their *devguru* has been described in the seventh chapter. The extraordinary Narayan chest-shield *(kavach)* of Lord Vishnu has been described about in the eighth chapter, which was provided to gods by Vishwaroop as a result of which gods had defeated demons in the battle of *Devasur*.

The famous stories of execution of Vishwaroop by Devraj Indra, emergence of Vritasur and defeat of gods by Vritasur, making of *Vajra* by gods with the bones of Dadhichi muni, and execution of Vritasur have been described from the ninth through twelfth chapters. After that, describing the account of the previous birth of Vritasur, there is mention of the curse invoked on king Chitraketu by Goddess Parwati. In the eighteenth chapter, there is detailed description of the progenies of Aditi and Diti and the emergence of Marudagna.

The nineteenth chapter of this *skandh* is very important and useful to public due to the detailed procedure of *Punsvan vrat*. A son with supreme qualities is born to those who observe this wish-fulfilling *vrat* methodically. With the consent of Maharshi Kashyap, Diti was the first to observe this *vrat* with a wish to have a son capable to assassinate Indra.

Beginning in the *Shukla paksh* (phase) of the month *Margshirsh*, women generally undertake this *vrat* with the consent of their husbands. In this, Lakshmi-Narayan is worshipped with a special *prasad* and *Agni* (the god of fire) is offered twelve consignments. This process goes on for 12 months and women observe fast on the last day of the month of *Kartik*. The next day the special *prasad*, prepared under the guidelines of the cooking rules, is given to the woman, which brings the desired result to her.

This *vrat* is very dear to Lord Vishnu. They achieve the desired objects who complete this *Punsvan vrat* methodically. The women who observe this *vrat* earn luck, affluence, wealth, progeny, fame etc. Besides, her husband lives longer. The men who chant it during post-funeral rites, their forefathers and deities provide them desired results.

7. The Seventh *Skandh*

The story of curse invoked on councillors of Lord Vishnu named Jai-Vijay, as told by Devarshi Narad against a query by King Yudhishthir, has been narrated in brief in the beginning of this *skandh*. After that, the story of demon Hiranyakashipu and his son Prahlad, the Vishnu devout, has been narrated from the second to seventh chapters. The episode of the emergence of Lord Nrisingh and execution of demon Hiranyakashipu is detailed in the eighth chapter. The extremely noble story of gutting Tripur by Mahadev with the blessing of Lord Shri Vishnu has been described in the tenth chapter.

In the following chapters *manav dharma*, *varna dharma*, *stree dharma*, *ashram dharma*, *yati dharma*, *moksha dharma*, and domestic etiquettes have been established. In the thirteenth chapter of this *skandh* the tastelessness of materialistic pleasure and the process of engaging and disengaging oneself from deeds have been established by means of dialogue between *Avadhoot* Lord Dattatreyaji and Prahlad. Therefore this chapter has been called very important and educative from the point of view of spirituality.

Dattatreyaji says in it, "*Jeev* has to wander in different *yoni*s due to addiction to materialistic pleasures. The deeds that man do for attaining material pleasure put him in the illusory bond of the cycle of life and death. Thus, although they do something for attaining happiness and ending their sorrow, yet they receive the opposite result of it. They fall into deeper misery."

8. The Eighth *Skandh*

The four *manvantar*s namely *swayambhoo*, *swarochish*, *auttam*, and *tamas* and various histrionics performed by Lord Vishnu during these *manvantar*s have been introduced in brief at the beginning of this *Skandh*. The story of an elephant being caught by an alligator and his salvation by Lord Vishnu on his pitiful call has been narrated from the second to fourth chapters. After this there is description of the famous mythological stories of the churning of ocean, drinking of poison by Lord Shiv, emergence of nectar, and distribution of the nectar among gods by Shri Vishnu taking Mohini *avatar*. After that, *devasur* (gods and demons) battle and Lord Shiv's attraction towards the beauty of Mohini have been described. After that the responsibilities of Manu etc have been enumerated.

The episodes of demon king Bali's victory over paradise, Lord Vishnu in his Vaman avatar demanding three steps of land from Bali in donation, and Bali moving to *Patal* (the world under the earth) have been described. Finally this *skandh* has been concluded describing Lord Vishnu's fish *avatar*.

9. The Ninth *Skandh*

Vanshanucharit (documentation of succession) is an important distinction of *Purans*. Whether *Purans* have five distinctions or ten, the description of *Vanshanucharit* is a must in them all. Like other *Purans*, mythological dynasties have also been described in this *skandh* of *Shrimad Bhagwat*. First of all there is detail of Vaivaswat Manu and descent of his five sons. After that the brilliant royal dynasties of Ikshwaku, Nimi, Chandra, Sharyati, Raji, Bharat, Panchal, Kaurav, Puru, Magadh, Yadu, Anu, Magadh, Turvasu, and Vidarbh have been described.

Introducing *Vanshanucharit*, numerous mythological stories have been described which are related with Sudyumn, Maharshi Chyavan, Ambareesh, Saubhari Muni, Parshuram, Pururava, Trishanku, Harishchandra, Rantidev, Sagar, Bhagirath, Saudas, Shri Ram, Yayati, Dushyant, and Jarasandh.

10. The Tenth *Skandh*

Along with being a very important section, the tenth *skandh* is the base of this *Puran*. Comprising 90 chapters, this *skandh* is the longest *skandh* of this *Puran*. The histrionics related with Shri Krishna *avatar* of Lord Vishnu have been described in it. All the mythological incidences from birth of Lord Shri Krishna to his departure to *Golok* have been compiled in it.

The author of this *Puran* has divided this *skandh* in two parts – namely first half and second half – in order to present the character of Shri Krishna in a systematic manner.

First of all, in the first half, there are episodes of the wedding of King Vasudev of Yadu dynasty and Devaki, their incarceration by Kans, and assassination of Devaki's six sons. After that there are episodes of entering of Sheshji in Devaki's womb as her seventh child, his removal from Devaki's womb and planting him in the womb of Rohini executed by Yogmaya on the command of Lord Vishnu and planting herself in the womb of Yashoda, the wife of Nandbaba at Gokul. After that, there is episode of Lord Vishnu planting his fraction in the womb of Devaki and his prayer rendered by Shiv, Brahma, Indra and other gods. The intriguing gist of spiritualism has been presented in this prayer by means of nature like tree and God like bird.

In the third chapter, there is story of the *avatar* of Lord Shri Krishna on the eighth day of the month of *Bhadrapad* during *Krishna paksh* in the *Rohini Nakshatra*. After his birth, God appears in his real form and recalls the previous birth of Vasudev and Devaki. In the previous birth, Vasudev was a *Prajapati* named Sutapa and Devaki was his wife named Prishni. Having undergone arduous *tapasya*, they had asked from Lord Vishnu to give them a son like him. Since there is no one else like Lord Vishnu, therefore he took *avatar* in their house in the name of Prishnigarbha. Then Sutapa and Prishni became Kashyap and Aditi respectively in their next birth. Lord Vishnu was born from the womb of Aditi that time with the name of Upendra. His body was very small in this *avatar*, and hence he became famous as Vaman.

In this chapter, there are episodes of Vasudev leaving Shri Krishna at Yashoda's place and bringing her daughter to Mathura.

The episode of Yogmaya going into the sky escaping from the evil Kans's hand and assuming the form of goddess with eight hands and making a forecast is described in the fourth chapter. An extremely delightful description has been made of the birth ceremony of Lord Shri Krishna at Gokul in the fifth chapter.

The childhood playful acts (*lila*) of Lord Shri Krishna begin from the sixth chapter. There is the story of the execution of demoness Putana by Shri Krishna in this chapter. The stories of the salvation of Shakatbhanjan and Trinavart are narrated in the seventh chapter.

In the eighth chapter there is investiture of the nomenclature of Lord Shri Krishna and Balram by Gargacharya, the family *guru* of the Yadu clan. During the naming ceremony, Gargacharyaji says, "Hey Nand! This dark complexioned son of yours assumes a physical form in every *yug*. In the previous *yugs* he had accepted three colours – white, sanguine, and yellow respectively. He has born dark in this birth. Therefore hey Nand! His name will be Krishna. This child was earlier born with Vasudevji, hence those aware of this secret would also call him 'Shriman Vasudev'. Enemy will never be able to win those who love him.

After that there is beautiful description of the histrionics of Shri Krishna stealing butter, eating earth, and Yashoda looking at the universe in his mouth.

The stories of Yashoda tying Shri Krishna with *ukhal* (stub), Devarshi Narad invoking curse on Nalkubar and Manigriv, and their salvation by Shri Krishna, tied with *ukhal*, are described in the ninth and tenth chapters.

There is context of the departure of Shri Krishna to Vrindavan and salvation of Vatsasur and Vakasur in the eleventh chapter. The story of demon Aghasur is narrated in the twelfth chapter. In the thirteenth and fourteenth chapters, there is story of disappearance of the *gwal-bal* along with cows by illusioned Brahmaji and therafter Shri Krishna playing histrionics for one year by transforming himself into *gwal-bal* and cows.

The histrionics of the salvation of Dhenukasur and crushing the inflated ego of the Kalia snake by Lord Shri Krishna have been described in the fifteenth and sixteenth chapters. Thereafter there is the incident of the salvation of demon Pralambasur by Balramji and swallowing of *dawanal* (the jungle fire) by Shri Krishna to save the residents of Braj. Narrating the rainy and winter season, extraordinary illustration of the beauty of Vrindavan has been made in the twentieth chapter.

In the twenty-first chapter, describing the sweet ripples of sound from Lord Shri Krishna's flute, it has been said that the flute sound of Shri Krishna was enough to infuse love for God and produced longing to meet him. *Gopis'* hearts filled with love on listening to it and seeing their darling Shri Krishna, they were swept away in the sweet notes of the flute.

The histrionics of stealing the clothes of *gopis* has been described in the twenty-second chapter. The description of Shri Krishna becoming benign on the wives of Brahmins, offering solution to Indra's *yajna*, lifting mountain Govardhan for protecting the people of Braj, Nand informing *gopis* about the might of Lord Shri Krishna, and felicitation of Shri Krishna by *Devraj* Indra and Kaamdhenu has been made from the twenty-third to twenty-seventh chapters.

After that Nand being captured by Varun and bringing him back from the *Varunlok* by Shri Krishna has been detailed.

In the twenty-ninth chapter, an extremely delighting *raslila* of Lord Shri Krishna has been narrated. On floating the sweet note from the flute by Lord Shri Krishna, the eagerness to meet Shri Krishna among *gopis* has been presented with great emotions. The episode of *gopis* meeting their darling Shri Krishna suspending all their work expresses the principle of giving everything to God by the devotee. After this, Lord Shri Krishna has established various forms of love from the point of view of spirituality. The *maharas* enacted between Shri Krishna and *gopis* at the holy bank of river Yamuna has been described in the thirty-third chapter. This chapter presents the amorous face of Lord Shri Krishna.

After that the episode of the salvation of erudite Sudarshan and the councillor of Kuber named Shankhchood has been narrated. The chorus song sung by *gopis* is described in the thirty-fifth chapter. Therafter, there are stories of the salvation of demon Arishtasur, Devarshi Narad revealing to Kans the secret of the birth of Krishna, and Kans sending Akroor to Braj. In the thirty-seventh chapter the salvation of Keshi and

Vyomasur by Shri Krishna and the prayer of Shri Krishna by Devarshi Narad have been described.

After this there are episodes of the departure to Mathura of Shri Krishna and Balram along with Akroorji, blessings on gardeners Kubja and Sudama, breaking of the bow of Shiv, salvation of the elephant named Kuvalayapi, warrior like Charur etc. with the evil Kans.

In the forty-fifth chapter, there are episodes of *yagyopavit* (baptism) of Lord Shri Krishna and Balram, going to Ujjain to Saandipani muni for studies, and the salvation of demon Panchjan. After that there is description of Uddhav's journey to Braj at the command of Shri Krishna and presentation of *bhramar* song by *gopis* before him. Thereafter the first half of the tenth *skandh* concludes with Shri Krishna felicitating Kubja and Akroorji and sending Akroorji to Hastinapur to know the well-being of Pandavas.

The second half of the tenth *skandh* begins with the story of king of Magadh, Jarasandh attacking Mathura, his defeat by Shri Krishna and release alive, and construction of Dwarika. After that comes the story of Kalyavan turning to ash and King Muchukund of Ikshwaku dynasty.

In the fifty-second chapter there are episodes of the marriage of Balram and Rewati, and Rukmini sending marriage proposal to Shri Krishna. After that there are episodes of Shri Krishna kidnapping Rukmini, leaving Rukmi alive after defeating Shishupal and other evil kings, and celebrating marriage with Rukmini at Dwarika.

In the fifty-fifth chapter, there is description of birth of brave Pradyumn from the womb of Rukmini, his kidnapping by Shambarasur, and execution of Shambarasur. Thereafter is the story of *Syamantak mani* (gem) and, there is episode of marriage of Shri Krishna with Jambvati, the daughter of Jambvat and Satyabhama, the daughter of Satrajit. Thereafter there is story of the theft of Syamantak and the salvation of Shatdhanva by Shri Krishna.

Message of the Purans

The marriages of Shri Krishna have been briefly introduced in the fifty-eighth chapter. Then the execution of Bhaumasur, the son of earth and Shri Krishna's marriage with sixteen thousand princesses have been described. In this context, there is detail of Shri Krishna bringing in the divine tree of *Kalp* to fulfil the wish of Satyabhama. Thereafter there is description of the progenies of Lord Shri Krishna, meeting of Usha and Aniruddh, the battle between Shri Krishna and Banasur, and the salvation of King Nrig. After that there are the episodes of the salvation of Paundrik, *Kashinaresh*, and Dwivid Vanar and the marriage of Samblakshmana.

Description of the organization of *Aswamedh-yajna* by Pandavas, the salvation of Jarasandh and Shishupal, the king of Chedi, and the grand worship of Lord Shri Krishna has been made from the 71st to 75th chapters. The episodes of the execution of Shalva, Dantvaktra, Vidurath, and Balval are present from the 76th to 79th chapters.

The story of Lord Shri Krishna's friend Sudama has been described in the 80th and 81st chapters. While, this story represents the pure feelings of devotee and his deep reverence for the God, it also shows the affection of Lord Shri Krishna for devotees. Thereafter are the stories of Shri Krishna preaching the *brahmgyan* (the divine knowledge) to his father Vasudev, and arranging for his mother Devaki the visit to her six dead sons.

In the 86th chapter there are episodes of kidnapping of Subhadra, and Shri Krishna visiting Janak, the king of Mithila, and the Brahmin named Shrutdev at the same time. In the 87th chapter God's bodily form has been hailed through Shrutis by the means of dialogue between Devarshi Narad and Lord Narayan.

In the 88th chapter there is description of the execution of Vrikasur by Lord Vishnu and thereby saving the life of Lord Shiv. Thereafter are the episodes of examination of the trinity by Maharshi Bhrigu and resurrection of the dead son of the Brahmin by Lord Shri Krishna. With the detail of the of Lord Shri Krishna's excursion, the last chapter and this *skandh* come to end.

11. The Eleventh *Skandh*

A very brief introduction of the battle of *Mahabharat* has been given in the first chapter of this *skandh*. Thereafter is the description of the curse of *Yaduvansh*'s destruction invoked by *rishi-muni*s angered by the misdemeanour of *Yaduvanshi* princes. Telling Vasudev the dialogue between King Nimi and nine *yogishwar*s, Naradji has established in the second and third chapters the illusion (*maya*), way to get rid of the illusion, and *Brahm* and *Karma yog*. Histrionic *avatars* of the God have been briefly described in the fourth chapter. After this, the end of those men who are devoid of devotion, and the method of the God's worship have been described.

There is description of various *guru*s and the education obtained from them by Lord Shri Krishna through *avadhutopakhyan* which has been described from the 7th to 9th chapters. Some important *guru*s and the education related with them are as under:

Guru	Education and Knowledge Acquired
Earth (Prithvi)	: Man commits numerous misdeeds on the earth but it neither takes revenge nor cries under grief. Therefore we should learn the lesson of patience and forgiveness from the earth. It is required of man never to lose patience and also never to be furious.
Air of Life (*Pranvayu*)	: *Pranvayu* teaches that as it desires meal and gets satisfied on having it, similarly the goal-seeker should only take so much materialistic pleasure as would not disturb his mind and would not spoil his intelligence.

Space (*Akash*)	: Like the space remains untouched and undivided by fire, rain, crop of grain or its destruction, similarly man should consider soul as indivisible and isolated.
Water *(Jal)*	: Water is inherently clean, sweet, and pure. People become sacred merely by visiting Ganga and such pilgrim spots, touching and uttering their names. Therefore the goal-seeker should take the lesson from the water of being pure, clean, sweet in speech, and beneficial for the society so that the one who visit, touch or take his name become sacred.
Fire *(Agni)*	: As the fire does not get influenced in spite of eating everything, likewise the goal-seeker should keep his senses under control while enjoying any kind of materialistic pleasure. He should not acquire the evils.
Ocean *(Samudra)*	: One gets education from the ocean that the goal-seeker should always remain happy and serious. The goal-seeker should be peaceful like an ocean without tides and waves.
Moon *(Chandrama)*	: Moon always remains static though its crescent grows and recedes due to the influence of time. Likewise, from birth to death, all the stages belong to body; it has no relation with the soul. Only the body perishes; the soul always remains static.
Sun *(Soorya)*	: As sun evaporates water and rains the same at due time, similarly the goal-seeker should enjoy the materialistic pleasure but should desert it when the time comes.

Pigeon (*Kapot*)	: A pigeon lived with his family in a jungle. A hunter caught his family in a net when he had gone to fetch grain. Seeing this, that silly pigeon became very sad and, due to attachment with his family, jumped into the very net himself. This fable educates that he, who gets added to family and material objects, never gets peace. Like the pigeon, he suffers with his family.
Python (*Ajgar*)	: The persevering person should not make effort for meals, like a python does not make any effort despite having no meals and lies hungry for many days. One should live life eating whatever comes by unasked for.
Wasp (*Patanga*)	: A wasp is attracted to the fire and dies being burnt. Similarly the man who cannot control his senses is attracted to women and falls into the darkness of ignorance and is destroyed like the wasp.
Honeybee (*Madhumakhi*)	: The honeybee teaches that a persevering person should not accumulate alms for the evening or, for that matter, for the next day.
Elephant (*Gaj*)	: The hunter uses a wooden female-elephant to catch an elephant. While trying to touch it, the elephant is caught by the hunters. Similarly a saint should not touch a woman even made of wood. Otherwise he perishes.
Snake (*Sarp*)	: A persevering person should wander alone like a snake. He should not make a family or relation.

Honey-collector *(Madhuharta)*	: Honey-collector teaches that as he steals the honey accumulated by honeybee, similarly some other man enjoys the wealth of those men who do not use or donate their accumulated wealth.
Deer *(Mruga)*	: Deer teaches that a saint should never listen to the sensuous songs. Otherwise as. deer falls prey due to being attracted to the hunter's song, likewise a persevering person falls into the bondage of materialism by listening to sensuous songs.
Child *(Balak)*	: A persevering person should not bother about his respect or disrespect; this is the teaching one gets from a child. One should remain engaged in one's own soul like a child.
Fish *(Meen)*	: Like a fish loses her life in the greed of a piece of a flesh attached with a hook, similarly the man who is greedy for taste embraces many sufferings. Therefore a persevering person should keep his sense of taste in check.
Prostitute *(Pingala-Veshya)*	: There lived a prostitute named Pingala in the city of Mithila. She was very beautiful. One day she was waiting at her door for some rich man to come. Thus the midnight passed by. At last she lost hope and went to sleep. This story preaches that hope is the worst sorrow and hopelessness is the best happiness.
Kurari (Bird of prey)	: Once a Kurari bird had a piece of flesh. At that time another bird attacked her with its beak to snatch the piece of flesh.

Message of the Purans

Finally he got solace when he threw the piece below. This story preaches that a devotee should not go for undue accumulation, otherwise he suffers like the Kurari bird.

Maiden girl *(Mumari Kanya)* : Once some guests came to the house of a young girl. Her family members had gone somewhere. Therefore, to prepare meal, she began to beat paddy at an isolated place. As a result the bangles of her hands began making sound at high pitch. Acknowledging that the guests would come to know that she herself was beating the paddy, she broke her bangle leaving just two in each hand. But even they started making sound. Then she broke one more bangle from each hand. With just one bangle in each hand, finally there was no noise. Similarly when two persons live together, there always is some friction. Therefore a persevering person should always wander alone.

Maker of bow-arrow *(Baannirmatha)* : Once a bow-arrow maker was so busy in making bow-arrow that he remained unaware of the king's procession that passed by sounding drums and instruments. In the same way a persevering person should control his mind by concentration, practice, and detachment.

Spider *(Makali)* : Spider weaves web according to her desire and wanders in it and does not get entangled. Similarly, despite living in the illusory world, man should not be trapped into it.

Message of the Purans

Hornet *(Tataiya)* : *Tataiya* captures *illi* (caterpillar) and imprisons it in her hole and then lays egg on it. In her imprisonment, *illi* adopts her shape just by contemplating about it. In the same way a person becomes the same by which thought – say fear, love, envy, hatred – he contemplates someone. Therefore a persevering person should only contemplate God to meet him.

Lord Shri Krishna in the 10th chapter has established the tastelessness of physical and metaphysical joys. Explaining the oneness of soul and the supreme-soul, Shri Krishna says, "The oneness of soul cannot be realized until *jeev* resorts to the ego of 'I' and 'my'. *Jeev* lives under the influence of *kaal* (time) and deed in absence of this realization. The soul is recognized by various names as *kaal, jeev,* nature (*swabhav*), *dharma* etc. due to lending false pride in the body arisen out of ignorance. Therefore one should experience the oneness of soul. The truth is that there is nothing other than me."

The description of the sign of bonded, freed, and devoted, glory of interaction with seers (*satsang*), the method to do away with deeds, discourse delivered by swan-like God to Sanakadi *munigana,* glory of *Bhaktiyog*, method of meditation, and various *siddhi*s (accomplishments), and their names and signs have been made in the 11th to 15th chapters.

From the 16th to 28th chapters achievements of God, *varnasram-dharma,* means of devotion (*bhakti*), knowledge (*gyan*), and regular routine and rules (*yam-niyam*), *gyanyog, karmayog, bhaktiyog,* the shapes and secrets of the order of virtues and vices, *sankhyayog, kriyayog,* elements, and the symptoms of three virtues have been enumerated.

Establishing the *Bhagwat dharma* in the 29th chapter, Lord Shri Krishna says, "Devotees are supposed to do all the deeds for me and gradually increase their practice to remember me. With this, in a few days, their mind and soul will be surrendered to me. They should live at those sacred places where saints live and should follow the actions of my dedicated devouts – be it god, demon, or human. A devotee is supposed to see me in all the living beings and substances of the universe because I am soul and am placed in everyone equally. The person who does so and looks upon all with equal feeling is truly called the supremely learned (*param gyani*). Envy, malignity, dejection, ego, anger, and competition are removed from the mind of a persevering person by this way. 'I am great and he is bad', persevering person should reject such feelings besides the feeling of social cowardice. As long as he does not experience such divine feeling, he should continue my worship through mind, voice, and resolutions and actions of body. When the *brahm*-knowledge is practised in this way, he achieves the knowledge in a few days and he witnesses everything as a form of Brahm. His entire doubts end and he witnesses me and thus realizes me. This discourse of mine is very sacred. The devotee who would read it for others everyday, all of his sins will be destroyed. The devotee who will listen it everyday will become free from the bondage of deeds and will realize me." After this, there is description of Uddhavji's departure to Badrikashram.

Thereafter the episodes of destruction of *Yaduvansh* in the *prabhas* region, departure of Balramji to his *lok,* targeting an arrow on his feet misunderstanding Shri Krishna for a deer by a hunter named Jara, and departure of Jara to heaven by the blessings of Shri Krishna have been described in the 30th chapter.

Very beautiful and grand illustration of the daparture of Shri Krishna to his abode has been made in the 31st chapter. Subsequently with the brief description of Arjun's departure to Indraprashtha along with remaining people of Dwarika and submerging of Dwarika under water by the ocean, this *skandh* comes to an end.

Message of the Purans

12. The Twelfth *Skandh*

This *skandh* begins with the description of the royal families of *Kaliyug*. Narrating the *dharma* of *Kaliyug*, Shukdevji says, "As the *Kaliyug* would appear on this earth, so would diappear *dharma*, truthfulness, holiness, forgiveness, compassion, life, power, and memory from here. He would be considered, elite, noble, and sacred who will have money in this *yug*. He, who will have power with him, will change the *dharma* and justise in his favour. Family, virtues, ability etc. will have no importance. The Brahmin will be recognized by *yagyopavit* (baptism) and not by his virtue and nature. *Brahmchari* and saints will be recognized by stick, pail (*kamandalu*), and clothes. People will practise *dharma* only for earning fame. The wicked people will rule the earth. Kings would be cruel and greedy. There will be no difference between them and robbers. Stealing, lying, violence and other evils will increase among men. Listening, hymning, meditation, and prayer to the appearance, virtues, name, and histrionics are the only ways to save from the evils of *Kaliyug*. Destroying all the sins, he makes them supremely sacred in this way."

The glory of hymning the name to save from the evils of *Kaliyug* has been mentioned in the third chapter. The four kinds of annihilations have been described in the fourth chapter. After this, there is narration of the ultimate end of Janmejaya, Janmejaya's (snake)-*yajna*, and the difference of the branches of *Vedas*.

The branches of *Atharvaved* and the distinction of *Purans* have been clarified in the seventh chapter. The stories of the *tapasya* of Maharshi Markandeya, offering him vision by Nar-Narayan, and offering of boon to Markandeya muni by Lord Shiv have been described from the eighth to ninth chapters.

There is description of the armours of the God, and that of twelfth *Suryagana* in the eleventh chapter. This *skandh* has been concluded with the counting of *Puran's* verses and description of the glory of *Shrimad Bhagwat*.

The Glory of *Shrimad Bhagwat*

This section has been narrated after the twelfth *skandh* to glorify *Shrimad Bhagwat*. The secret of Shri Krishna's histrionics narrated by Shandilya muni and the glory of the land of Braj have been described. After that there is description of the dialogue between Yamuna and the wives of Shri Krishna, Uddhavji's appearance during the celebration of hymns, the glory and tradition of *Shrimad Bhagwat*, the realization of the abode of God to the listeners of *Bhagwat*.

This *puran* ends with establishing the form, identity, sign of listener and orator, method of reading and listening and its importance of *Shrimad Bhagwat*.

Story from *Shrimad Bhagwat Puran* : Freedom from the Yoni of Ghost

It is a story of the ancient times – there was situated a beautiful town at the bank of Tungbhadra. Its citizens were religious and engaged always in noble deeds. A Brahmin named Atmadev lived in the town. He keenly observed *dharma*, and good conduct and was kind by nature. He was respected by all due to practising *dharma* regularly.

His marriage was solemnized with a beautiful girl named Dhundhuli who belonged to an elite family. But opposite to her great beauty, she was contumacious, cruel, envious, greedy, and evil natured. Her behaviour was rude and pugnacious. In spite of that, the life of Atmadev and Dhundhuli was passing peacefully. Several years passed by thus. But they did not get the joy of progeny. They performed various sacred deeds but their desire remained unfulfilled. Hence Atmadev started living in grief.

One day, the aggrieved Atmadev set off from home with determination to die. He sat for a few moments by a pond, sighting it on the way. At that time, a saint came there. His face was as radiant as sun.

Seeing Atmadev in grief, he went to him and said, "Son!

What are you doing in this jungle? What is your woe that your body has weakened so much? Tell me without hesitation, son."

Atmadev experienced supreme peace and happiness on hearing the compassionate words of the saint. He caught the feet of the brilliant saint and explained in sad voice his story about being childless.

The saint was very kind and a master of *yog*. His heart flooded with compassion on hearing Atmadev's story. He said after gazing at the lines on his forehead for a few moments, "Son! You should leave the idea of having a child. You cannot have a child by virtue of your past deeds. Therefore concentrate your mind on the devotion to God leaving the worldly attachment and illusion. This would secure happiness for you in *lok* and *parlok* (the other world)."

But Atmadev was determined on his resolve. At last the saint gave in before his determination. He offered him a divine fruit and asked to feed it to his wife. Then he went away from there. Atmadev gave the divine fruit to his wife Dhundhuli to eat.

'I would become pregnant by eating this fruit and my health would deteriorate. Further it is beyond my capacity to follow the rules till the child is born. A woman with child always carries the worry of nursing the child. Infertility of woman is a more comfortable option. I will not eat this fruit.' With this thought Dhundhuli kept the fruit in hiding and informed Atmadev that she has eaten the fruit.

One day, Dhundhuli's sister Mriduli came to meet her. Dhundhuli narrated her the whole detail. Mriduli counselled her, "Do not worry, sister! I am pregnant at present. I will hand over my child to you. Until then you carry on pretending to be pregnant. We would devise some method so that everyone would believe that my child died soon after birth. After that I would visit you everyday to nurse the child. Now you feed this fruit to some cow without delay so that your husband could not get even an inkling of this plan.

Accepting Mriduli's advice, Dhundhuli fed the fruit to a cow and started pretending to be pregnant.

After some time Mriduli gave birth to a child. Immediately, with the help of her husband, Mriduli sent the child at Dhundhuli's house and spread the news in her neighbourhood that her son died after birth.

On this side, after receiving the child, Dhundhuli gave the news of the birth of child to her husband Atmadev. Coming to know about the birth of his son, Atmadev became overwhelmed with joy and started donating grain and money among beggars.

Seeing her husband extremely happy one day, Dhundhuli said lovingly, "Master! How can I foster this child, as I am too weak? My sister gave birth to a child but it died soon after birth. Hence, if you deem fit, send for her to stay here. She can nurse our child better. This will also alleviate her grief." Atmadev went himself and brought Mriduli to his home for nursing his son. The child was named Dhundhukari based on the name of Dhundhuli.

On the other side, the cow, which was fed the fruit by Dhundhuli, by grace of god, gave birth to a human-like child after three months. The boy was very beautiful, divinely radiant, and fair skinned. Atmadev became very happy seeing him. The ears of the child were like that of cow; hence Atmadev named him Gokaran.

When both the children grew up, Atmadev sent them to *gurukul* (school). Soon, Gokaran became supremely learned after acquiring the learnings of *Vedas* and scriptures but Dhundhukari remained illiterate for not paying due attention towards studies. He totally lacked characteristics suitable to a Brahmin. Anger always reigned his head. Gathering unworthy objects, stealing, create differences among people, and inflicting harm on the weak and sufferers were his cherished acts. Donning weapon, he used to wander for hunting. He paid no attention to prayer and worship. He considered it a petty and trifle job. By and by he fell in the trap of prostitutes.

Message of the Purans

His addiction destroyed Atmadev's entire prestige and property. Seeing this Atmadev became grief-stricken.

Then, offering the discourse of detachment, Gokaran said, "Respected Father! This entire world is meant to trap the living beings in the ocean of grief and whirlpool of attachment. Son, wife, money – all these are the bond of attachment and whoever falls into the trap of these bondages suffers with many sorrows. Man under its influence always burns in the devastating fire of grief. *Muni*s are the only ones who achieve happiness. Therefore you too leave the ignorance of attachment. Ensnared in such attachment, man has to go in a horrible hell. The body, after death, disintegrates into five elements and the soul alone survives. Therefore go to the jungle leaving the illusion and attachment behind and free yourself from the cycle of life and death through devotion to God."

Atmadev's eyes of wisdom opened on listening to Gokaran. A divine light spread in his inner self. Delightfully, he said, "Son! I was so dimwit and ignorant; how come I remained trapped in the bondage of illusion and attachment for so long! The human body is merely an illusion. You have salvaged me today by ending my darkness of ignorance. I am ready to depart for the forest this very moment. But tell me in detail what I will have to do there."

Gokaran said, "Father! This body is made of five elements. Stop looking at it as 'I'. Think of the world as momentary and not permanent. Turning away from all kinds of materialistic joy, dedicate yourself in the devotion of *parbrahm* Lord Shri Krishna."

Thus Gokaran provided Atmadev with the wisdom of detachment (*vairagya*). Atmadev went to the forest and began praying and worshipping Lord Shri Krishna in order to secure his blessings. At last he realized the abode of Lord Shri Krishna due to chanting Shrimad Bagwat regularly.

After the departure of his father Atmadev to the forest, Dhundhukari became absolutely free and his misdeeds increased day by day. He started intimidating Dhundhuli for money. Panicked by his misdeeds, Dhundhuli finally jumped into a well and died. After the death of mother and father, Gokaran set off for pilgrimage. Now, Dhundhukari began to live with prostitutes. His intelligence was spoiled in the worry of arranging the objects for pleasure. He started committing crimes.

Once he executed a theft in the royal palace. Then the prostitutes thought, "This man steals everyday. Today he has made a theft in the palace. We will also be punished if he would be caught. Hence taking all the money after killing him, we should move away. Nobody will come to know about this."

With this thought, they tied Dhundhukari when he was asleep and beagn strangulating him. When he did not die with this, they threw burning coal on his face. Dhundhukari died struggling in the flame of fire. They buried him in a pit. Due to his misdeeds, Dhundhukari became a ghost and started wandering there.

One day Gokaran visited his town and went to his house to sleep during night. Seeing him there, Dhundhukari, donning a dreadful appearance, began frightening him. Gokaran was quick to understand that this was some degraded *jeev*. Thinking so, he asked the ghost to give his introduction.

When Gokaran asked with great affection, the ghost said in tears, "I am your brother Dhundhukari. I had ruined my Brahminhood through my misdeeds. The women whom I loved the most tortured me to death. Since then I am repenting by roaming in this ghost *yoni*. Brother! You are very kind, *tapaswi, yogi,* and learned person. You alone can free me from this *yoni* through your divine powers (*tapobal*). Have mercy on me. Make me free."

Then Gokaran assured Dhundhukari to free him from the ghost-*yoni*. Dhundhukari went away happily. Hither Gokaran remained pensive on this matter for the whole night. But he could not devise any remedy. Having heard the news of his arrival, many learned and knowledgeable persons came to see him in the morning. Gokaran told them in detail about the incidence occurred during night and inquired about a solution. They fathomed through *Vedas* and scriptures but could not find a remedy to his freedom. Finally, Gokaran decided to put his inquiry before lord Sun.

Gokaran said humbly to Lord Sun, "Accept reverence of this trifle in your feet. Lord! You remove the darkness of this world with the light of your rays. O abode of compassion! Now you please tell the solution of freedom of Dhundhukari and salvage him from darkness, O god."

Then Lord Sun said, "Son! Your brother's freedom is possible through listening to *Shrimad Bhagwad Puran* only, hence you listen to it for a week. This would benefit other living beings as well along with Dhundhukari."

Gokaran agreed upon discoursing *Shrimad Bhagwat* for the salvation of Dhundhukari and the benefit of other living beings. Many people from nearby villages, towns and states began to assemble there on hearing the news of oration of *Bhagwat-katha*. Soon a huge crowd congregated there. When Gokaran placed himself on the seat of *guru* to deliver the *katha* (discourse), Dhundhukari also came there and began searching for a place to sit. Then he noticed seven bamboos supported in the earth. He sat into one of the bamboos and started listening to the discourse.

Gokaran started discourse (*katha*) of *Shrimad Bhagwat*. When the discourse came to halt in the evening, one bamboo burst open making a loud noise. Another bamboo burst open on the evening of the next day. Thus all the seven bamboos burst open by the end of the *katha*. Due to listening the holy *katha* of *Shrimad Bhagwat*, Dhundhukari got freedom from the ghost-*yoni* and appeared before everyone in a divine form. His body was adorned with divine radiance, clothes, ornaments, and crown. At that time a divine plane descended there with the councillors of Lord Shri Krishna.

The councillors boarded Dhundhukari on the plane. Seeing this Gokaran asked in surprise, "Gentlemen! Many listeners are present here. Why did you not bring planes for them too?

All the listeners have heard the *katha* in the same way, why then there is such a distinction in the distribution of reward?"

The councillors said, "Hey *munivar*! The difference in reward lies in the difference of listening. True that everyone has listened the discourse of *Bhagwat* in the same way but no one has reminisced it like this ghost. That is why there is this difference in the reward despite listening the *katha* together. This ghost listened to this *katha* observing fast and keeping control over his senses for seven days. More so, he kept reminiscing the *katha*. Therefore he became the rightful claimant of the supreme position of Lord Shri Krishna." Saying this, they went away to *Golok* along with Dhundhukari.

Then Gokaran began discoursing the *katha* once again and the audience listened it once again. Lord Shri Krishna came there himself on the conclusion of the *katha*. Gods began showering flowers on Gokaran. After that, Lord Shri Krishna went to Golok along with Gokaran and all the listeners.

Thus all the devotees realised the supreme status of Lord Shri Krishna by listening to *Bhagwat katha*.

●●●

6

NARAD PURAN

Introduction

'*Narad Puran*' is called as *Vaishnav Puran* because like *Shrimad Bhagwat* and *Vishnu Puran*, its theme also is devotion to Vishnu. The gist of all of the eighteen *Purans* is narrated in this *Puran*. Besides there is detailed analysis of mythological and educative descriptions, the stories related with the important *vrat*s of the twelve months, its method of worship, glory of *ekadashi* (eleventh day of a month) *vrat*, the science of *mantra* and astrology, the glory of holy Ganga and pilgrim spots situated at her bank, etiquettes and *dharma* of *varnashram*, stories inspiring devotion, and the spiritual philosophy.

This *Puran* begins with the five questions raised before Sootji by *rishi-muni*s:

1. Which is the easiest method to please Lord Vishnu?
2. What is the benefit of devotion and what should be the appearance of the devotees of God?
3. How can man attain emancipation (*moksha*)?
4. What is the actual form of *varnashram*?
5. How should guests be received?

The gist of the answers of these questions as offered by Maharshi Lomharshan Sootji is as follows:

1. The easy way to realize Lord Vishnu lies in observing reverence, devotion, and good conduct.

2. Lord Vishnu's blessings are obtained through devotion. This is the greatest reward of life. Those have been said to be true devotees who observe selfless devotion to Lord Vishnu.
3. Man can achieve closeness to God which means that he can attain emancipation (*moksha*) by dedicating his mind in Shri Vishnu's feet through selfless devotion by regulating his senses.
4. There have been said to be four *varna* – Brahmin, Kshatriya, Vaishya, and Shudra; and there have been said to be four *ashrams – brahmcharya, grihastha, vaanprastha,* and *sanyas*. The duty of Brahmin is to do *yajna* and rituals, Kshatriya has to protect people, for Vaishya business etc., and Shudra has to serve the three class of the people mentioned above. Among *ashrams, brahmcharya* should be observed with special strictness and the *grihastha* should take care of the men in other three *ashrams*.
5. Guest should be given great reception as if he is the real God.

It is evident from the above statements that the human values, the related rules, actions and *dharma* have been analysed in detail in the *Narad Puran*. Besides Vishnu's worship, there is description of method of *mantra* and worship of Shri Ram, Hanuman, Krishna, Kali, and Shiv in this *Puran*.

Number of Verses and Sections

There are twenty-five thousand (25,000) verses in *Narad Puran*. The total *Puran* is divided into two sections – first part and second part. There are one hundred and twenty-five chapters in the first part and eighty-two chapters in the second part. Thus the entire *Narad Puran* is narrated in two hundred and seven (207) chapters.

The Gist of *Narad Puran*
1. The First Part

The glory of *Narad Puran* and devotion of Lord Vishnu has been established in the first part. After that the mythological and geographical situation of India and the glory of Prayag, Kaashi, Ganga, and Gayatri have been described in detail. In the 16th chapter, the *vrat* on every twelfth day of the dark phase (*Krishna paksh*) of months from *Margshirsh* to Kartik have been described with the details of *Vishnu mantras*, worship, and method of completion.

Extremely beneficial and provider of materialistic pleasure, affluence, and emancipation after ending all the problems, the rare *Haripanchak vrat* has been described in the 19th chapter. This *vrat* is very dear to Lord Vishnu. Lord Vishnu, becoming pleased, fulfil all the desires of the devotees who observe this *vrat* with reverence. After this the description of various hells along with procedure for post-funeral rites has been made as well as the benevolence from the point of view of spirituality and philosophy has been defined through the dialogue between Jadbharat and the king of Sauveer. Thereafter there is description of eighteen *Purans* and the respective number of verses in it.

2. The Second Part

The discourse of Maharshi Vashishtha and Mandhata rishi is narrated in this part. *Vedang*s have been described from the 46th to 53rd chapters of the second part. *Vedang* means the subject matter of *Ved*. Education, *kalp*, grammar, *nirukt*, astrology, and paragraph – these are the six subjects of *Vedas*. For the deep study of the knowledge in the *Vedas*, it is extremely essential to know about these *vadang*s. In the second part these six subjects of *Vedas* have been described in detail in simple and easy language.

Under 'education', the first subject of *Ved*, voice has been said to be the primary. Describing the seven notes, its pronunciation and method has been established. Seven voices, three *gram*, fifty-nine *taan*, and twenty-one *murchhan* – these collectively are called 'the spectrum of voice (*swarmandal*)'. In addition to the signs of *swarmandal*, there is description of the voices delivered from the mouth of gods, demigods (*gandharva*s), and different living beings.

Message of the Purans

Hawan and *yajna* like rituals have been described under the second subject of *Vedas* named '*kalp*'. Besides this there is mention of position and speed of *nakshatra*s, the prayer of gods, forefathers, and *rishi*s, the method of post-funeral rites, and *tarpan*, and the counting of time period.

The third *Vedang* 'grammar' has been described in the 52nd chapter. The form of the words according to grammar and their importance etc has been established in it. After that the fourth subject of *Vedang* '*nirukt*' has been described. Having given a deep thought to the selection of words, the orthodox, compound, and combination of orthodox and compound forms have been explained in it.

Under 'Astrology', mathematics that is principle, the effect of planets and *nakshatra*s, the speed of planets, *hora* in relation to *jatak*, the nature of planets' ascendence, *rajyog*, the effect of *grahgochar*, time, *dasha-antardasha*, the effect of twelve *Bhawgat* planets, *bhaumchar* etc. have been described in detail.

After that the sixth and the last *Vedang* that is 'paragraph (*chhand*)' has been described. *Vedic* and physical *chhand* and its signs have been described in this. There cannot be any progress in *Ved* without *chhand* and therefore it is called the feet of *Ved*. *Vedas* are also called *chhandas* because verses of the *Ved* cannot be recited without *chhand*s. *Gayatri*, *Shakwari*, and *Atishakwari* are the signs of *Vedic chhand*s; *matrik*, and *varnik* are the signs of physical *chhand*. These *chhand*s have been described in simple language in this *Puran*.

Thereafter deep secrets related with *mantra*, its shortcomings, the correction of these shortcomings, the procedure for anointing the *mantra*, the prayer of Panchdev, and the autorities of *Shrikanth matrika*, *Ganeshmatrika*, *Matrikanyas*, and *Kakamritika* etc. have been described.

In the 68th chapter, *mantras* related with Lord Vishnu such as *Astakshar* and *Dwadashakshar* have been described along with the procedure of observance. After this there is detailed narration of the useful *mantras* of Lord Ram, and Devi Sita. In the 74th chapter there is mention of *mantras* related with the worship of Hanumanji, the Rudra incarnate and the *mantras* to destroy the ghosts and spirits. In it, there is also method of observing these *mantras*. After that there is description of methodical observance of various *mantras* of Shri Krishna and the *sahstranamstrota* of the couple of Radha and Krishna.

After that the glory of holy Ganga has been explained through the dialogue between Mohini and Vasu. Finally this *Puran* has been concluded with the description of the holy sites of Prayag, Kaashi, Badrikashram, Awanti, and Mathura and the glory of reading, listening, and reminiscing *Narad Puran*.

Story from *Narad Puran*: Descent of Ganga on the Earth

It is a tale of ancient time. A very famous king named Sagar came into being in the Ikshwaku dynasty. He was extremely learned, knowledgeable, *tapaswi*, brave, intelligent and truthful king. He had two beautiful queens named Keshini and Mahati.

One day, offering his blessing to him, Maharshi Aurva said, "one of your queens will bear sixty thousand sons while the other will have just one. But the one son from the other queen will be the heir to the dynasty. Therefore either of your queens may choose one of the two boons." Then queen Keshini accepted the boon of one son and Mahati accepted the boon of sixty thousand sons.

Queen Keshini gave birth to one son after some time whose name was Asmanjas. A sachet full of seeds was produced from the womb of queen Mahati. There were sixty thousand eggs of the size of seed in it. King Sagar arranged to put them in pitchers full of ghee and appointed sixty thousand maids to nurse them. Sixty thousand children were produced from it at the proper time. All the children were very brave, strong, and aggressive warriors.

Once, the thought of organizing *ashwamedh yajna* developed in the mind of King Sagar. He ordered his counsellors to prepare for the *yajna*. The *yajna* started at an auspicious time. The horse of the *yajna* was released. But, changing into the form of a demon, Devraj Indra stole the *yajna*'s horse and hid it in the *ashram* of Maharshi Kapil, the fraction incarnate of Lord Vishnu.

On the disappearance of the horse, *rishi-muni* said to Sagar, "King! There has developed impediment in the *yajna* due to disappearance of the horse of the *yajna*. Therefore arrange to search the horse soon; otherwise it would cast bad omen."

Sagar sent his sixty thousand sons to search for the horse of the *yajna*. Then they searched the entire earth, but they saw the horse of the *yajna* nowhere. Then they started digging the earth with their strong arms. Along with earth, the habitants of that place namely snakes, demons, and other living beings started screaming in panic due to their massive strike.

Digging the land, the sons of Sagar arrived near the *ashram* of Maharshi Kapil. They saw the horse of the *yajna* tied there. Assuming that Kapil muni had kidnapped the horse of the *yajna*, they hurled derogatory words on Maharshi Kapil, the fraction *avatar* of Lord Vishnu. Then, outraged Kapil muni turned them into ash.

Sagar drowned into the sea of sorrow on hearing his sons being turned into ash. Then his grandson Anshuman placated Maharshi Kapil by praying him. Pleased, Maharshi Kapil returned the horse of the *yajna*. Seeing that the *Maharshi* was pleased, Anshuman asked him the method of salvation of the dead sons of Sagar. He said that the sacred stream of Ganga alone could salvage the sons of Sagar.

King Sagar engaged himself into an arduous *tapa* in order to bring Ganga on the earth according to the advice of Maharshi Kapil. After his death, Anshuman, and his son Dilip after him performed arduous *tapa* for many years. But they did not succeed to bring Ganga on the earth. At last, Bhagirath, the grandson of Anshuman, performed arduous *tapa* of Lord Vishnu to bring Ganga on the earth. Pleased with his arduoud *tapasya*, Lord Vishnu appeared before him in real.

Message of the Purans

Having seen the appearance of Lord Vishnu, Bhagirath started praying him with deep reverence. Then, pleased Lord Vishnu said to Bhagirath, "Son! I am extremely happy with your rigorous *tapa*. I have appeared here to give you your desired boon. Ask your desired boon without hesitation."

Bhagirath said, "God! Kapil muni had turned my ancestors into ashes many years ago. My ancestors are roaming in the *prêt-yoni* since then. Maharshi Kapil had said that if Goddess Ganga descend on the earth and anoint them with her holy water, they will be salvaged from the *prêt-yoni* and they will become worthy of your supreme abode. O God! My great grandfather Sagar, grandfather Anshuman, and father Dilip underwent arduous *tapa* for many years. But they did not succeed and had lost their lives while doing *tapasya*. Then I started doing arduous *tapasya* to complete their task. O abode of compassion! If you are pleased with my *tapasya*, be kind to send Goddess Ganga on the earth."

On listening him, Lord Vishnu said to *Goddess* Ganga, "Ganga! Go to the earth right away in the form of a river and salvage all the sons of Sagar. All those princes will get my ultimate abode by your touch. All the sins would be destroyed of those evildoers who would bathe in your water. People bathing in your water on festivals and special auspicious dates would earn happiness, prosperity, pleasure, and affluence and would attain emancipation (*moksha*) after death. People bathing in your holy water during solar eclipse would earn *punya* (holy reward) and happiness. The entire sorrow and troubles of living beings would end merely by remembering you."

Having heard this Ganga spoke with folded hands, "God! I obey your command. But how long will I have to stay on the earth? The evildoers will give their sins to me. In such a situation how will I get rid of those sins? Abode of compassion! You are omniscient; aware of past, present, and future. No information of this world is hidden from you. Therefore you may clear my doubt."

Lord Vishnu spoke, "Hey Ganga! You will stay on the earth in the river form. My fraction form ocean will be your husband. You will be the most superior, auspicious, and holy among all rivers. Hey goddess! You have to stay on the earth during the five thousand years of *Kaliyug*. All the living beings will pray and worship you like a goddess. Man who will worship you with dedication will achieve rewards equal to *Ashwamedh yajna*. The entire sins of the past lives of the devotees would end who will chant the name Ganga continuously, and after death they would earn my supreme abode Vaikunth."

When Lord Vishnu quelled all the doubts of Ganga, she addressed Bhagirath, "King! I am ready to come with you to the earth due to the command of Lord Vishnu and your strict *tapa*. But king! When I will descend from heaven to earth, I will have enormous momentum. The earth would be thrown into *Patal* (the region below the earth) due to my forceful impact. Therefore king! If you wish to fulfil your desire, first solve this problem."

Listening to Ganga, Bhagirath pleaded Lord Vishnu to solve this problem. Then Lord Vishnu said to Shivji, "Mahadev! Only you can solve this problem of Bhagirath. You may hold Ganga, descending on the earth at a high speed, in your huge locks of hair. Thus Ganga's momentum will come down and the earth would be saved from collapsing into *Patal*."

Shivji happily became ready for this. Then Goddess Ganga paid obeisance to Lord Vishnu and started off towards the earth in the form of a river. Her speed increased immensely while moving towards earth. It seemed as if annihilation was approaching. The clouds began thundering. The earth shook up seeing Ganga's momentum.

At that point, Shivji came in the way by the inspiration of Lord Shri Vishnu and Ganga disappeared with her full momentum in the locks of Shivji. After that Lord Shiv disentangled one lock of his hair and released one stream of Ganga towards earth. Ganga began flowing on the earth at a slow speed. Thus, the earth was saved from collapsing to the *Patal* due to decrease in her momentum.

Soon the Ganga arrived on the surface of the earth, King Bhagirath said praying her, "Hey supremely beneficial Goddess Ganga! The holy goddess who washes sins of evildoers! I salute you millions of times. Mother! May your blessing give progeny to the infertile ones. May all the bondages of the people open up. May the sins of evildoers change into *punya*. Give these blessings."

Worshipping and praying Ganga in this fashion, Bhagirath arrived with Ganga at the place where his ancestors had burnt into ash due to the fury of Kapil muni. They all departed to *Vaikunthlok*, receiving the touch of holy Ganga.

Thus the holy Ganga arrived on the earth. Since the holy Ganga could come on the earth by the effort of King Bhagirath she is also called Bhagirathi.

•••

7

MARKANDEYA PURAN

Introduction

There is dialogue of Maharshi Markandeyaji with Jaimini, the disciple of Vyasji, in the *Markandeya Puran*; therefore this *Puran* is called *'Markandeya Puran'*.

First of all this *Puran* was told to Maharshi Bhrigu by Brahmaji, Bhrigu told it to Chyavan *muni*, Maharshi Chyavan told it to *Brahmarshi*s, and *Brahmarshi*s told it to Daksh Prajapati. After that Daksh Prajapati told it to Maharshi Markandeya. Later it was Maharshi Markandeya only who narrated this *Puran* to Jaimini and other *rishi-muni*s and spread it among common man. Thus this *Puran* got related with Maharshi Markandeya.

Markandeya Puran has been said to be the *Puran* of *'Shakt'* customs. The main reason for this is the detailed description of the story of Bhagwati Durga, and *Durga Saptshati*. This *Puran* is very popular among the common man due to incorporation of all the three mythological discourses of *Durga Saptshati*.

People have been made to be careful about the *dharma*, and deeds with the help of short parables. An interesting and detailed description of fourteen Manu and *manvantar*s is not found anywhere else to read. Where the ruling section has been taught the lesson of lawful governance through the example of faithful Madalsa, the subtle description of post

Message of the Purans ●●121

death end of *jeev*, tourture at the hell, rebirth etc. have been made by the example of Subuddhi and Sumati.

Prior to this, there are some questions and answers on the important topics of *'Mahabharat'* discussed between four birds and Jaimini muni, the dear disciple of Maharshi Vyasji and famous philosopher. The four divine birds were not only spiritually enlightened but also the scholars of scriptures. They were *rishi*s in their previous birth and were born in the bird-*yoni* out of a curse. Actually this entire *Puran* is written in conversation style, in which Jaimini muni asks questions and the four birds reply to his questions. Thus the series of stories get interlocked with one another.

Several brave, learned, religious, and adventurous kings have been described about in the *Markandeya Puran*. Human soul becomes sacred listening to the character of those kings.

Number of Verses and Sections

Markandeya Puran is very brief in comparison to the other *Purans*. About nine thousand (9,000) verses are described in this *Puran*. The total number of chapters in the *Puran* is one hundred and thirty seven (137).

The Gist of *Markandeya Puran*

This *Puran* begins with the questions raised by Jaimini rishi about the doubts related with *Mahabharat*. These four questions are:

1. Why did *Parbrahm* Lord Shri Krishna, the fosterer of universe, omnipresent, and formless, take *avatar* in the human form?
2. How did Draupadi get the sacred place among the *Panchkanya* (Sita, Mandodari, Draupadi, Kunti, and Tara) in spite of being wife of five Pandavas?
3. How did Balramji, the elder brother of Lord Shri Krishna, become free from the effect of a sin like Brahmin's assassination (*brahm-hatya*) in the context of pilgrimage?
4. How did Draupadi's five warrior sons, whose fathers were very brave Pandavs and on whom Lord Krishna was so kind, get killed at the hands of Ashwathama like orphans?

After that there is the story of Jaimini rishi, on the advice of Maharshi Markandeya, going to the *Dharma* birds inhabiting mount Vindhyachal. In this context, there is description of invoking curse on Vapu, the court dancer (*apsara*) by Durwasa muni, birth of Vapu in the bird-*yoni* by the name of Tarkshi, Tarkshi's freedom from the curse by the arrows of Arjun during the war of *Mahabharat*, nursing of the four eggs of Tarkshi by Maharshi Shamik, and narration of their previous birth by the birds emerged from the eggs at the instance of *rishi* named Vipul Swan and his four sons.

Pingaksh, Vibodh, Suputra, and Sumukh – these four *dharma* birds say in response to the first question raised by Jaimini rishi that Lord Shri Krishna is placed in four forms according to his characteristics. The first form of Lord Shri Krishna is of Vasudev, which is infinite, invincible and free from envy. The other form of his is Sankarshan. Embracing *tamoguna*, this form of Lord resides in *Patal* by the name of Sankarshan. Lord Shri Krishna's third form is of Pradyumn, which embraces *satoguna*. The fourth form of the Lord is Aniruddh, which embraces *rajoguna* and creates universe. Lord Shri Krishna is present in every atom of the universe and he takes *avatar* in the body form to end unrighteousness (*adharma*) and injustice.

Replying to the second question of Jaimini rishi about Draupadi and his five husbands, the *dharma* birds say that once in the ancient time Devraj Indra had assassinated Vishwarup, the son of a Prajapati named Twasta, scared of his arduous *tapasya*. As a result, Indra became acused of the assassination of a Brahmin and a fraction of his radiance dissolved and transferred into Dharmaraj. Another time Devraj Indra again became acused of assassination of a Brahmin when he killed Vritrasur, also son of Prajapati Twasta, and a fraction of his radiance dissolved further and transferred into *Vayudev* (the god of air). After this, disguising himself as Gautam rishi, Devraj Indra copulated with Gautam rishi's wife,

Ahilya. As a result of this sin, his beauty and brilliance receded and dissolved and went into Ashwini Kumars. When demons took birth in the form of numerous kings and it became unbearable for the earth to bear their sins, gods took birth in human form to end unrighteousness (*adharma*), and injustice on the command of Lord Shri Krishna. In this process, Indra's radiance transferred into Dharmaraj gave birth to Yudhishthir, the radiance transferred into *Vayu* gave birth to Bhim, Arjun from the radiance of Indra himself, and Nakul and Sahdev were born from the radiance of Indra present in Ashwini Kumar. Shachi, wife of Devraj Indra, herself took *avatar* in the form of Draupadi and appeared from the fire of *yajna*, and became wife of Pandavas. Thus, despite being wife of five Pandavas, she remained wife of one Indra because all the five Pandavas were the fraction *avatar* of Indra.

In answer to the third question, the *dharma* birds have established the evils of alcoholic drinks. They say that the person who consumes alcohol loses his wisdom and intelligence. In the state of drunkenness, Balramji also had murdered Sootji; as a result of which he suffered with the sin of assassination of a Brahmin (*brahmhatya*). Subsequently, coming to senses, he felt great remorse for his severe sin. Then he decided that he will propitiate his evil deed observing a *vrat* for twelve years so that everybody could acknowledge the evils of drinking alcohol. Thus Balramji became free from the accusation of *brahmhatya* due to repenting with true heart.

The *dharma* birds narrated the story of Harishchandra in response to the fourth question related with the sons of Draupadi. They say that when Harshchandra was going away with his wife and son from their town after donating his kingdom, Vishwadevs criticized and termed as sinful the behaviour of Vishwamitra on observing his cruel and bitter behaviour. Angered with the criticism of Vishwadevs, Maharshi Vishwamitra invoked curse on them to take birth in the human-*yoni*. The five Vishwadevs were born as Draupadi's sons due to this curse and, on completion of the duration of the curse, became morsel of death through the hands of Ashwathama and regained their divinity.

The *dharma* birds have told therafter the story of Sumati, the son of Bhargava. The description has been made through this discourse of rebirth and the principle of emergence of *jeev*, position of *jeev* after death, various forms of hells.

After that, the birth of Lord Dattatreyaji from the womb of Anusuya, the wife of Maharshi Atri, has been described. In this context, there is mention of execution of demon Jrimbhasur and boon of one thousand arms to King Sahsrarjun by Dattatreyaji.

After this the story of King Alark is narrated. In the beginning of this, having described the previous birth of King Ritdhwaj through sons of snakes (*naagputra*) there is description of disturbance in the *yajna* of Maharshi Galav by a dreadful demon named Patalketu, Lord Sun offering a horse named Kuvalaya to Maharshi Galav, execution of demon Patalketu by prince Ritdhwaj riding the Kuvalaya horse, marriage of Ritdhwaj and *Gandharva's* daughter Madalsa, and killing of Madalsa by trick by demon Talketu, the brother of Patalketu. After this, resurrection of Madalsa through pleasing Lord Shiv by Ashwatar, the king of snakes, and his brother Kambal has been described.

After marriage, Madalsa bore three sons named Vikrant, Subahu, and Arimardan. Madalsa gave them extraordinary discourse on detachment, oneness of soul and supreme soul (*parmatma*), and the fragility of the world. The three sons followed the path of detachment due to this.

King Ritdhwaj got worried seeing the detachment in his sons. Then, according to his wish, Madalsa provided her fourth son Alark with deep secret of politics, conduct towards *dharma*, *varnashram*, and post-funeral rites.

After this the episodes of the departure of Ritdhwaj and Madalsa to the forest, and attack on King Alark, drowned in

Message of the Purans

the materialistic pleasure, by his elder brother with the help of the king of Kashi with a purpose to preach him the essence of knowledge *(tatva)* have been described. In this context, the dialogue between Alark and lord Dattatreya is also described by way of which *yog*, the obstacles in the way of *yog* and methods to save from it, remedies of diseases, seven concepts, eight affluences, freedom of *yogi*, and the signs of death have been analysed in deapth.

Subsequently, there is episode of Alark dedicating himself in the devotion of God leaving his governance and kingdom.

Thus, describing about spiritualism and philosophy through the story of Alark, the difficulties of the *jeev*s who assume the materialistic pleasure as supreme and way to freedom from it have been analysed.

After that, the creation of the universe, position and systematic development have been described through the dialogue between Markandeya muni and Kraustuki.

The story of Bhagwati Durga and the complete *Durga Saptshati* has been described in this Puran. The emergence of Bhagwati Durga, the execution of the demons named Mahishasur, Madhu, Kaitabh, Shumbh, Nishumbh, Raktbeej etc. by her, and obtaining boon from Bhagwati Durga by King Surath and Samadhi Vaishya are the stories that are described in the *Durga Saptshati* comprising seven hundred verses and thirteen chapters.

After this the emergence of Vaivaswat and the fourteen Manus and the stories about their consecration to the designation of Manu and a very beautiful description of the Jumbu and the other seven islands have been described. Thereafter emergence of Lord Sun from the womb of Aditi, the wife of Maharshi Kashyap, defeat of demons by him, and his prayer and worship by gods have been described.

Finally, this *Puran* has been concluded with the description of the characters of the kings named Rajyavardhan, Sudyumn, Nabhag, Khanitra, Aveekshit, Marut, Narishyant, Dum etc. along with the glory of the *Markandeya Puran*.

Story from Markandeya Puran: Righteousness of Vipashichat

It is a tale of old time: A famous king named Vipashichat happened to be in the Janak's dynasty. Vipashichat was a very religious, noble, and kind king. He had never shown his back in the battlefield. He never returned a mendicant disappointed. He enjoyed the worldly pleasures for many years. Subsequently, in his old age, he transferred the kingdom to his son and went himself to the forest and engaged himself in arduous *tapa*. He spent his life through *tapasya* while in the meditation of God.

Vipashichat was sent to the hell after death where he was put to great sufferings. A messenger of Yam (the god of death) came there one day. King Vipashichat spoke seeing him, "Messenger of Yam! Please tell me what sin did I commit during my life that I am made to suffer in such a horrible and painful hell? I organized several *yajna* in my kingdom. Ruled the earth by *dharma*. Offered enough donations to beggars. Fostered my subjects well. Having earned so much of *punya*, why did I come to this hell?"

The messenger of Yam said, "King! All that you have said is correct. But you had committed a small sin too. Your wife Peewari was going through the days of conception once but you did not cooperate with her at that time because you were attracted towards princess Sushobhana. She remained devoid of the pleasure of your touch. You are suffering in this hell because of breach of cooperation. The man who, under influence of lust, does not cooperate with his wife during her period of conception comes in this hell. Your sin is this much only. Other than this you have committed no sin. You have completed the retribution of your sin here. Therefore now you come with me to enjoy the fruit of you sacred deeds."

Hearing the messenger of Yam, Vipashichat asked him about the sinful deeds, its retribution, and different *yoni*s awarded as a result. The meesenger of Yam explained in detail

Message of the Purans

about this. After that Vipashichat pleaded to tell the distinction between sinful and sacred men.

The messenger of Yam said, "Emperor! Condemning, ungratefulness, disclosing others' secrets, heartlessness, cruelty, lying, disrespecting mother, father, and teacher, mouthing of bad words against them, adultery, robbing others' money, living unclean, killing innocent beings, condemning gods and disrespecting *Vedas*, using intelligence for bad deeds, and engaging in other despicable deeds – these are the signs of men returned from the suffering of the hell. Being kind to living beings, speaking nice and truth, performing noble deeds for *parlok*, respecting teacher, gods, mother, father, and saints, doing noble deeds, being friendly with everyone, and doing all the deeds which are noble – these are signs of men returned from the comfort of heaven. King! I have answered all your questions. Now, please take pain to come along with me."

Vipashichat was about to go with the messenger of Yam when the other inmate sufferers of the hell said crying, "King! Please have mercy on us by staying here a little longer. The air that comes to us touching your body ends our suffering, disease, and sorrow and is providing us happiness."

Listening to them Vipashichat said, "Messenger of Yam! How do these people get happiness from my presence here? What is the deed that I have done which rains happiness on these sinful men?"

Messenger of Yam said, "King! You have taken your meal only after offering it to gods, forefathers, guests, and Brahmins. You have served them by your body, mind, and wealth. Therefore the air that blows touching your body provides happiness. That is why the torture of hell does not affect these sinners. Their sufferings have ended by the radiance of you *punya*. Now come, let us move from this place. The door of heaven has opened for you. Leaving these sinners here, you enjoy the comfort of heaven earned by you through *punya*."

Vipashichat said, "Hey messenger of Yam! Men in heaven or *Brahmlok* cannot experience the joy, which one derives from freeing the suffering persons' sorrow and providing them peace. If they feel nice in my proximity, I will stay here forever. He can never achieve peace who ignores grief-striken persons and indulges in pleasure himself. I do not want anything other than their happiness. You return back leaving me here."

At that very time, a divine aircraft appeared there, from which alighted Lord Vishnu, Indra, Sun, Dharmaraj, and other gods. They had come to take King Vipashichat with them to heaven.

Dharmaraj spoke first of all: "King! You have observed your *dharma* (duty) quite well. Happiness or sorrow – you have never disregarded me. We have come to take you to heaven due to those sacred deeds of yours. Kindly board the plane."

Vipashichat said, "God! Be kind to free these *jeev*s from the hell first, if you wish to take me to the heaven. I am prepared to donate all of my *punya*s to salvage them."

Then Devraj Indra spoke, "Hey King! Your *punya* are infinite – like drops of water in ocean, stars in the sky, and the streams of rain are infinite. Your *punya* has multiplied millions of times due to being kind to these *jeev*s languishing in the hell. You have attained even more higher place due to your generosity. Pleased with your kindness and righteousness, I free all of these *jeev*s from the torture of hell."

Saying this, Devraj Indra freed all of those *jeev*s languishing in the hell. A rain of flowers began to shower upon King Vipashichat and Lord Vishnu ushered him to the plane himself and took him to his divine abode.

•••

8

AGNI PURAN

Introduction

'*Agni Puran*' is a very old *Puran*. There is description of the prayer and worship of sun and trinity – Brahma, Vishnu and Mahesh. Many scholars have said it to be the encyclopaedia of Indian culture on account of the subjects and topics covered in it. This *Puran* is a storehouse of a variety of experiences related with man's life.

The *Puran*-like visage of Lord Vishnu has been described in *Padm Puran*. In that, the eighteen *Purans* have been said to be the 18 parts of the Lord's body. According to that *Puran*-like description, '*Agni Puran*' has been said to be the left feet of Lord Vishnu. The orator of this *Puran* is lord of Fire (*Agnidev*); therefore it is called '*Agni Puran*'. First of all, lord of Fire (*Agnidev*) narrated this *Puran* to Maharshi Vashishtha. All the disciplines of knowledge have been incorporated in this *Puran* in spite of being too brief. From this viewpoint it becomes even more special and important. *Agnidev* himself clarifies the imporatance of '*Agni Puran*' through the following verse:

"आग्नेये हि पुराणेऽस्मिन् सर्वा विद्या: प्रदर्शिता: ।"

Which means that all the disciplines of education are described in the *Agni Puran*.

Number of Verses and Sections

There are narrated a total of fifteen thousand and four hundred (15,400) verses in the *Agni Puran*. Not divided into *skandh* or section, this has been divided into three hundred and eighty three (383) chapters.

The Gist of *Agni Puran*

Along with all the subjects of learning *'Ramayan'*, *'Mahabharat'*, *'Gita'*, and *'Harivansh Puran'* have been introduced in this *Puran*. Several famous and mythological discourses related with *lilaavatar* of lord Vishnu named Matsya, Koorm, Varah, Nrisingh etc. are described in this *Puran*. Besides, the appearance of God by the name of Harivansh, all the festivals of *Mahabharat*, and the description of the clan of Lord Shri Krishna are the important distinctions of this *Puran*.

Description of universe, procedure for worship during evening, procedure for holy offering to fire (*homam*), signs of postures, procedures for teaching and felicitation, method of observing different types of tents, tying of holy thread, method of *Adhiwas*, preparation for the process of emancipation, the art of temple building, commemoration of a project, signs of the idols of gods, characteristics of *prasad*, characteristics of *ling* and *pindika*, method of worshipping deities, method of infusing life in the stone idol, practice of art, practice of education, practice of peace, worship of man-made structure (*vaastu*), learning of base knowledge, astronomy, glory of pilgrimage, post-funeral rites, and astrology etc. are described in detail in the *Agni Puran*.

Similarly the deep secret of the theory of victory in battle, theory of hypnotism, theory of epidemic, names of *sanvatsars*, *varnashram dharma*, *mantra*, medical science, different sins and their respective penitence, monthly *vrat* (fast), weekly *vrat*, daily *vrat*, donation, earthen lamp *vrat*, glory of charity, the *dharma* of a king, description of different dreams, good and bad omen, examination of gems, archery, good behaviour, table manners, method to quell misadventure have been clarified in this *Puran*.

Subsequently, details of *Siddha* medicines and syrups, medical treatment of horse, medical treatment of elephant, Ayurved of trees, proven *mantras*, category of snakes and the medical treatment for snakebite, child *tantra*, planetary mechanism, Narsingh *mantra*, *Trailokyamohan mantra*, Lakshmi worship *mantra*, salvation *mantra* for Aghorastra, mollifying Pashupat, mollifying Rudra, art of poetry, art of drama, vocabulary, grammar and figure of speech, identification of different poetry, description of *yog*, knowledge of Brahm, description of heaven and hell, description of annihilation, *karmvipak*, meaning of *Bhagwat Gita*, glory of *Yam Gita* etc. have been established in detail in this *Puran*.

The concept of 'soul' and 'body' has been explained separately in this *Puran*. According to this, the body made of five elements (*panchbhoot*) is totally separate from the soul. The senses of *jeev* are like a machine, which is run by the soul situated in the heart. The soul resides in the heart of living beings.

The dissolution of the speed of *jeev*-mind in Brahm is termed as *yog* and unification of soul and supreme soul is said to be the ultimate goal of life in this *Puran*.

Story from Agni Puran : *Matsyavatar*

It is a tale of old time: A brave, adventurous and brilliant king named Satyavrat ruled a country named Dravid. He was a dedicated devotee of Lord Narayan. His mind was perpetually dedicated to the devotion of Shri Vishnu.

One day he was offering oblation in the river named Kritmala. At that very time a small fish fell into his hands. Satyavrat dropped it back in the river out of compassion. At this, the fish said in pitiful voice, "Hey king! You are very kind. You are aware of the fact that the large creatures of water feed on the smaller species of their kind. Why are you leaving me here then? I am in your shelter out of their dread. Therefore protect a trifle creature like me."

On hearing the entreaty of the fish, Satyavrat said, "Fish! Do not worry. The one who comes to my refuge does not return disappointed. I promise that I will protect you. My *kamandalu* (holy pail) itself has enough space to accommodate a small fish like you; you can live in it without fear. You will not require to move anywhere else." Saying this, Satyavrat took resolve to protect the fish and allowed her to live in the *kamandalu*.

But the size of the fish grew so huge that the *kamandalu* was not adequate to accommodate her. Then she said to Satyavrat, "Hey king! You had selected the *kamandalu* to accommodate me but this *kamandalu* has become very small for me. I cannot live in it. Therefore you should arrange a larger space for me where I could live happily."

King Styavrat removed the fish from the *kamandalu* and placed her in a large pitcher. But in a few moments her size grew so large that the pitcher too turned small for her. She said to Satyavrat again, " King! This place too is very small for me. Therefore please put me in a large water pond so that I could live there happily."

King Styavrat transferred the fish into a large pond. But her size grew so large in a few moments that even the pond turned small for her. Then she pleaded again, "Hey king! This pond too is very small for me. Therefore put me in a larger water reservoir so that I could live there happily."

The fish was growing so fast in size that Satyvrat was amazed with the phenomenon. But, without a word, he brought her out of the pond and transferred her into the sea. Entering the sea, the fish acquired the size of a huge fish and came to Satyavrat and said, "King! You had promised to protect me, why then have left me amid these violent water cratures? Do not leave me here."

Ashamed King Satyavrat spoke then, " Hey huge fish! I am a dimwit who, despite being aware that the entire universe is created by Lord Vishnu, who is its fosterer, protector, and destroyer, resolved to give you shelter out of ego. Nothing is possible in this universe without the wish of Lord Vishnu. God! Who are you to have granted me wisdom in the fish incarnate, which grew so large in size in a matter of few moments? I have neither seen nor have heard of a water borne

Message of the Purans

creature with such a divine capability. Certainly you are the omnipotent Lord Narayan. You incarnate time to time only to bless devotees. Although all of your *avatars* are meant to benefit the human being, yet I am curious to know the purpose of your this *avatar* of fish."

Then the fish incarnate of Lord Vishnu spoke being pleased, "Hey Satyavrat! The time for annihilation has arrived. All the *lok*s including *bhulok* (earth) will drown in the sea of annihilation on the seventh day from today. A large boat will come to you at that time. Taking the subtle bodies of all the *jeevs* of the earth, and the seeds of small and big grain etc. you board that large boat along with *saptrishi*s. When the boat will start shaking due to violent blow of storm, I will come there appearing in this fish form and you would tie the boat through Vasuki snake with my fin. After that I will float in the sea pulling the boat till the end of annihilation."

Saying this Lord Matsya disappeared and Satyavrat began waiting eagerly for the annihilation.

Right on the seventh day, clouds began raining horrifically and the water of the sea started rising breaking past the shores. In a matter of time, the entire earth submerged under the water. A boat came there at that point of time. He boarded the boat with the subtle bodies of all the species, and seeds of grains etc. along with *saptrishi*s. When the boat started shaking due to terrific tides of the sea, Satyavrat started remembering Lord Vishnu. At that time, Lord Vishnu appeared in *matsya* form. Satyavrat tied that boat through Vasuki snake with the large fin of the Lord Matsya and prayed him to provide the divine wisdom. Then, floating with the boat in the sea, Lord Vishnu gave discourse to Satyavrat of the entire divine *Puran* full of knowledge, devotion, and *karmyog*. The discourse that Lord Vishnu, in the fish form, delivered to Satyvrat during this time period is called *Matsya Puran*. Later, by the blessing of Lord Vishnu, Satyavrat was born in the house of Lord Sun and consecrated by the designation of Vaivaswat Manu.

•••

9

BHAVISHYA PURAN

Introduction

Written by Maharshi Vedvyas, *Bhavishya Puran* has secured the ninth place among the eighteen *Purans*. This is also called *'Saur Puran'* or *'Saur Granth'* due to the detailed description of the glory of Lord Sun, his appearance, and the method of his prayer and worship. Sacred *vrat* and fast, its procedures, and related mythological and educative discourses and dialogues are described in detail in this *Puran*.

Besides this *samudrik* science which means the physical distinctions of male and female, procedure for the examination of different gems and stones, a number of *stotra*s, numerous effective medicines and well elaborated description of snake related knowledge is made in the *Bhavishya Puran* which is not available in any other *Puran*. The detailed description of various royal families, Indian religious culture, the then socio-religious system, education system, and architecture has been made in it.

There is exact description of 2000 years in *Bhavishya Puran*. The future events have been pointed in it by giving systematic description of Nand and Maurya dynasty along with Shankaracharya, Taimur, Babar, Humayun, Akbar, Aurangjeb, Prithviraj Chauhan, Chhatrapati Shivaji and other kings. Queen Victoria rising to become the empress of India in 1857 and extinction of Sanskrit language due to expansion of English language are such events that are also described in this *Puran*. That is the reason why this *Puran* has been said to be the mirror of future.

Number of Verses and Sections

Although, according to the ancient scholars, *Bhavishya Puran* has been said to comprise fifty thousand (50,000) verses, yet only twenty-eight thousand (28,000) verses are available in it at present. Which means that scholars are still unaware of those mysterious occurrences which are described in the remaining half of this *Puran*. The entire *Bhavishya Puran* is divided into four parts – *Brahm parva, Madhyam parva, Pratisarg parva,* and *Uttar parva*.

The Gist of *Bhavishya Puran*

1. *Brahm Parva*

Brahm parva is the first section of *Bhavishya Puran*. This section begins with the dialogue between Sumantu rishi, the disciple of Maharshi Vedvyas, and King Shataneek. In the first and second chapters of this section, a detailed description has been made of the glory of *Bhavishya Puran*, the emergence of the four *Vedas* and the eighteen *Purans*, the five distinctions of *Purans*, counting of period and number of *yugs*.

After this a brief description from conception to the tradition of *yagyopavit* (baptism) has been made. Describing the scriptural procedure for taking meal, it is said that one's age, wealth, truth, and family increases by facing East, West, North, and South direction respectively while eating. Man should not eat after finishing his meals once. This fact has been clarified in the story of *vaishya* named Dhanvardhan. Subsequently the rituals undertaken by right hand have been explained which have been said to be the real five pilgrim spots. These pilgrim deeds are as follows:

Deeds	*Pilgrimage*
Donation to Brahmin etc.	Like God's pilgrimage
Offering water and post-funeral rites	Like father's pilgrimage
Ablution etc.	Like Brahm pilgrimage
Lagnhotra etc. during wedding	Like *prajapatya* pilgrimage
Worship for God	Like *saumya* pilgrimage

After the description of five pilgrimages, a brief description has been made of the study of *Vedas*, importance of chanting *Onkar* and *Gayatri mantra*, procedure for obeisance, the greatness of mother, father and teacher, and auspicious and inauspicious signs of marriageable girls.

Eight kinds of weddings, distinctions of faithful women, and five great *yajnas* (*brahm yajna, pitra yajna, dev yajna, bhoot yajna,* and *atithi yajna*) have been established from the 15th to 16th chapters. After this the glory of *Gauri vrat* and *chaturthi vrat* has been described. In the context of the story of *chaturthi vrat*, writing the distinctions of male and female by Kumar Kartikeya, creating obstacle in his work by Ganeshji, fighting between Kartikeya and him, throwing the text of Kumar Kartikeya into the sea by furious Lord Shiv, and command by Lord Shiv to the sea to re-write the text are the episodes that are narrated. Therefore the text that tells about the distinction between male and female is called *samudric* text. After detailed description of auspicious and inauspicious signs of women, men, and royal men, different dimentions of the worshipping of Lord Vinayak has been established.

Explaining the reward of *naag-panchami vrat*, Sumantu muni says in the 32nd chapter, "Hey king! The only remedy from the snakebite is to observe *naag-panchami vrat* and fasting along with ritualistic completion. 12 *naag panchami*s occur in a year. Anant, Vasuki, Shankh, Padm, Kambal, Karkotak, Aswatar, Dhritrashtra, Shankhpal, Kaliya, Takshak and Pingal – these 12 snakes (*naag*) govern the 12 *panchmi*s. A snake image made of wood or earth or gold should be prepared in the night of *chaturthi* for the sake of completion of this *vrat*. Its prayer and worship should be performed with reverence and devotion on the fifth day during the *panchak* of *naag*. Subsequently Brahmins should be given a feast. Thus, on the completion of 12 months and cosequent prayer of each *naag*, a total completion ceremony should be observed and a feast should be given to the Brahmins along with donation of the image of the snake. The man who bathes snakes with milk, his entire clan becomes free from the fear of snake."

In this context, Sumantu muni has described the symptoms of men suffering from the snakebite, the intensity of the poison of snakes, transfer of the poison in the body, its effect, and the treatment of snakebite. After this the *Pashthi vrat* has been analysed.

The glory of Lord Sun has been explained in great detail in this section. Explaining the character of Lord Sun, there is detailed mention of the extraordinary and miraculous stories about him and procedure of his worship. In this context, there is episode of Lord Shri Krishna telling to his son Samb about the procedure of Lord Sun's worship, the list of names of twelve *aditya*s, and narration of the glory of *rath saptami vrat*. In the following table, it has been clarified what the twelve forms of Lord Sun are and which of his form should be worshipped during which month:

Twelve Months	Twelve Forms of Lord Sun
Maagh	Varun
Falgun	Surya
Chaitra	Vaishakh
Vaishakh	Dhata
Jyeshtha	Indra
Ashad	Ravi
Shravan	Nabh
Bhadrapad	Yam
Ashwin	Parjanya
Kaartik	Twashta
Maargshirsh	Mitra
Paush	Vishnu

The supremely beneficial and fruitful *stotra* of Lord Sun is narrated in the 71st chapter. After this, the other important *vrat* related with Lord Sun, methods of his prayers and worships, and the story of Suryastavraj are written there.

Finally this *parva* has been concluded analyzing the glory of *Marich saptami*, *Bimb saptami*, and *Arksamputika saptami vrat*.

2. Madhyam Parva

The *Madhyam parva* of the *Bhavishya Puran* clarifies special characteristics of many mythological and religious rituals. The description of the emergence and position of universe and different *lok*s, and the glory of *grihasthashram* as well as the importance of mother, father, and teacher have been delineated in this *parva*.

After this, different deeds have been analysed in it. The detailed description of the reward earned by planting different trees has also been made in it.

Clarifying the importance of tree plantation, it is said that the leaves, flowers, and fruits of tree serve our forefathers everyday. The trees that give shadow and fruit and flower salvage forefathers from their sins. Trees planted in temple and along the road provide with fame and auspicious results. Those without progeny get children and the poor acquire affluence by planting trees. One achieves emancipation by planting Peepal tree and the grief ends by planting Ashok tree. Planting of the blackberry *(Jamun)* tree provides with money and wealth, the *Anjeer* tree wife, pomgranate tree provides beauty, and the *viplav* tree provides age. *Vakul* and *Vanjul* trees destroy one's sins and provide strength and intelligence. Mango tree fulfils all the wishes. Guwak tree gives accomplishment and Kadamb tree provides fame. In the same manner, one attains paradise by planting trees of Shimshipa, Jayanti, Havparak, Shrivriksh, Kinshuk etc.

Man should never plant such trees as Samidh, Kantaki, Kush, Drum, and Jalaj. Becoming devoid of affluence, men suffer massively by planting them. Planting of tamarind tree invites loss and planting of jackfruit and *kevanch* causes loss of progeny.

The four months, namely Vaishakh, Asharh, Shravan, and Bhadrapad, are very conducive for planting trees. Planting trees in these months fulfils all the wishes. Contrary to this the months of Jyestha, Ashwin, and Kartik are very inauspicious for planting trees. Man loses power, intelligence, progenies, wealth, respect, and honour by planning trees in these months.

Subsequently, there is description of the methods of the worship of fire (*agni*) and different shapes of utensils used in *yajna*. Ten types of *yajna*-places (*kund*s) namely lotus-shaped, moon-shaped, semi-moon shaped, square, circular, vagina-shaped, pentagonal, septagonal, octagonal, and nanogonal have been described in this *parva*. Thereafter rewards obtained by seeing different birds and various religious rites related with *yajna-hawan* etc. as narrated by Sumantu *muni* have been enumerated.

After that the glory of the four kinds of months namely *chandra* month, *saur* month, *nakshatra* month, and *shraavan* month have been described. Describing these four months, it has been said that the first day of *shukla* phase to the dark phase is called '*chandra* month'. The post-funeral rites of forefathers should be performed in this month only. The period when sun travels from one *sankranti* to another *sankranti* in one sign (*rashi*) is called '*Saur* month'. There is system of performing weddings, fasting, *hawan*, *yajna*, holy bath and such religious rites during this month. '*Nakshatra* month' occurs between Ashwin and Rewati *nakshatra*. There is tradition of performing the rites of forefathers during this month. A thirty-day period or a period from some day to the date occurring after thirty days is called '*Shraavan* month'. Such deeds as first weaning (*annaprashan*), worship of *mantras*, confession, paying the royal tax, and counting of the days for *yajna*s are executed in it.

Besides the above-mentioned four months, there is one more month called 'the month of *Mal*'. Auspicious deeds are prohibited during this month. The month having no chance of full moon and no chance of *sankraman* is called *Mal* month. This month returns after a gap of two and a half years. No *sankranti* of sun occurs during this period.

The good rewards of the specific deeds performed during different dates have been described under the title of 'Description of Dates'. For example, the husband of the woman who prays Shri Vishnu keeping fast on the second day of the months of Asharh and Shraavan when sun is placed in the Gemini and Cancer signs gains longevity. If it is the third day of the month of *Vaishakh* with the good occurrence of *Swati nakshatra*, or it is the third day of the month of *Magh* with the good occurrence of *Rohini nakshatra*, the donation of jaggery and camphor offered on these dates destroys all the inauspicious and unfortunate happenings.

Later the glory of different gardens, ponds, grazing grounds, *ashwatth*, *pushkarini*, *tulsi*, sanctum sanctorum (*mandap*) etc. are described in this *parva*.

3. *Pratisarg Parva*

Pratisarg Parva of the *Bhavishya Puran* presents an extremely beautiful combination of the historical and modern incidents. Incidents have been described in chronological order in this *parva*. The birth of Jesus Christ, his journey to India, advent of Mohammad Saheb, imperial growth of Queen Victoria etc. have been described in it.

Pratisarg Parva begins with the dynasties of the kings of *Satyug*. Thereafter there is description of the kings of *Suryavansh* and *Chandravansh* of *Tretayug*, the kings of *Dwaparyug*, the kings-to-be in the *Kaliyug* and their languages. Subsequently, description of the story of the deluge of 'Nooh', the king of Magadh, Nand, the Bauddh kings and the kings of Chauhan and Parmar dynasties are found in this *parva*.

Betal-pachchisi and Vikram-Betal are described in detail in this *parva*. The ideals of human lives have been inspired to be established by means of various educative stories narrated to king Vikram by Betal. In this context, the stories of King Roopsen and Veervar, Hariswami, King Dharmavallabh and councillor Satya Prakash, Jeemutvahan and Shankhchood, Gunakar, and four dimwits and middle son are described. Besides being interesting, these stories are very educative and knowledge-enhancers. Very popular, holy, auspicious, and supremely beneficial *'Shri Satyanarayan Vrat Katha'* has been described in detail along with the procedure of worship from the 23rd to 29th chapters. In the context of the *Satyanarayan vrat*, the glory of the *vrat* has been demonstrated by means of the stories of Shatanand Brahmin, King Chandrachud, the woodcutter, the businessman named Sadhu and his son-in-law.

After that there are stories of the three characters of Goddess Durga as described in *saptshati*, *Katyayan* and *Mahanand*, the king of Magadh, and defeat to Katyayan by Maharshi Patanjali with the blessing of Goddess Saraswati.

Thereafter the history of India post-1000 AD has been described. Appearance of Jesus Christ and his journey to India has been detailed in it on the basis of mythological evidences.

The stories related with Prophet Mohammed, Shankaracharya, Krishnachaitanya, Prithviraj Chauhan, Akbar, Jaichand, Taimurlang, Ramanuj and Quatubuddin Aibak are described in this *parva*.

In this *parva*, Shankaracharya and Ramanuj have been said to be the fraction avatar of Lord Shiv and Lord Vishnu respectively and the debate between them that took place at Kaashi has been described.

4. Uttar Parva

The last *parva* of the *Bhavishya Puran* comprises 136 chapters. *Bhuvankosh* has been described in the first and second chapter of it. There is episode of disillusionment of Devarshi Narad due to the illusion created by Lord Vishnu in the third chapter. After that there is episode related with the character of Chitralekha. The glory of the *Tilak vrat* of *sanvatsar pratipada* which ends the bad effects of ghost, *pishach*, witch, and planets has been established through this discourse.

The glory of *Ashok vrat* observed on the first day of *Shukla paksh* (phase) of the month of *Ashwin* and *Karvir vrat* (worship of the tree of Kaner) observed on the first day of *Shukla paksh* (phase) of the month of *Jyeshtha* have been detailed in the 9th and 10th chapter. After that supremely secret and immensely fruitful *Kokila vrat* has been described. The love between husband and wife strengthens due to the influence of this *vrat*. Besides, several fortune enhancing *vrat*s such as *Rama Tritiya*, *Madhook Tritiya, Lalita Tritiya, Aviyog Tritiya, Ramya Tritiya, Harkali Tritiya* etc. are described in this *parv*.

The story of Pipplad is described in the 114th chapter. The glory of *Shani vrat* for remedy from the ordeal inflicted by the planet Saturn is described in it. Thereafter this *Puran* has been concluded with the narration of *Prakirn vrat*, Rudra bath, eclipse bath, Magh bath, and the celebration on full moon.

Story from *Bhavishya Puran*: Story of Sadhu Banik

In the ancient time, there was a king named Chandrachud who was intelligent, truthful, and had mastered his senses. There was no one else parallel to him in doing the religious deeds, donations and noble deeds. He used to visit temple everyday and would bring to end the suffering and sorrow of several poor men by offering donations to them there. He was hailed throughout the kingdom. Chandrachud's wife too was faithful and generous by nature.

Once Chandrachud along with her wife observed the *Satyanarayan vrat* at the bank of Bhadrasheela river and organized a grand religious festival. All the people present there were listening to the hymns of God. A rich businessman named Sadhu Banik came there. Surprised by seeing the king and queen praying Lord Vishnu, Sadhu Banik inquired about the details of worship from King Chandrachud.

Chandrachud said, "Gentleman! We are praying and worshipping Lord Satyanarayan. The wellbeing of our kingdom and us depends on his blessings. All the griefs end merely by remembering him. Lord Satyanarayan provides money to poor, child to childless, youth to old ones, power to weak persons. All the sins of his devotees are destroyed merely by his kind sight and opens for them the doors of emancipation."

Message of the Purans ●●143

Sadhu Banik said humbly listening to Chandrachud, "King! Kindly tell me too about the method to observe this *vrat*. I wish to secure the kind sight of Lord Satyanarayan by observing this *vrat* within due guidelines. If Lord Satyanarayan provides child to childless, he would certainly provide the childless me with progeny." Chandrachud told Sadhu Banik the complete procedure of the *Satyanarayan vrat*.

On returning home, Sadhu Banik told his wife Lilawati about this *vrat*. Thereafter he resolved under vicarious witness to Lord Satyanarayan that he will observe the *vrat* the same day when a child would take birth in his home. Lilawati got pregnant by the blessings of Lord Satyanarayan and gave birth to a girl in due course. The girl was named Kalawati.

After the birth of the girl, Lilawati reminded her husband Sadhu Banik about his resolve and told him to observe the *Satyanarayan vrat*. Ignoring her advice, he said, "Dear! I remember my resolve and I will meet it definitely. But I am overburdend with work right now. The business is growing day by day and I will have to go out of town for work. Therefore I will observe the *Satyanarayan vrat* only after our daughter's marriage." Saying this he ignored the advice of his wife.

By and by, several years went by. Kalawati had become young then. Seeing his daughter good for marriage, Sadhu Banik wedded her with a youth named Shankhpati. Then he involved him in his business. After Kalawati's marriage, Lilawati reminded her husband about his resolve but he again ignored her reminder. Lord Satyanaran got angry seeing the dejection of the *Satyanarayan vrat* by Sadhu Banik and he invoked curse on him to suffer with deep suffering. Some days later while doing business, Sadhu Banik and Shankhpati arrived at a town named Ratnapur situated near a sea. Chandraketu was the king of this town. Both of them stayed there to carry on with their business.

Once a thief stole money from the royal treasury and ran away and arrived at the place where Sadhu Banik and

Shankhpati had stayed. The king's soldiers were following the thief. Terrified, the thief carefully placed the stolen money near Sadhu Banik and ran away from there himself.

Seeing the king's money near Sadhu Banik, the soldiers caught them assuming them the thieves and produced them before the king. Awarding the punishment of strict imprisonment to both, King Chandraketu ordered them to deposit their entire money in the royal treasury. A variety of torture began to be inflicted on them according to the order of the king.

Hither, the home of Sadhu Banik was also robbed. Thieves took away his entire capital. There was acute shortage of food, money and clothes in his house. The mother and daughter both started spending their days by securing alms.

Disturbed with hunger and thirst, Kalawati went to a Brahmin's house one day to procure alms. Lord Satyanarayan's *vratkatha* was going on there. Kalawati heard the entire *katha* (discourse) sitting there. The Brahmin offered her *prasad* after the *katha*.

Kalawati narrated the detail of *Lord Satyanarayan vrat* to her mother. Then Lilawati said in sad voice, "Daughter! Your father had resolved to observe the *Satyanarayan vrat* before your birth. But he did not fulfil his resolve. Our suffering is perhaps the result of that."

Listening to her mother, Kalawati said, "Mother! If father forgot to observe the *Satyanarayan vrat*, we will observe the *vrat* and would thus fulfil his resolve. I have strong faith that Lord Satyanarayan who is extremely kind will accept our prayer and will be kind upon us."

Understanding the thought of Kalawati, Lilawati with her close relatives performed the prayer and worship of lord Satyanarayan and said in humble voice, "God! We had forgotten you in our selfishness. Kindly forgive our mistakes. Abode of compassion! Keep your kind sight upon us always." Lord Satyanarayan got happy by observance of *vrat* in such a manner. Appearing in the dream of King Chandraketu the same night, he explained the truth and commanded him to release Sadhu Banik and Shankhpati.

Chandraketu begged pardon from Sadhu Banik and Shankhpati in the morning for his mistake and returned all of their money and sent them off from his town respectfully. Sadhu Banik and Shankhpati happily began to put their money in the boat to depart for their town.

But Sadhu Banik was still unaware of his resolve. Then Lord Satyanarayan appeared there in the disguise of a hermit and said to Banik, "O kind gentleman! What is kept in this boat?"

In the disguise of a Brahmin, Lord Satyanarayan was examining the generosity of Sadhu Banik. Sadhu Banik said to him that there was leaves of *bale* only in the boat. The Brahmin-in-disguise, Lord Satyanarayan said '*tathastu*' (as you say) and went away to sit at a distance.

Sadhu Banik felt that the load of he boat had gone. He found there *bel* leaves only on looking closely. Seeing this Sadhu Banik fell on the feet of the hermit and started praying humbly.

Then the hermit made him recall that he had beseeched for a child during the *katha* of Lord Satyanarayan at King Chandrachud several years ago. But he did not show gratitude towards Lord Satyanarayan despite receiving the reward and affluence. Sadhu Banik came to recall his resolve on listening to the hermit. He promised the hermit to fulfil his resolve. His boat again filled with the money due to the blessing of the hermit. And he arrived at his town in a week.

Hither Lilawati and her daughter Kalawati were busy in the *katha* of Lord Satyanarayan. Receiving the information of the arrival of her husband, Lilawati proceeded to welcome her husband leaving the responsibility of worship upon her daughter Kalawati. Longing to meet her husband, Kalawati too followed her mother disregarding the *prasad* of Lord Satyanarayan.

The boat of Sadhu Banik submerged into water alongwith Shankhpati due to the disregard to the *prasad*. Seeing this sight, Lilawati and Kalawati started praying Lord Satyanarayan and started begging for their mistake. Then there came a voice from the sky, "they both go back home and receive the *prasad* of Lord Satyanarayan. Thus alone their husbands will be resurrected."

They did as was told. Sadhu Banik and Shankhpati reached their home. From that day onwards the family began praying and worshipping Lord Satyanarayan on the day of every full moon.

•••

10

BRAHMVAIVART PURAN

Introduction

Brahmvaivart means the size of Brahm. The elementary form of Brahm is 'nature'. Different dimensions of nature only have been established in the *Brahmvaivart Puran*.

The detailed analysis of Shri Krishna *avatar* of Lord Vishnu has been made in this *Puran* only next to *Shrimad Bhagwat Puran* among the eighteen *Purans* written by Maharshi Vyas. Therefore this *Puran* has been placed in the rank of *'Vaishnav Puran'*. Lord Shri Krishna has been said to be the form of supreme Brahm whose fraction produces this entire universe.

Parbrahm Parameshwar Shri Krishna had provided the knowledge of this *Puran* to Brahmaji at *Golok*. At Pushkar, Brahmaji provided this knowledge to Dharmaraj, Dharmaraj to his son Narayan, and Lord Narayan offered this knowledge to Devarshi Narad. Later Devarshi Narad provided this knowledge to Maharshi Vyas and Vyasji provided it to his disciple Sootji. At last this knowledge reached Shaunak and other *rishi-muni*s through Sootji.

Brahmvaivart Puran facilitates mortal pleasures to pleasure-seekers and emancipation to the men who seek freedom from all bondages (*moksha*). For Vishnu devotees, this *Puran* provides devotion and is like *kalp* tree. The seed form of this universe has been established in this *Puran* which is prayed and meditated by all the *yogis* and seers.

Besides the emergence of the universe, stories of main goddesses – Durga, Lakshmi, Saraswati, Gayatri, Savitri, Tulsi, Ganga, etc.– the birth of Lord Ganesh and the mythological stories related with him, and various histrionics related with Lord Shri Krishna have been described.

Number of Verses *(Shlokas)* and Sections

Brahmvaivart Puran comprises eighteen thousand (18,000) verses. The complete *Puran* contains two hundred and eighteen (218) chapters which are divided into four sections. These sections are – *Brahm Khand, Prakriti Khand, Ganapati Khand,* and *Shri Krishna janm Khand.*

The Gist of *Brahmvaivart Puran*
1. *Brahm Khand*

This first *khand* (section) of the *Brahmvaivart Puran* comprises 29 chapters. This *khand* begins with the description of universe. There is described the birth of universe by *Parbrahm* Lord Shri Krishna and emergence of Narayan, Brahma, Shiv, Kaamdev, Suryadev, Chandradev, Saraswati, Lakshmi, Rati, Moorti etc from the different parts of his body.

There is the story of the emergence of Radhaji in the 5th chapter who had appeared from the left part of Lord Shri Krishna. Thereafter there is episode of the emergence of *Gopo*s from the papillae of Lord Shri Krishna and *Gopi*s from the papillae of Radha. After that there is story of the birth of Devarshi Narad in the *Gandharva yoni* by the name of Upbrihan as a result of a curse invoked by Brahmaji, wedding with fifty *Gandharva* girls by him, and invoking of curse again on Upbrihan and birth of Devarshi Narad in *Shoodra yoni* due to the curse. In the context of this story, the medical science and different secrets of Ayurved have been described in detail by Lord Narayan in the disguise of a Brahmin before Malawati, the wife of Upbrihan. The sixteen texts written by sixteen scholars are said to be the basic pillars of Ayurvedic medicine. These texts and their authors are introduced in the following table:

Sr. No.	Author	Text
1.	Suryadev	*Ayurved Samhita*
2.	Dhanvantari	*Chikitsa Tatvavigyan*
3.	Divosan	*Chikitsa Darpan*
4.	Kaashiraj	*Divya Chikitsa Kaumudi*
5.	Ashwinikumar	*Chikitsa Saartatva*
6.	Nakul	*Vaidyak Sarvasva*
7.	Sahdev	*Vyadhi Sindhuvimardan*
8.	Yamraj	*Gyanarnav*
9.	Chyavan	*Jeevdaan*
10.	Janak	*Vaidya Sandehbhanjan*
11.	Buddh	*Sarvasar*
12.	Jaabaal	*Tantrasaar*
13.	Jaajali	*Vedangsaar*
14.	Paail	*Nidan Tantra*
15.	Karath	*Uttam Sarvadhar Tantra*
16.	Agastya	*Dwait Nirnaya*

After that the episodes of Krishna armour *(Kavach)* named *Brahmandpavan* and *Sansarpatan*, the glory of Shivstavraj, nomenclature of Brahmaji's son, and the importance of domestic life (*grihastha dharma*) narrated by Brahmaji to Devarshi Narad are described. Finally this holy *khand* has been concluded analysising the glory of Lord Shri Krishna and the goddess nature.

2. Prakriti Khand

This *khand* of *Brahmvaivart Puran* comprises 47 chapters. It begins with the description of the five-goddess forms of nature (*prakriti*) – Durga, Lakshmi, Saraswati, Gayatri, and Radha. *'Pra'* means superior and *'kriti'* means creation. Which means the goddesses equipped with superior abilities who are capable in creation are called *'prakriti'* (nature). The *parbrahm* produced himself in the two forms namely *purush* and *prakriti* at the beginning of the creation. After that a fraction of *prakriti* separated to become Durga according to the wish of Lord Shri

Krishna and became dear to Lord Shiv. The embodiment of all the power, Bhagwati Durga is ruler of all the accomplishments. Worshipped by gods and *rishi-munis*, goddess Durga salvages them who take refuge in her and provides them fame, affluence, *punya*, and emancipation.

Emerged from the fraction of *prakriti*, and the force behind Lord Vishnu, Goddess Mahalakshmi is the ruler of wealth. Mahalakshmi is called Swarg Lakshmi for residing in paradise, Rajlakshmi for residing at kings, and Grihlakshmi for residing in houses.

The goddess of intelligence, education, and knowledge, Saraswati is said to be the voice of supreme soul (*paramatma*). This goddess provides intelligence, wisdom, brilliance, and memory, and provides the power of imagination through enlightening the difference between principles and its meaning.

Goddess Gayatri has been said to be the fourth *prakriti* goddess. She is the mother of Bodhgamya, Ved-Vedang, Chhand and scriptures for *Brahmin*s, *Kshatriya*s, and *Vaishya*s. Dear to Brahmaji, Gayatri has another name– Savitri. This goddess, identical to *parbrahm*, grants emancipation.

The fifth and last *prakriti* goddess is Radha who is dear to Shri Krishna and lives on the left side of Lord Shri Krishna. She is identical to *parbrahm* in virtues and is revered in all the *lok*s. She is said to be the goddess of *ras* (romance).

Thus these five goddesses are complete in themselves. There are various forms of these goddesses namely main fraction, important and histrionic fraction. For example, Ganga, Tulsi, Vasundhara, Manasa, Mangalchandi, Khashthi (Devsena), and Mahakali etc. have emerged from the main fraction of the five goddesses; Dakshina, Deeksha, Swaha, Swadha, Swasti, Tushti, Dhriti, Kshama, Rati, Mukti, Pratishtha, Kirti, Priya, Daya, Mithya, Shanti, Lajja, Buddhi, Medha, Smriti, and Murti etc. have emerged from the important fraction of the five goddesses; and Sita, Rukmini, Rohini, Tara, Lopamudra, Arundhati, Ahalya, Ansuya, Devbhuti, Prasuti, Ahuti, Varunaani, Mena, Shachi, Damyanti,

Yashoda, Devaki, Kalawati, Draupadi, Gandhari, Saivya, Kaushalya, Subhadra, Rewati, Satyabhama, Renuka, etc. are said to be the histrionic fraction of the five goddesses.

After the brief introduction of the wives of all the main gods, there is description of the method of worship of Saraswati, the world-winning armour of Saraswati, and the prayer of Goddess Saraswati by Maharshi Yagvalkya. Thereafter the episode of Saraswat, Ganga, and Lakshmi invoking curse upon one another and descend of Saraswati and Ganga on the earth as river as the result of the curse is described. In this context, the episodes of birth of Lakshmi as Tulsi on the earth as a result of the curse of Saraswati, marriage of Tulsi and Shankhchud, assassination of Shankhchud, to attack upon the faithfulness (*satitva*) of Lakshmi, and Shri Vishnu staying back on the earth as tree and Shaligram rock are described. After that there is description of the worship, meditation, *namashtak* and *stavan* of Tulsi.

The story of Goddess Saraswati has been described in the 23rd chapter. Worship of Goddess Savitri (Gayatri) by King Ashwapati and his wife Malati, and detailed analysis of the glory of Gayatri by Maharshi Parashar has been made in it. There are episodes of fraction of Goddess Savitri taking birth from the womb of Malati, the wife of Ashwapati, marriage of Savitri and Satyavan, resurrection of Satyavan by Yamraj pleased by the faithfulness (*pativrat*) of Goddess Savitri. In this Puran there is description of the holy *vrat* alongwith the method of worship observed by Savitri for fourteen years.

After the glory of Savitri, the story of the emergence of Mahalakshmi from the left part of Lord Shri Krishna and her departure to Vaikunthlok with Lord Vishnu has been told. In this context, the mythological stories of disrespect of Durwasa muni by Devraj Indra, invocation of curse on Indra by furious Durwasa muni and, as a result of curse, disappearance of Goddess Lakshmi and her reappearance during the churning of the ocean are described.

After that there are stories of producing *Swaha* for fire (*agni*), *Swadha* for forefathers, and *Dakshina* for *yajna-purush* by Lord Shri Krishna. In this very sequence, the stories related with Goddess Shashthi, Manasa, and Mangalchandika have been cited.

Describing the holy character of Radha-Krishna, the method of worship, meditation, *shodshopchar*, nursing, *pariharstav* worship, ant the glory of the very benevolent armour named *Jag-Mangal* of Shri Radha have been described in detail from the 49th to 56th chapters.

Finally there is description of the famous sixteen names of Bhagwati Durga, method of worship, the story of King Surath and *vaishya* named Samadhi, the special *nakshatra* for the worship of goddess and her *stotra* named *Durg Nashan*.

3. Ganapati Khand

The third section of *Brahmvaivart Puran* is called *Ganapati Khand* due to the mention of the details of mythological histrionics related with Lord Shri Ganesh. This *khand* comprises 40 chapters. The *Ganapati Khand* begins with the episodes of the story of Sati, wedding of Shiv and Parwati, birth of Kartikeya, and invoking of curse on all the gods by incensed Parvati. In this discourse Lord Shiv explains the glory of the *Punyak vrat* to Parwati when she asks the way to get progeny.

After that there are episode of Parwati observing *Punyak vrat*, and, by the influence of the *vrat*, Shri Krishna emerging at Parwati's home in the form of Ganesh.

Thereafter sighting by Shanidev at the child Ganesh on the insistense of Goddess Parwati at the birth ceremony of Ganeshji and, as a result, Ganeshji's head falling away from his body have been described. Seeing his son dead, when Goddess Parwati began crying with grief, Lord Vishnu replaced the head with that of an infant elephant. Ganeshji holds the first right to be worshipped among all the gods due to a boon of Lord Vishnu. The first worship and prayer of

Ganeshji at any occasion or auspicious act represents freedom of the work from all the hurdles.

In this story there is episode of Shri Vishnu and Indra addressing Ganesh by eight names while worshipping and praying him. These eight holy names of Lord Ganesh are – Vighnesh, Ganesh, Herambh, Gajanan, Lambodar, Eikdant, Shoorpkarna, and Vinayak.

Why did Lord Ganesh, the destroyer of hurdles, get beheaded? This important question has been answered through a story narrated in the 23rd chapter. In this story there is description of the execution by Suryadev of demons named Mali and Sumali who were devotees of Shiv, incensed on the execution of his devotees, Lord Shiv executed Suryadev by Trishool, and invoking of curse on Shivji by Maharshi Kashyap.

After that there is description of the armour and *stotra* of Suryadev and Mahalakshmi. Thereafter there is the description of the episode of assassination of Maharshi Jamdagni by King Sahasrarjun and execution of Sahasrarjun by Parashuram, the son of Maharshi Jamdagni. In the context of this episode Durga's armour, Kaali's armour, and the discipline of Dashakshari are described. After that there is the incident of breaking of a tooth of Ganeshji due to the attack of the weapon called *farasa* of Parashuram. Lord Ganesh was known as *Eikdant* due to loss of one tooth.

Finally the prohibition of Tulsi leaf during Ganesh Puja has been established through the help of the episode of lord Ganesh and Tulsi.

4. *Shri Krishna Janm Khand*

Shri Krishna Janm Khand of the *Brahmvaivart Puran* is more elaborate than the other three sections. Comprising 101 chapters, there is detailed description of the histrionics related with Lord Shri Krishna. Though there is detailed description of the character of Lord Shri Krishna in the *Shrimad Bhagwat*, yet some special incidents related with him are cited in this *khand* which has found insignificant or negligible mention even in the *Shrimad Bhagwat Puran*.

This *khand* begins with the description of *Golok*. Thereafter the entire story from Shri Krishna's incarnation to taking him to *Gokul* by Vasudev has been described in sequence. The detail of the previous birth of Nand and Yashoda are made in this context in which Nand was a Vasu named Drona and Yashoda was her wife named Dhara. After that a beautiful childhood-histrionics of Shri Krishna from his birth onwards at *Gokul* has been made.

There is description of Shri Krishna armour *(kavach)* in the 12th chapter which destroys physical, spiritual, and material fear completely. Man becomes free from all kinds of fear by framing this beneficial armour in a gold *yantra* and wearing it on the neck or arm. Lord Shri Krishna bestows kindness upon him.

In the 13th chapter, there is the episode of the nomenclature of Lord Shri Krishna and Balram by Garg muni, the family guru of Yaduvanshi. List pertaining to 33 names of Lord Shri Krishna and 9 names of Balramji has been given in it. A detail of sixteen names of Radhaji has been given to Devarshi Narad by Lord Narayan in the 17th chapter. The lists of the names of Lord Shri Krishna, Balramji, and Radha follow as under:

The 33 Names of Lord Shri Krishna		
Krishna	Pitambar	Brahm
Govind	Kansdhwansi	Yashodanandan
Vishtarshrawa	Devakinandan	Shreesh
Hari	Sanatan	Vishnu
Achyut	Sarvesh	Garudadhwaj
Sarvaroopaddak	Sarvadhar	Sarvagati
Sarvakarankaran	Radhabandhu	Radhikatma
Radhika Sahchari	Radhamanaspurak	Radhadhan
Radhikang	Radhikasaktmanas	Radhapran
Radhikesh	Radhikaraman	Radhikachitchor
Radhapranadhik	Prabhu	Paripoornatam

Message of the Purans

The 9 Names of Balramji		
Sankarshan	Rauhineya	Haldhar
Shitivasa	Hali	Anant
Baldev	Revati Raman	Musali

The 16 Names of Radhaji	
Radha	Krishnapriya
Krishnaa	Krishnaswaroopini
Krishna Pranadhika	Krishnavamangsambhoota
Raasvasini	Paramanandroopini
Rasikeshwari	Raseshwari
Vrinda	Vrindavanvinodini
Vrindavani	Chandrawali
Chandrakanta	Sharacchandra Prabhanana

Besides, the list of those hundred materials and occasions which enhance good fortune merely by seeing it has been given. The special holy benefits from bathing at different pilgrim spots on special dates have been described in this *khand*.

After that the glory of the donation of grain has been established. Lord Shri Krishna proclaims in it that there is no greater donation than the donation of grain. Man can earn more and more *punya* by donating grain. The donation of grain must be made to the person suffering from hunger (irrespective of the caste or creed he belongs to).

Following it is the detailed analysis of the effect of dream and the solution to quell bad dreams, ensuing the prescription of edible and nonedible food for man. The eleven names of Lord Shri Krishna – Krishna, Keshav, Narayan, Harey, Ram, Anant, Mukund, Madhusudan, Vaikunth, Kansarey, and Vaman – have been termed as provider of *punya* and the destroyer of the sins of the previous birth.

The description of the *Raslila* in this *Puran* played by Lord Shri Krishna with *gopis* is entirely different from that of *Shrimad*

Bhagwat. Whereas the *Raslila* of *Shrimad Bhagwat* presents the devotional form of Lord Shri Krishna and *gopi*s, there is predrminance of romance in the *Raslila* of *Brahmvaivart Puran*. In the love of Lord Shri Krishna and *gopi*s, the element of pleasure has been given prominence in it.

The details of the previous birth of Dhenukasur and Usha, the daughter of Banasur, and turning of his wife Kandali into ashes by Maharshi Durwasa have been depicted in this *khand*.

Finally this *Puran* has been concluded with the names of *Purans*, its five distinctions, number of verses, glory of reading, listening, and thinking of *Brahmvaivart Puran*.

Story from *Brahmvaivart Puran*: Glory of the Reward of Action

Lord Shri Krishna was performing histrionics alongwith Balramji at Vrindavan. Once he noticed that his father, Nand, and all the *gops* of Braj were preparing for some special *yajna*. Different kinds of materials were being gathered.

Lord Shri Krishna is omniscient and is capable to know what lies in one's heart. Nothing is hidden from him. Even then, like an ordinary child, he went to Nand to quell his curiosity and asked, "Father! I am observing for several days that the residents of Braj and you are involved in the preparation of some grand *yajna*. Which *yajna* is that? What is its reward? Who and by what means and by which purpose do the *yajna* is organized? I have great curiosity to know that. Father! I also want to know if the auspicious act that you are going to perform has approval of scriptures or is just wordly. Kindly tell me something about it."

Nand Baba started to speak trying to make Shri Krishna understand, "Son! Lord Indra is the ruler of clouds. The clouds rain the life-providing water on the earth on his command. We pray and worship the very lord Indra, ruler of clouds. The material used in the *yajna* is the same that is produced by the water rained by him. We use the grain for our sustenance,

Message of the Purans

which is left over after the *yajna*. It is Lord Indra who gives us the reward of our labour. The clouds would stop raining water if he would become angry and a dreadful famine would ensue. Therefore this auspicious act is performed every year according to our family tradition to secure his blessing. He never gets merciful with those who shun this noble act out of selfishness or greed."

Listening to Nand Baba, Lord Shri Krishna said, "Father! A person is born according to his actions and meets his death according to his deeds. He experiences happiness, grief, good luck, bad luck and fear etc. according to his deeds. Therefore what is the need of Indra if all the beings are experiencing the reward of their actions? What is the relevance behind pleasing him if he cannot change the rewards of the action of the previous birth or cannot change one's luck? Man is governed by his nature. He only follows it. The entire universe, be it gods, demons, or humans, is based on the theory of reward of action. *Jeev* adopts superior or inferior bodies according to his deeds. Deeds are man's friend, enemy, and guru. Father! The entire world is governed by *parbrahm* God. Clouds rain on the earth acoording to his arrangement. That produces grain and the grain maintains the livelihood of all the people. What is the role of Indra in it then? What can he do then?"

Nand said, "Son! Your satement is correct and we agree by it too. But we have resolved to perform the *yajna*. All the material has also been arranged. Now we have no other option but to perform the *yajna*. The entire material will go waste if the *yajna* will not be performed. Besides, we all will become liable to commit the sin for not performing the *yajna* in spite of taking resolve for it."

Shri Krishna said amusingly, "Father! Neither we rule a country nor we control large cities. Even the village and house are not our own. Therefore we will worship cows, Brahmins, and Govardhan, the king of mountains. You organize this *yajna* with the same materials which have been collected for Indra's *yajna*. Various types of delicacies should be prepared. *Hawan* should be performed methodically by the superior Brahmins and they should be donated grain, cows, and money. After offering ample donation, cows should be offered food. After that, Govardhan, the king of mountains, should be offered feast and then circumambulate it on feet. Do so if you find my advice proper. I have firm belief that this *yajna* will be dear to gods alongwith all the creatures."

Since the intention of Lord Shri Krishna was to break the ego of egoist Indra, he had planned the drama. Nand Baba and other *gops* happily accepted his advice.

First of all, Govardhan, the king of mountains, was prayed and worshipped chanting *Ved-mantras* by Brahmins. Then, having donated amply to Brahmins, cows were fed with green grass. When the occasion to feast the Govardhan, the king of mountains, came, then the *gops* began thinking that Govardhan is in the form of mountain. How could he be fed? The *yajna* shall remain incomplete if we could not offer feast to Govardhan.

Lord Shri Krishna acknowledged the doubt in the mind of *gops*. Then he made a fraction of himself turn into a giant god who appeared and said, "devouts! I am Govardhan, the king of mountains. Bring the feast to me and complete your *yajna*." Saying this he accepted the entire food product.

Along with the other residents of Braj, Lord Shri Krishna also bowed his own form and said, "The king of mountain (*giriraj*) has been immensely kind to have appeared in person. It can adopt any kind of appearance. He ruins the persons who disregard him. Come; let us properly worship the *giriraj* who nourishes our cattle and us."

Then, on being prompted by Shri Krishna, Nand along with all the *gops* prayed and worshipped Govardhan and circumambulated it along with cows. Pleased with the devotion of the residents of Braj, Govardhan, the fraction *avatar* of Shri Krishna, gave his blessing and disappeared.

When Indra came to know that *gops* had stopped worshipping him, he became outrageous because of ignorance. He gave command to the *gana* of annihilating clouds r amed

Message of the Purans ———————————— 159

Sanvartak, "how dare those milkmen disregard me Indra, the god of gods, carried away by the talks of a child named Krishna. In spite of being innocent, egoist and imprudent, Krishna considers himself very knowledgeable, strong, and clever. He himself is the morsel of death, yet these milkmen are ignoring me at his behest. While they are getting out of their mind in the pride of their wealth, Krishna is fuelling their wrong act. Those dimwits want to salvage themselves through this *karma-yajna*, I will certainly punish them. Sanvartak! March immediately to Vrindavan with your annihilating clouds and break the pride of those egoist milkmen. Kill their cattle. Along with brave warriors I also come after you to destroy Braj."

Having the command of Indra, Sanvartak reached with his annihilating clouds and started devastating the entire Braj by heavy rains. It started lightning everywhere. Clouds started creating horrible thunder by mutual collision. Huge trees began uprooting like straw due to terrible force of storm. The houses of the residents of Braj blew up into smithereens in a matter of time. It appeared as if the entire earth would submerge into water.

It started deluging heavily. Then all the residents of Braj went to the refuge of Lord Shri Krishna for protecting their lives. Lord Shri Krishna is extremely kind and has affection towards his devotees. How could he bear to see his devotees in suffering? He came to know the devilry of Indra. He uprooted mount Govardhan playfully for the benefit of the residents of Braj and placed it at the tip of his small finger as if it was a lotus flower. Then he said in cool voice, "the residents of Braj! Take shelter under this mountain along with your cattle, grain and other materials. No one can harm you here." Seeing this histrionics of Lord Shri Krishna, the residents of Braj started hailing him. Thereafter, all the residents of Braj along with their cattle gathered under mount Govardhan as per the command of Shri Krishna. Lord Shri Krishna held the mount Govardhan at on one finger for seven days.

Even Indra was baffled seeing this illusion. When he saw how Lord Shri Krishna raised Govardhan playfully to remove the trouble of the residents of Braj, his pride was broken. He felt shame by the thought that he competed with *parbrahm* God and he withdrew from there.

Lord Shri Krishna asked the residents of Braj to proceed along with their cattle from the shadow of Govardhan when he saw that Devraj Indra has accepted defeat and has returned. He placed the Govardhan at its original place once everyone came out of it. All the residents of Braj embraced him and hailed him.

To seek pardon for his misdemeanour, Devraj Indra with Kaamdhenu appeared before Lord Shri Krishna when he was sitting in peace and bowed his head at his feet and said, "God! Though you have no relation with this ignorant world, yet your fraction incarnates to protect *dharma* and end evil. You are personification of *kaal* (death) to punish the evildoers. You appear in a human body to fulfil the wishes of you devotees and destroy the ego of those sinners who presume themselves as *parbrahm* God and thus you perform various histrionics. Then shedding the false pride, ignorant beings like me come to your shelter. God! I was totally oblivious of your influence and power. Therefore, under influence of false pride of affluence and power, I dared to disregard you. Kindly forgive my mistake! Also bless me such that I never fall prey to such egoistic ignorance. Abode of kindness! I had unbound ego, but you have been kind to salvage me. Now you are my master, guru, and soul. God! I am at your refuge."

Listening to the humble prayer of Devraj Indra Lord Shri Krishna became pleased and said, "Devendra! The pride of affluence and power had corrupted you. Since you are my dear devotee, therefore, to help you, I have disrupted your *yajna* so that you could remember *Parbrahm* perpetually. Devendra! The man who becomes blind with the pride of affluence, wealth, and power, he forgets that I, the God in the form of *kaal* (death), always ride his head with the baton of punishment in my hand. I snatch away everything – affluence, wealth, and power – of those on whom I cease to be kind. Devendra! I am glad that you have accepted your mistake. This is a superior virtue in you. Now return to paradise and observe your *dharma* as per my command. Destroy your ego and always remember me. I will keep my kind sight upon you always."

After that Kaamdhenu prayed to him, "God! *Devraj* Indra had tried to kill me but you had saved me. Therefore you are the god I worship. Abode of kindness! I consider only you as my Indra, therefore be our Indra, and accept the position of Indra."

Saying this, Kaamdhenu by her milk and Indra by the water of Ganga fetched by Eirawat felicitated Lord Shri Krishna amidst chanting of *mantras* by *Devarshi*s and addressed him by the name of 'Govind'. Then they all returned to their *lok* after performing his worship and prayer.

•••

11

LING PURAN

Introduction

Having incorporated various mythological episodes, discourses, and incidents related with Lord Shiv in *'Ling Puran'*, the Shaiv principles have been enumerated in a natural, simple, and logical manner. Therefore this *Puran* has been said as *"Shaiv Pradhan Puran"*.

Though the literal meaning of *'ling'* is said to be the reproductive organ, yet *'ling'* does not mean reproductive organ but *Onkar* in this *Puran*. Inception of the universe is said to originate from *'Parbrahm'*, which neither has a shape nor form. That has no characteristic and is formless. The *'ling'* is the symbol of expression for the same *Parbrahm* that is devoid of any characteristic.

The description of the three forms of Lord Shiv – visible, invisible, and the dual form – is found in many texts. This idea has been expressed in the three forms of Lord Shiv in the *Ling Puran*:

एकेनैव हतं विश्वं व्याप्त त्वेवं शिवेन तु।
अलिंगं चैव लिंगं च लिंगालिंगानि मूर्तयः।।

It has been clarified in the above-written *shloka* that *aling*, *ling*, and *lingaling* respectively are the symbols of the three forms of Lord Shiv.

Lord Shiv is ever present in the invisible *ling* in the form of *parbrahm* even when the universe was not in the existence. After that it is he who appears in the form of visible *ling* and creates the universe. Thus Lord Shiv is present in the universe in both the forms – the invisible (no characteristic) and visible (with characteristic). His visible and invisible (dual) form is called *lingaling*. That is to say that the invisible form of Lord Shiv is presented by *aling*, visible form by *ling*, and the visible and invisible (dual) form by *lingaling*.

The Number of Verses and Sections

There are eleven thousand (11,000) verses and 163 chapters in this Puran. This Puran is divided into two parts – first half and second half. There are 108 chapters in the first half while the second half contains 55 chapters.

The Gist of *Ling Puran*

Consisting 163 chapters, the *Ling Puran* begins with the detailed description of universe. It is said in it that the universe has emerged from the *panchbhoot* namely atmosphere (sky), air, fire, water, and earth.

According to *Ling Puran*, when the thought of the creation of universe came into the heart of Brahmaji, first of all, he produced ego or *aham* (*avidya*). The five sensory characteristics (*tanmatra*) namely sound, touch, beauty, taste, and smell were born out of ego (*ahankar*). The five base elements (*panchtatva*) were produced out of these sensations. Sensation means characteristic of each element. Which means that sensations are subtle and the elements are said to be the bulk.

Explaining this principle in detail and in a simple manner, it is said that the sensory sound emerges from ego, the element of sky from the sound, the sensory touch from sky element, the air element from touch, sensory beauty from air element, fire from the sensory beauty, sensory taste from fire element, water element from taste, smell from water element, and the earth element from smell. The universe emerges in this very sequence of the emergence of elements and sensory characteristics.

The discourses about *yog* and *kalp* have been enclosed

after the description of universe. Thereafter there is description of the appearance of *ling* and its method of prayer and worship, the educative dialogues of Sanatkumar and Shail, the story of Maharshi Dadhichi, the establishment of *yugdharma*, and vault of universe (*Bhuvankosh*).

Thereafter, like other *Purans*, in this *Puran* too, having narrated the Sun dynasty and Moon dynasty, the five distinctions of *Puran* and the story of the execution of the demon named Tripur by Lord Shiv has been described. Lord Shiv had become famous by the name of Tripurari due to executing the demon named Tripurari. In the context of this story, the procedure of the installation of *'ling'* and Lord Shiv being known as Pashupatinath and the uncovering of the *pashu-paash* of gods have also been described.

After that there are descriptions of various holy *vrat*s, good conducts, and remorses etc. that bring blessings of Lord Shiv. Elaboratinging on the good conduct, it has been said in the gist that controlled, religious, kind, *tapaswi*, truthful, and nourishing the good thought for all beings are the men who are dear to Lord Shiv.

Explaining *dharma*, it has been said in this *Puran* that the moveable and immoveable world have been created by God only. Therefore, rejecting the narrowness of high-low, caste and creed, man should nurture the thought of affection and compassion for all the living beings. In fact that is the *dharma* of man.

After that there are the stories of the birth of Andhakasur and his defeat by Lord Shiv, salvation of the earth by Shri Vishnu through the Varah incarnation and the execution of the demon named Jalandhar.

After that, the description of the useful thousand-name *stotra* of Lord Shiv, the destruction of the *yajna* of Daksh Prajapati, the birth of Parvati, the burning of Kaamdev, the wedding of Shiv-Parvati, the birth of Ganesh, the *tandav* dance of Shiv, and character of Upmanyu and other mythological episodes are described. The procedure for the worship of Lord

Shiv, the method of *panch-yajna*, the method of dubbing one's body with ashes, the method of taking a bath, the cycle of astrology, description of India along with islands like Jumbu and Plaksh etc., the story of Kshup-Dadhichi, the story of Dhruv, and the glory of Kaashi – these are the important characteristics of *Ling Puran*.

Having narrated the useful form of Lord Vishnu in the first part of *Ling Puran*, the glory of *Eikadashi vrat* has been established through the story of King Ambareesh. Then there is the dialogue of Sanatkumar and Nandishwar in which the glory of *yajna* and donation, and the worship of sun have been discussed.

After that, the 28 *avatars* of Lord Shiv, the reverence of *aghor* form of Lord Shiv, the glory of Trayambak, the glory of Gayatri, and the educative analysis of the great study of Brajeshwari have been made. Finally, describing the importance of reading, listening, and thinking of the *Ling Puran*, it has been concluded.

Story from *Ling Puran*: Story of King Ambareesh

It is the story of olden times: King Nabhag had a brilliant son named Ambareesh. Ambareesh was a very brave, intelligent, and *tapaswi* king. The entire affluence and material pleasure of the earth were in his control. But the Vishnu devotee, Ambareesh, knew wealth and affluence is the pleasure of a few days but man, in the grip of its greed, falls into the deep hell. Therefore his mind was always dedicated to the lotus feet of Lord Vishnu and towards the service of his devotees.

After being crowned, King Ambareesh worshipped Lord Vishnu through performing several Ashwamedh *yajna*. Pleased with his devotion, Lord Vishnu had appointed his *chakra* for his safety. This *chakra* named Sudarshan destroys enemies and protects devotees.

Once King Ambareesh along with his wife decided to

observe *dwadashi pradhan eikadashi vrat* for one year. He worshipped Lord Vishnu and amply donated grain and money to Brahmins. At that time Durwasa rishi arrived there. Ambareesh welcomed him and made him sit on a higher pedestal. Then after praying Durwasa rishi, he gladly insisted on him to accept the feast. Durwasa rishi accepted his invitation. But first he went to the bank of river Yamuna for pre-meal freshening up. Focusing his meditation on the *Parbrahm*, he started taking bath in the water of river Yamuna.

Here *Dwadashi* was only a few moments away. Finding himself in this dilemma, King Ambareesh discussed with Brahmins, "Gentlemen! Eating without offering to the Brahmin as well as not eating before *Dwadashi* ends – both are the situations which render man sinful. Therefore tell me some way by which I do not become sinful."

Brahmins said, "King! Drinking water is equal to having meals as well as not having meals. Hence you complete the discipline of *Dwadashi* by drinking water." Having heard this, Ambareesh drank water and started waiting for Durwasa *rishi*.

On his return, Durwasa came to know by his power of *tapa* that Ambareesh had finished his meals. Hence he became furious and said bitterly, "Evil Ambareesh! You consider yourself too great under the false pride of money. You have dejected me. You had invited me for meals but have finished your meals before me. Now look how I punish you for your evil act."

Saying this Maharshi Durwasa pulled out a strand of his hair and produced a terrible giant Kritya (Devi Shakti) to kill Ambareesh. Kritya marched towards him with a sword in hand at the command of Durwasa rishi. But without being disturbed, he kept remembering Lord Vishnu in his mind. The moment Kritya attacked on him with the sword, the Sudarshan *chakra* of Lord Vishnu burnt him into ashes. When Durwasa rishi saw that the *chakra* was approaching him after burning Kritya into ash, he became terrified and ran away from there to save his life.

Durwasa rishi went to the sky, nether world (*patal*), the earth, the ocean, the mountains, forests etc. but Sudarshan *chakra* did not leave the chase. When he found shelter nowhere, he started praying Brahmaji for protection.

Expressing his inability, Brahmaji said, "Son! All the gods, Indra, sun, Prajapati, and I am bound within the rules made by Lord Vishnu. We do the good of this universe as per his command. Therefore protecting the enemy of his devotee is not in our control."

Disappointed by Brahmaji, Durwasa rishi went to the shelter of Lord Mahadev. Mahadev said, "*Rishivar*! This Sudarshan *chakra* is the weapon of Lord Vishnu and protects his devotees. Its radiance is unbearable for all. Therefore you go to the refuge of Lord Vishnu. He alone can save from Sudarshan *chakra* and will bless you."

Diapponted from there too, Durwasa *rishi* went to the refuge of Lord Vishnu and fell on his reverd feet and said humbly, "Lord! I am your culprit. I tried to kill your supreme devotee King Ambareesh for I was unaware of your influence. You are ocean of compassion. Kindly forgive my devilry and protect me. The living beings become free from trouble merely by remembering your name. Be kind on this devotee of yours too."

Lord Vishnu said, "*Munivar*! I am always in the control of my devotees. My simple and plain devotees have bound me with their love. I am the only shelter of my devotees. Therefore, other than them, I neither like myself nor goddess Lakshmi. How can I even think of leaving them who have come to me leaving their kith and kins and all the pleasure? You go to the refuge of devotee Ambareesh if you wish to save yourself from this trouble. You will automatically become free from this trouble if he will be pleased."

Following the advice of Lord Vishnu, Durwasa rishi returned to Ambareesh and started asking for forgiveness catching his feet. Ambareesh became very compassionate seeing this tragedy of Maharshi Durwasa. Then he hymned the *chakra* to go back. Sudarshan *chakra* returned pleased with his prayer and Durwasa rishi became free from its fear.

King Ambareesh had not taken food since Durwasa rishi had gone from there. But, first of all, seating Durwasa rishi with honour, he prayed him methodically and feasted him heartily. Pleased by the behaviour of King Ambareesh, Maharshi Durwasa blessed him and went away from there.

Ambareesh righteously ruled the earth for many years. When he grew old, he handed over the kingdom to his sons and went himself to forest to do *tapasya*. He surrendered all the pleasures and transcended into *samadhi* meditating Lord Vishnu. At last he met the supreme abode by the blessings of *Parbrahm* Lord Shri Vishnu.

•••

12

VARAH PURAN

Introduction

First of all, Lord Varah had told this *Puran* to the earth; therefore this *Puran* is called *'Varah Puran'*. In fact it was Lord Vishnu who had incarnated as *Varah avatar* to salvage the earth. Hence, for the description of Lord Vishnu in the form of *Varah* (pig), this *Puran* is said to be *'Vaishnav Puran'*.

In this *avatar*, Lord Varah, having executed the demon named Hiranyaksh, supported the earth on his vast mouth for one thousand years. Subsequently placed back on her designated spot, and presenting her curiosity about the form of Lord Varah, Lord Varah gave her discourse of the ancient and deep knowledge. The same divine knowledge offered to the earth by Lord Varah has been analysed in detail in this *Puran*.

The Number of Verses and Sections

Varah Puran is the essence of ten thousand (10,000) verses (*shlokas*). This holy *Puran* is one long text instead of being divided into sections or *skandh*. There are a total of two hundred and seventeen (217) chapters in the entire *Puran*, which present in order the discourse given to goddess earth by Lord Varah.

The Gist of *Varah Puran*

The birth of universe and its step-by-step development has been described at the beginning of this *Puran*. After that there is description of the glory of *Brahmpar stotra*. 'Action is supreme between knowledge and action', this statement has been clarified with help of the story of a hunter named Nishthur. After that, the holy *stotra* named Pundareekaksh derived from the story of Raibhya muni, and the importance of *shraadh-tarpan* at pilgrim spots have been established. Subsequently, the emergence of *swarg* (paradise), *patal* (subterranean zone) and other *loks*, along with the glory of Trishakti, the mythological episode of the protection of *Vedas* by the *matsya-avatar* of Lord Narayan, the glory of Shakti and the glory of Triprakar *stotra* have been analysed.

Clarifying the glory of Triprakar *stotra*, it is said that keeping it at home in the written form shuns away all troubles, illness, and impediments. The devotees earn special rewards for reading this *stotra* on the eighth, ninth, and fourteenth day of a month.

After Lord Shiv's *vrat* named *Kapalik* and the story of Satyatapa of Bhrigu dynasty, the method of worship of Lord Vishnu on the twelfth day of a month (*dwadashi*) and the glory of donations of *jaldhenu, rasdhenu, gurdhenu, sharkaradhenu, madhudhenu, navneetdhenu, lavandhenu* etc. through the story of king Shwet has been described.

After that, the description of the mistakes committed against Lord Vishnu, and number of forefathers and the dates of *shraadh* have been analysed. The time of inception of Uttarayan and Dakshinayan, the moonless night (*amavasya*) when *nakshatra*s named Vishakha, Anuradha, and Swati converge, and the moonless night when the nine *nakshatra*s converge and the dates of *ashtaka* are great dates for *shraadh*.

After the description of *shraadh*, there are the descriptions of the episodes of the birth of a son named Durjay at the house of king Supritak, defeat of gods by Durjaya, Lord Vishnu offering Chintamani to a *rishi* named Gaurmukh, snatching of the Chintamani from Gaurmukh muni by Durjay, and turning of Durjay to ashes by Lord Narayan. The Sudarshan *chakra* of Lord Narayan had taken just a *nimish* of time (sixty

Message of the Purans

nimish is equal to one second) to turn Durjay along with his army into ashes; therefore that place became famous by the name of *'Nimisharanya'*.

Various holy *vrat*s and the related stories are depicted from the 20th to 50th chapter. The special dates and the stories of the emergence of their ruling gods and their character are described in the date *(thithi) vrat*s. By praying and worshipping the ruling gods on the special dates provides great rewards. These special dates and its governing deities are as follows:

Special Dates	Ruling God	Special Dates	Ruling God
Pratipada (1st)	Agnidev (Fire)	Dashami (10th)	Dishaa
Dwitiya (2nd)	Ashwinikumar	Eikadashi (11th)	Kuber
Tritiya (3rd)	Gauri	Dwadashi (12th)	Shri Vishnu
Chaturthi (4th)	Ganesh	Tryodashi (13th)	Dharma
Panchami (5th)	Naag (Snake)	Chaturdashi (14th)	Rudra
Shashthi (6th)	Kaartikeya	Amavasya	Pitragana
Saptami (7th)	Surya (Sun)	(Moonless Night)	
Ashtami (8th)	Maatrikaa	Poornima	Chandrama
Navami (9th)	Gaayatri	(Full Moon)	(Moon)

In this *Puran*, there is description of the stories of the ten incarnations of Lord Vishnu corresponding to the *Dwadashi* (twelfth day of the month) *vrat* of the twelve months:

The Month of Dwadashi	The avatar of Shri Vishnu
Maargsheersh	Matsya (Fish)
Paush	Koorm
Maagh	Varah
Falgun	Nrisingh
Chaitra	Vaman
Vaishakh	Parashuram
Jyeshtha	Shri Ram
Ashaarh	Shri Krishna
Shravan	Buddh
Bhadrapad	Kalki (Yet to happen)

After the glory of the *Dwadashi vrat*, the mythological description along with various methods of worship has been established of several holy *vrat*s namely Kaanti, Avighna, Dhanya, Shanti, Saubhagya, Arogya, Kaam, Shaurya, Putreshti, Saarvbhaum, and Raudra etc.

After that, the bringing of Ganga on the earth by Maharshi Gautam, the glory of Trinity, and the seven islands such as Jumbu and Saptdweep etc. are narrated.

After that, explaining the method of worship of Lord Vishnu, narrations about various pilgrim spots namely Kokamukh teerth, Karveer teerth, Agni teerth, Vayavya teerth, Shukra teerth, Taptsamudrak teerth, Manasar teerth, Poornmukh teerth, Maya teerth, Kubjamrak teerth, Manas teerth, Haridwar, Saarvakaalik teerth, Akhetak teerth, Gridhvat teerth, Chakra teerth, Vaivswat teerth, etc. and the related stories, worship method, the importance of bathing and donation at such pilgrim spots, and the great rewards earned from it have been analysed. Within this context, the procedure of the *Bhagwati deeksha* that removes the illusory bondage of life and death, and the geographical, cultural, and historical description of Mathura have been presented.

Characterisation of Ganesh, characterisation of Kartikeya, description of regions of Rudra, characterisations of Sun, Brahmaji, and Lord Shiv, description of their prayer and worship, the discourse as mentioned in *Vedas* between Devshuni-Sharma and Nachiketa are the other distinctions of this *Puran*. The sinful deeds have been discussed in detail in the discourse of Nachiketa. Besides, in this *Puran*, *Karmvipaak*, glory of faithful woman (*pativrata*), glory of Gokarneshwar and Shukreshwar, *panchratracharya*, *varnashram* dharma, devotion to God, praise of self-realization (*atmagyan*) etc. and such subjects have been established in detail.

Men have been preached of virtues of helping others, selfless service, truth, compassion, good conduct, reverence, forgiveness, etc. through several educative discourses narrated in this *Puran*.

The making of idols of different gods with different metals

or material, description of their method of installation, and expression of the glory of *Shaligram* and *Shivling* has been made in the *Varah Puran*.

Finally this *Puran* has been concluded with the description of different sinful deeds and the different hells met as a result and the glory of reading, listening, and contemplating about *Varah Puran*.

Story from *Varah Puran*: *Chandal* and *Brahmrakshas*

This story belongs to the old times: A *Chandal* used to live in a beautiful city named Avanti (Ujjain) situated at the bank of river Kshipra. He was very humble, truthful, intelligent and skilled in music. Sustaining his family by earning money through noble deeds was his motive. He was great devotee of Lord Narayan. He observed fast on the eleventh day (*eikadashi*) of every month and sang hymns at the temple of Lord Vishnu. He would return home the next day after bowing to God and would eat meals after offering food to his family. Thus the major part of his age was spent meditating at the lotus feet of Lord Narayan.

Once, on the *eikadashi* of *Krishna paksh* (dark phase of the moon), the *Chandal* went to the forest to collect flowers to worship Lord Narayan. A dreadful *Brahmrakshas* used to live in that forest. The *Brahmrakshas* was very cruel and sinful by nature. He would kill and eat every man who trespassed the forest. When the *Chandal* was collecting flowers for the worship of Lord Vishnu then *Brahmrakshas* caught him and said with loud laughter, "It seems as my luck is in my favour today, that is why I have got my food without exerting myself. Now I will eat it in peace."

Then the *Chandal* beseeched, "the king of demon! Do not eat me today. Spare me. I will return to you tomorrow morning. Tonight I have to pray and worship Lord Narayan and have to sing his hymns. You should not become impediment to it. I promise that I will surrender myself to your service at the break of the dawn. I would hail dreadful hell if I could not fulfil my words."

The *Brahmrakshas* was in awe on listening to the *Chandal*. He allowed him to go and sat down there to wait for him to return. The *Chandal* rushed to the temple and gave the flowers brought from the forest to the priest to offer at the lotus feet of Lord Vishnu. Then sitting at the door of the temple and singing hymns remained awake all night. In the morning the *Chandal* took bath and bowed to Lord Narayan. Then started for the demon to fulfil his promise.

On the way, seeing him heading towards the forest, a known Brahmin interrupted him, "Look! Today is *dwadashi* and you should be returning to your home after keeping awake the whole night for Lord Vishnu. Why, then, are you going towards the forest?"

The *Chandal* told him the complete story. Then the Brahmin said, "This body is the sole means of the four endeavours namely *dharma, arth, kaam,* and *moksha*; hence man should always look for its well-being. Man can attain emancipation (*moksha*) only on being alive. Therefore leave this foolishness and return to your home."

Listening to the Brahmin, the *Chandal* said humbly, "Brahmindev! It is only the truth that is permanent and holy in this world. All the happiness and affluence possible on the earth are achieved by truth. Man attains *dharma, arth, kaam,* and *moksha* by truth only. Truth is *Parbrahm*. Even among *yajnas*, the truth is the superiormost; therefore man should never leave the truth." Saying this the *Chandal* moved on towards the forest and arrived at the demon soon.

Seeing the *Chandal*, the *Brahmrakshas* said with surprise, "Sir! You are the true observer of the truth. It appears from this deed of yours that you are not a *Chandal* but a truthful Brahmin who observes his *dharma*. You have proved true to your words by coming here. I, too, am curious to know what you have done at the Lord Vishnu's temple which makes you look so happy? How long it has been for you in his devotion?"

Message of the Purans

Chandal said, "Hey demon! Having gone to temple I sang hymns of Lord Vishnu and remained awake the whole night singing his praise. Waking the whole night on the eleventh day of every month, I have spent twenty years."

Brahmrakshas said, "Sir! You are the supreme devotee of Lord Narayan. If you offer me the reward of waking one night, I will free you and go away from here."

Chandal said, "King of demon! I have offered you my body, therefore leave the useless talk and make me your meal."

Brahmrakshas said humbly, "Sir! At least provide me the reward of the last hymn that you sang about Lord Narayan when the night was about to pass by so that my salvation could be possible."

Then *Chandal* said, "Hey king of demon! I can offer you the reward of my one hymn if you promise not to kill anybody henceforth or you can eat me."

Brahmrakshas happily accepted the condition of *Chandal*. Then the *Chandal* offered him the reward of waking half the night and hymning. *Brahmrakshas* became very happy on receiving it and bowed to the *Chandal* and moved away towards a pilgrim spot named Prithudak. *Brahmrakshas* stopped eating there and eventually left his life. With the reward of hymn, his *punya* was increased and as a result he was born in the Brahmin *yoni* after getting freedom from the *rakshas yoni*.

Hither, after this episode, the *Chandal* also became detached. Transferring the responsibility of his wife on his sons, wandering around the earth, he arrived at a pilgrim spot named *Paapmochan*. He took bath there and became free from all the sins and attained the great status and secured place in *Vaikunth*.

•••

13

SKAND PURAN

Introduction

The *'Skand Puran'* is the lengthiest among the eighteen *Purans* written by Maharshi Vedvyas. The mythological discourses, educative discourses, and intriguing mysteries related with the universe have been presented in this great *Puran* in more detail than other *Purans*.

Skand Kumar is the eldest son of Lord Shiv and Bhagwati Parwati. Another famous name of him is Kartikeya. *Skand* means 'execution'. Skand Kumar has been established as the executional power of gods in the *Purans* and other religious texts. Kumar Kartikeya, in his childhood, had executed the demon named Tarkasur along with his army for the benefit of the universe, therefore he received the name *'Skand'*. In the context of *Skand Puran*, the word *Skand* means the power of execution. But the knowledge itself described in this *Puran* has been said to be the power of execution, which destroys ignorance residing in the heart of man, *adharma*, and injustice.

Though the *Skand Puran* is a *Puran* predominantly promoting *Shaivmat* yet the glory of Vishnu, Brahma, and such gods besides Lord Shiv has been duly established. There is detailed description of the character of Lord Shri Ram in this *Puran*.

The Number of Verses and Sections

This *Puran* comprises eighty-one thousand verses (*shlokas*). The entire *Puarn* is divided into six sections. These sections (*khand*) are : *Maaheshwar khand, Vaishnav khand, Brahm khand, Kaashi khand, Avantika khand,* and *Reva khand.* Although some people divide the *Avantika khand* into *Tapti khand* and *Prabhas khand* and thus make it a *Puran* of seven *khand*s, yet its six divisions only are acceptable.

(Although *Skand Puran* is included among the eighteen *Purans* written by Maharshi Vedvyas, yet there is a sub-*puran* (*up-puran*) by this name too. According to the *Soot Samhita,* this sub-*puran* has been divided into six parts namely *Sanatkumar Samhita, Soot Samhita, Shankar Samhita, Vaishnav Samhita, Braahm Samhita,* and *Saur Samhita.* The division of the *Samhita* provides the separate identity to the sub-*puran* named *Skand Puran.*)

Gist of *Skand Puran*

1. *Maaheshwar Khand*

Maaheshwar Khand is divided into three subsections (*upkhand*) – *Kedar, Kumarika,* and the glory of *Arunachal.* The essence of these subsections is described here with the main text.

Maaheshwar Khand begins with the Shiv-*katha.* The mythological episodes where furious Daksh Prajapati invokes curse on Shivji and Nandi invokes curse on Daksh are described in it. In the same story, there are episodes of *yajna* organized by Daksh at Kankhal, self-immolation by Bhagwati Sati infuriated by the rejection of Shiv, emergence of Veerbhadra, battle between gods and Shiv *gana,* destruction of the *yajna* of Daksh, resurrection of Daksh Prajapati by Lord Shiv, a vast form attained by *Shivling,* removal of one head of Brahmaji by Bhairav at the command of Lord Shiv. In this context the curse to prohibit the flower of Ketaki for his worship by Lord Shiv and boon for the devotees engaged in the decoration of the Shiv-*mandap* have been described.

After that the episodes described are of the glory of the installation of *Ling* and the worship of *Ling*, advent of Ravan, rejection of the guru of gods Brihaspati by Indra, capturing of the governance of paradise by demons, the churning of ocean, drinking of poison by Lord Shiv, emergence of Lakshami, the *Mohini avatar* of Lord Vishnu, and the rift between *Chandra* (moon) and Rahu.

After that, the execution of Tarkasur by Kartikeya and Meru, Udaygiri, Mahendra, Shail, Vindhya, Shwetkut, Trikut etc. mountains transforming into the *Ling* form have been described. Narrating the glory of *Shivling*, lord Skand Kumar says that the *Ling* of Lord Shiv who is the ruler of all gods should be considered as the temple of Shiv (*Shivalaya*). *Ling* can be made of any metal or material. For example – sapphire, ruby, pearl, *padmrag*, *gomed*, silver, gold, *markat*, *chandra* and such metals may be used to make *Ling*. All the stones at the middle of the river Reva (Narmada) have attained the form of *Ling* by the blessings of Lord Mahadev. It should be worshipped by the method prescribed in scriptures. The kind sight of Lord Shiv always stays with the man who meditates and worships *Shivling*. The entire trouble of the devotee is removed who meditates this *'Om Namah Shivaya!'* mantra.

Describing the signs and *Nakshatra* it is said that when Brahmaji created the entire moveable and immoveable world along with cosmos, then the cycle of sign was born. The 12 signs and 27 *Nakshatra*s are present in this cycle of sign. The play of this world is governed by the time cycle of these signs and *nakshatra*s. This cycle of sign and *Nakshatra* governs creation, fostering, and destruction.

Thereafter, glorifying the donations made on the *Poornima* (the day of full moon) and *Amavasya* (the day of moonless night) and describing the special dates and its ruling gods, it is said that the midnight of the fourteenth day of *Krishna paksha* (phase) is famous as the date designated for Lord Shiv. This is called *Shivratri* (the month of *Shivratri*). To exemplify the glory of *Shivratri-vrat* there is a story of a *Chandal* who, due to observing *Shivratri-vrat*, became King Vichitraveerya in his second birth and was called Veerbhadra in his third birth emerging from the locks of Lord Shiv.

After that there is description of the Panchapsar pilgrim spot. Five pilgrims namely Mahakaleshwar, Kumaresh, Stambhesh, Varkareshwar, and Siddhesh spots are merging in the Panchapsar pilgrim spot. In the related stories, there is the episode of the devotees being asked to leave these pilgrim spots out of the dread of five alligators and subsequently their salvation by Arjun, the son of Pandu. In fact, these five alligators were five nymphs *(apsaras)* of paradise whose names were Varcha, Saurmeyi, Saameyi, Budbuda, and Lata and who were rendered free of their curse by Arjun.

The glory of donation has been established by the dialogue between Devarshi Narad and King Dharmavarma. Naradji says that donations should be made with full respect and capacity. He who donates despite shortage in family never gets happiness. The donation should always be made as per *dharma*. Someone's deposit, the money kept for emergency and borrowed money should never be donated. *Dharma, arth, kaam, kreeda, harsha,* and *bhaya* – these are said to be the six types of donations. That is someone by greed, someone by desire of reward, someone by being glad to see some loved one, and some by the fear go for making donation. The *dharma* donation is the greatest and the most beneficial among all the donations which are offered without any expectation to someone who deserves. The good influence of the donation made to the noble men remains stable even in the *parlok*, whereas the reward of the donation made to evil men extenuates in this world only. One should not repent after making a donation otherewise its importance is weakened. The donation which is not made with due respect or the donation; which arouses anger never yield reward.

After that, there is description of the narration of the previous birth as told to King Indradyumn by Lomesh rishi and the glory of the worship of Shiv and *Mahisagar sangam* (confluence).

After that, describing the glory of the names of the eighteen rivers it is said that men earn happiness and luck by chanting it. These holy rivers are as follows:

Iravati	Ganga	Payovaha
Daatridaatri	Shubha	Shasyamala
Mahasindhu	Tamra	Prithustuta
Kshitijanma	Rasya	Indradyumn kanya
Mahiparna	Mahishringa	Pitrapritiprada
Rajnadi	Nadnadi	Pashchimvahini

Subsequently, establishing the glory of Shatarudriya by Bhatriyajna muni, the worship of *Shivling*, made of different metals and installed by gods, demons, kings, *nags* (snake), *rishi*s and *muni*s, has been described.

The installation of three *Shivlings* by Lord Skand Kumar (Kartikeya) and different mysteries of the worship of *Shivling*, 108 names of Skand Kumar, mythological geographical system, the system of the nine planets, the detailed description of seven *lok*s, hells, *kaalman*, and India *('Bharat')* and the story of Kumarika, the daughter of King Shatshring are the educative distinctions of this section *(khand)*. Several curiosities related with *shraadh* (post-funeral rites) have been clarified through the dialogue between Mahakaal and Karandham.

After that, there are described *Kaliyug* and different royal dynasties, expression of good conduct, establishing lord Sun (*Suryadev*) by the name of Mahaditya by Devarshi Narad and hymning him with 108 names, the signs of body by Kamadh, position of *jeev* at and after death, the marriage of Ghatotkach, and the story of the birth of Barbreek.

Describing the glory of Arunachal, Lord Shiv installed in the form of stable *Ling*, the glory of various Shiv pilgrim spots, and the forms in which Lord Shiv is placed there with Goddess Parwati, are detailed.

Message of the Purans

The two famous mythological episodes of Bhagwati Durga described in *Durga-Saptshati* – the story of the execution of the demons Mahishasur and Shumbh and Nishumbh – have been described in detail in this section.

Finally this section *(khand)* comes to an end explaining the birth of Khadagteerth by Vindhyavasini, the story of Kaladhar, and the glory of the worship of Arunachaleshwar by Vajrangad.

2. *Vaishnav Khand*

Vaishnav Khand is also divided into subsections (*upkhand*) like *Maaheshwar Khand*. The number of its subsection is eight. These eight subsections are – glory of Bhoomivarah or Venkatachal, glory of Utkal or Purushottam region, glory of Badrikashram, glory of the month of Kartik, glory of Maargsheersh, glory of *Shrimad Bhagwat*, glory of Vaishakh, and the glory of Ayodhya. Like *Maaheshwar Khand*, here too the essence of this section is present in one text.

In the beginning of this *Khand* (section), the glory of mountain Venkatachal (Tirupati Balaji) and the pilgrim spots situated there has been described in detail. Lord Varah says that Venkatachal is the abode of lord Narayan in the Kaliyug. Hence it is also called Narayangiri. The pilgrim spots namely Chakra teerth, Kumardharika teerth, Dev teerth, Papnashan teerth, Akashganga teerth, Pandav teerth, Swami Pushkarani teerth, Tumb teerth, Krishna teerth, etc, which are supremely rewarding and provider of great benefits are situated at this holy mountain.

Explaining the glory of holy dip on the auspicious dates at these pilgrim spots, it is said that when the sun stays in the Auarius sign in the month of Maagh then by taking a bath and donation of grain in the afternoon on the day of full moon during *Magha nakshatra* at the pilgrim spot named Kumardharika brings equal reward as taking regular dip in the river Ganga for 12 years. Similarly, the entire sins of previous births are destroyed by taking bath at the Paapnaashan teerth when the celestial arrangement be of Pushya or Hast *nakshatra* on the Sunday of *Shukla paksh* or *Krishna paksh* (phase) and the date being seventh *(Saptami)*. Man attains emancipation by taking bath in the Tumbteerth pilgrim spot situated at mountain Guha when the sun stays in the Piscean sign and there be *Uttarfalguni nakshatra*.

In this context, the journey of Venkatachal by Pandu's son Arjun, the performing of *tapa* by Hanumanji's mother Anjana and boon of becoming mother to a son offered to her by *Vayudev* (the god of air) are the episodes which have been described.

After the glory of Venkatachal, establishing the glory of Purushottam kshetra it is said that Lord Narayan resides here in the human form. The *punya* (the holy reward) amounting to all the pilgrims is obtained by living in this region. Setting eyes upon Lord Purushottam after taking bath in the water of ocean, and by living in the Purushottam region, the devotee attains emancipation.

It becomes clear from the story related with Purushottam teerth that King Indradyumn had installed the idols of Lord Vasudev, Balramji, and Subhadra in this region on the advice of Devarshi Narad. Vishwakarma himself had made these idols. Besides this, Vishwakarma had created a huge beautiful chariot run by a hundred horses. The chariot-celebration, the retiring celebration of Lord Narayan, the worship method of twelve Aaditya, and the stories of departure to Brahmlok of King Indradyumn have been described in detail in this Khand.

Subsequently, narrating the glory of Badrikashram, Lord Shiv says that the region named Badrikashram of Shri Hari is extremely holy and rewarding and rare. The entire sins of devotees are destroyed merely by rememberance of this region. Those devotees who have performed *tapa* in the other pilgrim spots are included itself in the Badrikashram teerth. Badrikashram teerth is superior and holy among all the pilgrim spots. The reward that one gets through performing one thousand *Ashwamedh yajna* and by surviving on air alone, comes by in a moment at Badrikashram teerth. The ablution at Badrikashram teerth provides emancipation in *Satyug*, pleasure and affluence in *Treta*, rewarding in *Dwapar*, and *punya* (holy reward) in *Kaliyug*. Therefore several great *rishi*s and *muni*s stay here permanently.

There are five holy rocks at the Badrikashram teerth, which fulfil all the desires of the devotees. These rocks are called Narad, Markandeya, Garud, Varah, and Naarsinhi.

A region named Brahm teerth is situated at Badrikashram, where Lord Vishnu had incarnated as Hayagreev and had protected *Vedas* from the demons named Madhu-Kaitabh. A beautiful pond is situated at the Brahm teerth. It is said that the water in the pond is a fraction of the radiance of *Vedas*.

After that the glory of the month of Kartik is described in detail. Brahmaji says that like Shri Vishnu among gods and Badrikashram among pilgrims are superior, similarly the month of Kartik is extremely rewarding among all the months. The donation made during this month remembering Lord Vishnu destroys all the sins. By observing fast during this month, man becomes free from confusion and ego.

The scriptural method of observing *vrat* in the month of Kartik and action done during this month and the rewards from it are also described in detail in this *khand*. After that the story of Vishnudas and King Chol, marriage of Tulsi, the procedure of Bhimpanchak *vrat*, and the discourse on the prayer and worship of Shri Vishnu have been given.

Elaborating on the glory of the month of Vaishakh it is said that the donation, *vrat*, and bathing in this month destroy all the sins. Gods themselves perform worship of this month. Like Sheshnaag among snakes, Garud among birds, Brahmin among *varn*, gold among metals, and Ganga among rivers are superior, similarly Vaishakh is superior among months for the purpose of *dharma*. The month is the symbol of love for Lord Vishnu. The person who takes bath before sunrise easily secures all the superior rewards. Oil massage, sleeping on the bed or charpoy, bathing in house, taking meal twice, or eating in the night – all these acts are prohibited in the month of Vaishakh.

Illustrating the glory of the monh of Vaishakh it is said that the nectar had emerged from the ocean on the eleventh day of this month; Lord Vishnu had protected it from the demons on the twelfth day; and the gods had the opportunity to drink the nectar on the thirteenth day by the blessing of Lord Vishnu. Salvation of Hemkant by *Chhatradaan*, observance of *Vaishakh dharma* by King Kirtiman, offering of a part from the month of Vaishakh to Yam by Shri Vishnu, and the transformation of Maharshi Valmiki from *munikumar* to lion and becoming *rishi* again from the lion are the stories that are narrated here.

After that, narrating the glory of Ayodhya, the geographical situation of Ayodhya, the birth placc of Lord Shri Ram, glory of river Saryu, Brihaspatikund, Sitakund, Urvashikund, Ghosharkkund, Ksheerodakteerth, Gayakoopteerth and Singhpeedh situated in Ayodhya have been described. In this context, the holy rewards obtained by taking bath and making donation here have been described. Thus this *khand* (section) has been concluded with the glory of Ayodhya.

3. Brahm Khand

Like the first and second *khands*, *Brahm Khand* is divided into subsections (*upkhand*) too. *Setu Mahatmya*, *Dharmaranya Mahatmya*, *Chaaturmasya Mahatmya*, and *Brahmottar Mahatmya* are the four subsections (*upkhand*) of this *khand*. The essence of all the four sub-sections described above is presented here in one text.

The *Vaishnav khand* begins with the glory of the region of Rameshwar. The *Shivling* made of sand by Lord Shri Ram and the Shivling brought from Kailash by Hanumanji are placed in this area. Ram teerth, Lakshman teerth, Sitasarovar teerth, Brahmkund, Vetalvarad teerth, Chakra teerth, Paapvinashan teerth, Agastya teerth, Shiv teerth, Hanumatkund, Shankh teerth, Koti teerth, Ganga teerth, Yamuna teerth, Dhanushkoti teerth, Agni teerth, Manas teerth, Jay teerth, Sadhyamrit teerth, Mangal teerth, Amritvapika teerth, Gaya teerth, Lakshami teerth, and Saraswati teerth –

these twenty-four extremely holy teerth (pilgrim spots) are situated here.

After that, there are the stories narrated of Ashwathama taking bath and making donation at the Dhanushkoti teerth after assassination of the sons of Pandavs, installation of the *shivling* at Rameshwar by Shri Ram and Sita, the installation of a *Shivling* named Hanumadeeshwar by Hanumanji, and birth of Mahalakshmi at the house of King Punyanidhi.

In the context of the glory of Dharmaran teerth, the episode of the incarnation of Shri Vishnu as Hayagreev has been narrated. Elaborating the glory of the *teerth*, it has been said that adorned as *tilak* on the forehead of the earth, this holy pilgrim spot is excessively dear to Goddess Saraswati. Brahma, Vishnu, Shiv, Indra and other gods, beautiful dancers of the paradise (*apsara*), *lokpaal*, *Gandharva*, *Yaksh* etc. stay in this teerth permanently. The person who dies here, in this *teerth*, meets good end. The entire sins of men are destroyed merely by a sight of the Brahmins who live here.

Subsequently, enumerating *dharma*, good conduct, and *Kaliyug*, the glory of the four-month (*Chaturmasya*) has been discussed. Brahmaji says that the emancipation for men is not difficult due to observing *vrat* of *Chaturmasya*. This *vrat* is very dear to Lord Vishnu as well. It is desired of men that they observe *vrat* of Lord Vishnu during *Chaturmasya*. He naturally provides emancipation to the devotees who observe this *vrat*. Taking bath in *Chaturmasya* provides, reward equal to taking bath during all the seasons.

If a man takes bath for one day at the Bhaskar region in the river Narmada or bathes for three days in the river Narmada during *Chaturmasya*, it destroys all his sins. The devotee who takes bath in the river Godavari (Gautami) for one *paksh* (fifteen days) secures place in the *Vaikunthlok*. During *Chaturmasya*, Lord Vishnu reside in the water and therefore the water of all the pilgrim spots become pure and holy by his radiance. Therefore the bathing of *Chaturmasya* holds great importance.

Finally, this *khand* is concluded with the story of Daarshaah-Kalawati and the glory of five-lettered (*panchakshari*) *Shaiva* study.

4. Kashi Khand

Kashi, Naimish, Kurukshetra, Ayodhya, Mathura, Gangadwar, Amarawati, Kanchi, Gangasagar, Sindhusangh, Dwarika, Godawari, Tatkalanjar, Prabhas, Badrikashram, Pushkar, Gaya etc. and several pilgrim spots have been described in this *khand*. Describing the glory of Kashi, it is said that Kashi is the king of all pilgrim spots. Devotees discover here all the endurances namely *dharma, arth, kaam,* and *moksha*. The pilgrim spot of Gaya is said to be providing freedom to forefathers.

Truth, forgiveness, contentment, control on senses, holiness, compassion, donation, and observance of celibacy have been termed as the pilgrimage of mind (*manas teerth*) in this *khand*. Speaking sweet, striving for learning, and patience have also been said to be the main pilgrimage of mind (*manas teerth*). The purity of mind has been said as the main *manas teerth*. It is said that man can live in several pilgrim spots but until he does not purge himself with the water of knowledge of *manas teerth* he cannot get the *punya* (the holy reward). Which means by keeping senses in control, and repudiating the lascivious pleasures, envy, ignorance and cunningness from mind and following generosity, compassion, contentment and patience etc. and then residing in the pilgrim spots only can fetch man the *punya*.

After glorification of pilgrim spots, the glory of Gayatri, rise of Vishwamitra from the position of *Rajarshi* to *Brahmarshi* with the blessing of Goddess Gayatri, and the main names of Lord Sun (*Suryadev*) and his *mantra* have been described. In this context, it is said that Lord Sun remains present in all the ten directions. He is worshipped with *Gayatri mantra*. The men who bow to *Suryadev*, become as radiant as him. The men who perform *yajna* after taking bath at the dawn on the day of Sunday in the month of Paush become free from lust, anger, and attachment. Those who perform *shraadh* (post-funeral rite) related with forefathers and feast Brahmins on this day secure the supreme position. Those who make worship of Sun during the period of *Sankranti* never face adversity.

When the Sun is eclipsed by *Rahu*, all the water becomes like the water of Ganga, Brahmins become like Brahma, and all the things offered as donation become like gold. All the religious rituals during solar eclipse, be it donation, chanting of hymns, *hawan*, taking bath etc., become the means to realize Brahm.

After the glory of the sun, the glory of Manikarnika region and the related mythological episodes have been described. It is said about Manikarnika that the holy reward (*punya*) obtained by taking bath in the entire set of the pilgrims collectively can be obtained singularly by taking bath in Manikarnika just once. One should methodically take a bath in the Manikarnika region and should offer water with reverence. The man who has conquered his senses should first take bath in silence and then should visit lord Vishwanath. He can easily secure the *punya* of his all the *vrats* by doing so.

After that, the mythological story of turning the sons of Sagar into ashes by Kapil muni and descent of Ganga on the earth by Bhagirath has been described. In this context it is said that the man, who uses the water of river Ganga, masters all the disciplines of *yoga*. Ganga is the only means of salvation in *Kaliyug*. Man gains the knowledge of *Vedanta* by living at the holy bank of Ganga.

Once Lord Shiv had said to Shri Hari, "Holy Ganga provides reward to devotees according to their inner perception. *Yajna*, donation, *tapa*, *yoga* etc. do not provide as superior rewards as can be secured merely by praying Ganga. Ganga is means of all – *atmagyan* (the knowledge of soul), *Brahmgyan*, and self-salvation. The real *Parbrahm* can be realized by praying Ganga. Ganga is a form of the core of fire of my radiance and is the manifestation of my semen. She burns all the evils and destroys all the sins. Therefore devotees must pray and worship Ganga."

Forefathers feel satiated by flowing the material made of ghee, jaggery, and sesame in Ganga during *shraadh* (post-funeral rites). Taking bath in the water of Ganga irrespective of the conduciveness of *Nakshatra* or date etc. removes sins.

After the detailed description of the glory of Ganga and establishing the glory of Varanasi, it has been said that Kashi (Varanasi) is very dear to Lord Mahadev. All the persons reside in this city in the devotional mood by the influence of Shiv. Man departs to heaven from here after realizing Mahalakshmi. If Vaikunth be placed on the one pan of a balance and Kashi on the other, then the Kashi would weigh more. According to *Purans* the inhabitants of Kashi have been said to be the councillors of Lord Shiv.

After that, the mythological stories related with *Gyanod teerth, Kapaalmochan teerth, Matsyodari teerth* etc. and taking bath and making donations there on the special dates have been described. Related with Lord Shiv, all these pilgrim spots are situated at Varanasi.

The glory of the bank *(ghat)* of *Yogakhyan* Dashashwamedh, description of the emergence of Trilochan, and Vyas pillar *(bhujstambh)* are the important distinctions of this *khand*. In the context of Dashashwamedh *ghat*, arrival of Brahmaji in Kashi in the disguise of a Brahmin, organization of *Ashwamedh yajna* by King of Kashi Divodas, and installation of a *Shivling* named Dashashwamedh by Brahmaji have been narrated. Finally this *khand* has been concluded narrating the glory of Lord Shiv by means of the discourse by Maharshi Vedvyas.

5. *Avanti Khand*

In the beginning of this *khand*, glory of the rivers named Ganga, Yamuna, Saraswati, Chandrabhaga, Narmada, Vitasta, Godavari, etc. and pilgrim spots named Amarkantak, Prabhas, Kurukshetra, Naimishyaranya, Pushkar, and Kedar have been described.

After that, *Markateshwar teerth* situated in Avanti (Ujjain) has been described. In relation to this pilgrim spot it has been said that the holy reward (*punya*) equivalent to donating a hundred cows is earned just by taking a bath here. Children become free of illness if they are fed black gram and red lentil mixed together here in this pilgrim spot. The *punyas* of men rise at this place by the blessing of mother Sheetala. Subsequently, the stories of Sumati's son Agnisharma becoming a robber and Agnisharma performing *tapa* as directed by *Saptrishis* have been described.

Agnisharma became famous by the name of Valimiki due to performing *tapa* in a cave named Valimik for thirteen years with the blessings of *Saptrishis*. Later Maharshi Valmiki undertook long meditation of Lord Shiv and, after obtaining the ability to write poetry, created *Ramayan*. Since then he became famous in Avanti (Ujjain) by the name of *Valmikeshwar*.

After that the episodes of the birth of Somdev (Chandrama), production of medicines through him, making of Somdev the king of medicines by Brahmaji, birth of Budh from the fraction of Somdev, and prayer and worship of Lord Someshwar by Somdev establish the glory of *Someshwar Shivling* in the *Someshwar teerth*.

In the context of glorifying the Kimpunakteerth situated at Avanti, describing the story of Brahmin named Vishwasuk, it has been elaborated that taking bath in this pilgrim spot destroys even sins like *brahmhatya*.

After that, emergence of river Kshipra from the blood spilled from the little finger of Lord Vishnu and the story of Banasur has been described. After that, describing Vishnu *stotra*, Lord Vishnu incarnating in Vaman *avatar* and the story of sending Bali to *Patal* and stationing himself there has been said to illustrate the glory of pilgrim spot named *Vaman kund*.

Daksh's story in the episode of Kutumbeshwar, Dharmasharma's story in the context of Akhandeshwar, and the story of establishing *Shivling* in Avanti bringing it from Lanka by Hanumanji in the context of *Shivling* have been described.

Lord Shri Krishna and Balramji had learnt *Ved* from Sandipani muni who had made his *ashram* at the bank of river Kshipra in Avanti. Having resurrected his guru's son, Lord Shri Krishna gave this boon to Avantipuri that the man who would meet his end in this city will be free from the dread of Yamraj and will secure the supreme position of Shri Krishna. Thus the devout face of Avanti, the provider of emancipation, comes to light by this story.

Describing the glory of *Rameshwar teerth* situated in Avanti it is said that Lord Ram had performed the *pinddaan* of his father Dashrath in Avanti on the advice of Maharshi Vasishtha. Lakshman had put up *Rameshwar Ling* at this place. Since then this pilgrim spot has been said to be the provider of all the *punya* (holy reward).

Lord Shiv incarnating as Mahakaal in Avanti and emergence of *Baagandhak teerth* through the story of Andhakasur, the glory of famous pilgrim spot of Gaya through the story of king named Yugaadi, and the glory of *Naag teerth* through the story of Maharshi Aasteek are the episodes that are narrated. Finally, the glory of the pilgrim spots of Nrisingh, Gangeshwar, Prayageshwar, Madhukulya, Pret Shila, Deveshwar etc. and the related stories have been described.

6. Reva Khand

Reva Khand is the last *khand* (section) of the *Skand Puran*. This *khand* begins with the count of *Purans*, their distinctions, and the number of verses described in it. After that the glory of river Reva (Narmada) has been described through the dialogue between Maharshi Markandeya and Yuddhishthir. According to this *khand*, the emergence of river Narmada has happened from the perspiration of Lord Shiv. According to a boon of Lord Shiv, he himself resides at the bank of this river. The *stotra* by which Brahmins had first prayed river Narmada is also described in this *khand*.

After that, the glory of river Kaveri has been described through the story of Kuber. Kuber had become the king of Yaksha due to performing *tapa* at the confluence of Kaveri and Narmada. Confluence of Kaveri and Narmada has been said to be a holy pilgrim spot. *Shivlings* named Amareshwar and Chandhast are put up at the bank of this confluence. These *Shivlings* have been installed as the guard of river Kaveri. Since Kaveri has emerged from the body of Lord Shiv, it is called Punyavati. The glory of *Shoolbhedteerth* situated at the bank of Narmada is also described in this *khand*.

After that, there are the episodes of survival of river Narmada and Maharshi Markandeya during the destruction of cosmos by Lord Shiv, wedding of Ravan and Mandodari, and installation of *Shivling* in the river of Narmada by Meghnad, the son of Ravan. As a result, the Meghnad teerth was established at the bank of Narmada.

After the Meghnad teerth, there is the description of the glory of Bhineeshwar teerth, Naradeeshwar teerth, Dadhiskand teerth, Kaamad teerth, Sauvarnsheel teerth, Madhuskand teerth, and Skand teerth. In the context of Skand teerth, the birth of Shiv's son Kartikeya has been narrated. After that Angiras teerth, Kotis teerth, Kedareeshwar teerth, Pishacheeshwar teerth, Jamadagni teerth, Sarp teerth, and Agni teerth have been described. Besides the stories related with Himalaya, Maharshi Shaaktayan, Parashuram, and Devarshi Narad have been described.

Finally, the *Skand Puran* has been concluded with the description of the glory of Lord Satyanarayan, method of worship, related holy stories, and the importance of reading, listening and thinking of this *Puran*.

Story from *Skand Puran*: Glory of Someshwar Teerth

Maharshi Atri had emerged from the heart of Brahmaji when, in the past, he wished to expand the universe. Maharshi Atri went to forest to perform *tapasya* at the command of

Brahmaji. There, he performed arduous *tapa* named *Anuttar* for three thousand divine years. Radiant by the influence of *tapasya*, his semen fell in his eyes in the form of water and started lighting all the directions. This radiance of his was called *Som* (moon). Brahmaji placed Somdev on his chariot for the benefit of the entire *loks*. Seeing Somdev on the chariot of Brahmaji, gods and *rishis* and *munis* hailed him. Due to this Somdev became radiant. Adorning the chariot, Somdev revolved around the earth for twenty-one times. During circling the earth, wherever his radiance spilled on the earth all types of grains and medicines came into existence there.

After that, Somdev performed ten thousand years of arduous *tapa* and pleased Brahmaji. Pleased with his *tapa*, Brahmaji made him the ruling god of seeds, medicine, water, and Brahmins.

Then by the command of Brahmaji, Somdev organized a large *Rajsuya yajna*. Along with the gods, all the *rishis* and *munis* were invited at this auspicious occasion. The attending members performed methodical prayer and worship of Somdev at the conclusion of the *yajna*. Daksh Prajapati married his twenty-seven daughters – Ashvini, Bharani, Kritika, Rohini, Mrigshir, Punarvasu, Pushya, Ashlesha, Hast, Adra, Magha, Poorva Falguni, Uttara Falguni, Chitra, Anuradha, Swati, Vishakha, Mool, Jyeshtha, Poorvasharha, Uttarasharha, Shravan, Shatbhisha, Dhanishtha, Poorva Bhadrapad, Uttara Bhadrapad, and Revati – with Somdev. On receiving so much respect, affluence and wealth, Somdev's heart developed ego. Considering himself superior to most due to this ego, he began ignoring other gods.

One day, Somdev's lustful sight fell upon Devguru Brihaspati's wife Tara. She was extraordinarily beautiful. Somdev was blind in the pride of his affluence, hence he abducted Tara. Seeing such an unethical deed, he received rejection from all the *loks*. Gods and *devrishis* tried to advise Somdev in many ways but he did not agree to return Tara.

Then, angry with his misdemeanour, the king of gods, Indra, along with other gods attacked him. A fierce battle followed between the two sides, but gods had to face defeat at the end.

On the defeat of gods, Devraj (the king of gods) Indra asked help from Lord Shiv. On their prayer, Mahadev riding on Nandi marched to punish Somdev.

Hither, when Somdev received the news, he too took his position on the battlefield.

When Brahmaji saw the temerity of Somdev, he spoke advising him, "Son! What kind of silly task have you undertaken? Lord Mahadev is *aadipurush*. That *parbrahm* cannot be defeated. Your hardihood will lead you to death. Therefore, you return Tara humbly and ask for his forgiveness. Lord Shiv is very kind. He will certainly grant you pardon."

On his advice, Somdev begged forgiveness from Lord Shiv and returned Tara. Tara was pregnant at the time. Hence she terminated the foetus on the advice of Brihaspati. The three *loks* became full of light by the radiance of that foetus and a divine child emerged from it. Responding to Brahmaji's query, Tara said that the child was born from the fraction of Somdev. Then Brahmaji named that brilliant son of Som as Budh (Mercury). Budh was very intelligent. Pleased with his arduous *tapasya*, Brahmaji gave him boon of a place among planets.

Since Somdev had committed the sin of copulating with the wife of *guru* (teacher), therefore, suffering from leprosy, he lost his brilliance. This created chaos in all the *loks*. Obstacle developed in the routine of creation. *Rishis*, *munis*, humans, *gandharvas*, *naags* (snake) – all became fearful and panicked.

Hither, suffering from leprosy, Som invoked Brahmaji and asked about the remedy from the suffering. Observing Somdev in pathetic state, Brahmaji said, "Son! This is result of your bad deeds. You have met this pitiful state because you have committed the sin of the evil deed with other's wife. Now, only Lord Shiv can rid you from this sin. Therefore, chanting the *Mahamrityunjaya mantra* at a region named Prabhas, you pray and worship Lord Bholenath. All of your sufferings would end by his blessings and you will regain your glory."

After coming to know through Brahmaji the solution of freedom from the sin, Somdev arrived at the Prabhas region. He installed *Shivling* there and started chanting *Mahamrityunjaya mantra* of Lord Shiv after performing his methodical prayer and worship. This chanting of *mantra* went on for six months. In these six months, Somdev chanted *Mahamrityunjaya mantra* for a hundred million times.

At last, pleased with the *tapasya* of Somdev, Lord Shiv appeared there and said, " Hey Somdev! I am happy with your *tapasya*. Ask me, what boon do you want? I promise to give you the boon of your desire."

Somdev forgot his sufferings on seeing Lord Shiv before him and, praying with the leaves of *Bel* tree and the water of Ganga, started chanting his *mantra*. Then he said, "Abode of compassion! Whatever evil deed that I have committed against Devguru Brihaspati's wife Tara has rendered its bad effect on me and I have lost my glow and I am suffering so gravely. You please be kind to free me from this suffering."

Listening to his request, Lord Shiv said, "Hey Somdev! A person has to necessarily bear the reward of his deeds. Therefore you will have to bear with the fallout of your sin. But since you have performed arduous *tapasya*, I grant you this boon that your glow will recede in the one phase (*paksh*) but will grow in the other phase."

Thus Somdev again got back his brilliant radiance due to the boon of Lord Shiv. To promote the glory of Som, Lord Shiv is called Someshwar and the place became famous in all the *loks* by the name of *Someshwar* (Somnath) *teerth* (pilgrim spot). It is said that dreadful diseases like leprosy etc. are cured by praying and worshipping Lord Shiv at the Somnath teerth.

•••

14

VAMAN PURAN

Introduction

According to the count, the *'Vaman Puran'* is placed fourteenth among the eighteen *Purans*. Although this *Puran* has been named after the *Vaman-avatar* of Lord Vishnu, and which is very important among his main ten incarnations, yet *Shaiv* ideology has got more prominence in it than *Vaishnav* ideology. Therefore this *Puran* has been said to be predominant in *Shaiv* ideology.

First of all Maharshi Pulastya had elaborated it while providing the knowledge of this *Puran* to Devarshi Narad. Hence Maharshi Pulastya has been said to be the first orator and Devarshi Narad has been said to be the first listener of this *Puran*. Subsequently, Devarshi Narad gave the knowledge of this *Puran* to Maharshi Vyas, who gave it to Lomharshan Sootji and he gave it to Shaunak and other *rishi-munis*. Thus this *Puran* reached to the common man by several *rishi-munis*.

Although, comprising all the distinctions, various mythological episodes and incidents are described in the *Vaman Puran* in the clear chronological order and logically, yet these episodes and incidents are slightly different in comparison to that of the other *Purans*.

The Number of Verses (*Shloka*) and Sections

Ten thousand (10,000) verses have been narrated in the *Vaman Puran*. This *Puran* is narrated in two *khand*s (sections)

– *Poorva* (First half) and *Uttar* (Second half). There are six thousand (6,000) verses in the *Poorva khand* and four thousand (4,000) verses in the *Uttar khand*. However, at present, like *Bhavishya Puran*, only the first half is available. Which means that we are totally ignorant of the knowledge and those extraordinary incidents which are narrated in the *Uttar* (second half) of the *Puran*. There are 97 chapters in the *Poorva khand* of *Vaman Puran*.

The Gist of *Vaman Puran*

This *Puran* begins with the queries of Devarshi Narad about the *Vaman-avatar* of Lord Vishnu and Maharshi Pulastya telling him the story of *Vaman-avatar*. The histrionic character of Lord Vaman and the benevolence of the king of demons Bali have been illustrated by means of this story. In spite of being tipped by the guru of demons, Shukracharya, that Lord Vishnu himself had come in the disguise of Vaman, Bali donated three steps of land to Lord Vaman and proffered his head when the land fell short for the third step; it is the episode which illustrates benevolence, religiousness, and nice-heartedness of Bali, the grandson of Prahlad.

After the description of *Vaman-avatar*, the extraordinary histrionic character of Lord Shiv and the advent of Jeebhootvahan have been described. According to the story narrated in the episode of Jeebhootvahan, Goddess Parvati asks Lord Shiv to build a house to be protected from the rain. But Lord Shiv ridicules the proposal and expresses his inability to build a house as he considers himself an inhabitant of the burial ground of the dead. After that, he covers the clouds when Goddess Parvati reiterates her demand so that the rainwater could not touch Bhagwati Parvati. Since then Lord Shiv became famous by the name of Jeebhootvahan (a name of Indra).

After that, the episode of beheading of Brahmaji, episode of Kapalmochan, and the stories of the destruction of Daksh's *yajna* have been described. The story of the destruction of Daksh's *yajna* is altogether different in this *Puran* in comparison to the other *Purans*. According to this *Puran*, Goddess Sati comes to know about Daksh's *yajna* through Jaya who was the daughter of Maharshi Gautam and granddaughter of Daksh Prajapati. Coming to know that Lord Shiv was not invited in the *yajna*, Goddess Sati sacrifices her life right there on the ground. Then Veerbhadra, by the command of Lord Shiv, along with *Shivgana* goes to destroy Daksh's *yajna*.

Thereafter the episodes of the deadly form (*kaal*) of Lord Narayan and burning of Kaamdev have been described. The story of the burning of Kaamdev is also differently narrated like the story of the destruction of Daksh's *yajna*. According to the story of this *Puran*, after being turned into ash by the fire of fury of Lord Shiv, Kaamdev had changed into five flower plants (*Dukmdhrist, Vakul, Champak, Jaatipushp,* and *Patalya*). After that, the war between Prahlad and Narayan and the description of Bhuvankosh has been made. In the context of *Durga Saptshati*, the stories of the execution of demons named Mahishasur, Shumbh, Nishumbh, Chand, Mund, and Raktbeej have been mentioned.

Within the description of Kurukshetra, the glory of the pilgrim spots namely Brahmsarovar, Kurujangal, Prithudak etc. has been described in this *Puran*. The glory of Brahmsarovar has been termed as Saromahatmya in it. This Saromahatmya is narrated from the 24th to 51st chapters that is spread in 28 chapters.

The birth of Parvati, the advent of Gauri, the story of demon Andhakasur, the character of Skandkumar, the execution of Tarkasur, the story of Jaabaali, the birth of Marudgana, the story of Lakshmi, the marriage of Chitrangad, the execution of Jambh-Kujambh, the execution of Dhundhu by Trivikram (Shri Vishnu), the discourse of ghost, and Nakshatra-Pùrushakhyan are the important distinctions of *Vaman Puran*.

The stories related with the *vrat*s of *Kayajjali* and *Kark-*

chaturthi, method of worship, and the glory of *vrat* have been discussed in this *Puran*. The glory of Ganga, the mental bathing in Ganga, *Dadhi Vaman stotra*, the glory of Venkateshwari, the glory of Varah, and the importance of pilgrimage have been illustrated. Describing the appearance of Lord Bholenath, the names of the snakes gracing his different parts as ornaments, various forms of Lord Vaman and his abodes and separate description of the vehicles of gods and demons have been made.

Like other *Purans*, in the *Vaman Puran* too, the detailed mythological knowledge is decribed about emergence of universe, its development, Jambu and other seven islands and the geographical situation of the earth, different mountains of India, famous rivers, districts and the people inhabiting it. Explanation on different sins and the resultant hells have also been established.

In the *Vaman Puran*, the character of demon kings has been narrated to be as well-cultured, religious, art-loving, and kind-hearted and their uncultured, evil, cruel, dreadful, and irreligious face has not been shown.

Lord Vishnu among all the gods, *atmgyan* (the knowledge of soul) among all the learnings, *Sudarshan Chakra* among all the weapons, river Ganga among all the holy rivers, Kurukshetra among all the pilgrim spots, *Matsya Puran* among all the *Purans*, and *Ashwamedh* among all the *yajna*s have been said to be superior according to this *Puran*.

The supremely beneficial discourse delivered by Vishnu-devotee, Prahalad, to his grandson Bali fills the devotion for Lord Vishnu in the hearts of all the people. In this context, the method of worship of Lord Vishnu as told to Bali by Prahlad, construction of Shri-Vishnu temple, and educating Bali with Vaishnavi tenets become the concluding episodes of the *Puran*.

Story from *Vaman Puran* : *Vaman Avatar*

It is an incident of old time: The king of demon, Bali, took control of paradise after defeating gods. Indra and the other gods went into hiding in forests, caves, and mountains. The mother of gods, Aditi, was quite sad at the poor condition of gods. Seeing her sons in grief, she also became sorrowful. Kashyap muni was performing arduous *tapasya* in the forest during that time. On completion of *tapa*, he went to his *ashram*. Then, narrating the detail of the poor condition of gods, Aditi asked him to tell the solution of their well-being.

Kashyap said, "Kalyani! You pray Lord Vishnu who resides in the heart of all the living beings and removes the sorrow of devotees. He is very kind and affectionate to devotees. Their devotion never goes vain who pray and worship him with true heart. I have full faith that Shri Vishnu will certainly fulfil your wish."

Listening to Maharshi Kashyap, Aditi said, "Lord! How should I worship *Parbrahm* Lord Vishnu so that he could fulfil my wish at once? Tell me some method of his worship by which he could become pleased soon and remove the sorrow of my sons."

Maharshi Kashyap gave Aditi the discourse on *Payovrat*. Observing this *vrat* properly for twelve days, Aditi meditated Lord Vishnu.

Pleased with her prayer and worship, Lord Vishnu appeared in person and said, "Goddess! I am fully aware of your desire. The enemies have snatched away the glory of your sons. You wish that gods regain their affluence, fame, and paradise. Kalyani! You have prayed me with devotion and respect. Therefore pleased with your action I offer you the boon that I will place my fraction in your womb and will incarnate. This will be known as my *Vaman avatar*. In this incarnation of mine, I will eleminate demons and will protect gods." Thus, after offering boon to Aditi, Shri Vishnuu disappeared.

Aditi became very happy with the thought that Lord Vishnu

will take birth from her womb. Maharshi Kashyap had divine sight; nothing was hidden from him. He came to know by the power of his *tapa* that through him, Lord Vishnu will take *avatar* from the womb of Aditi. Then he placed his radiance in the womb of Aditi.

When Brahmaji came to know that Lord Vishnu has placed his fraction in the womb of Aditi, then he said in prayer, "the fosterer of universe, God! I bow millions of times at your feet. The keeper of the entire knowledge of *Ved* in your heart, God! Actually you are present in this cosmos in the form of *Parbrahm*. Heaven, earth, and *Patal* – all these three *lok*s are placed in your navel. You are the beginning and the end of universe. You are the creator of the entire universe, people, and gods. You are the only refuge to the gods expelled from the heaven. Remove their suffering, God!"

Pleased with the prayer of Brahmaji, Lord Vishnu descended before Aditi and Kashyap *muni*. Lord Vishnu had four arms, which adorned conch, club, lotus, and *chakra*. His appearance was very attractive. Gods began praying him sounding conch, drum, and *dhol*. Aditi became very surprised and glad to see the supreme-*purush*, Lord Vishnu, born from her womb. Maharshi Kashyap began hailing Lord Vishnu.

Then, all of sudden, Lord Vishnu changed himself into *Vaman Brahmchari*.

*Rishi*s were very pleased seeing lord Vaman. Then goddess Gayatri offered him the discourse of wisdom. The guru of gods, Brihaspati, did his baptism (*yagyopavit*), Kashyap muni did *janeyu*, the earth gave the hide of Krisna-deer, Brahmaji gave *kamandalu*, Aditi gave clothes, the moon gave stick, Saptrishis gave *kush*, Saraswati gave the necklace made of *rudraksh*, and the gods gave the umbrella. Kuber gave him a pail for begging, and Bhagwati gave him alms. Thus Lord Vaman was graced with the divine items.

The king of demons, Bali, was performing *Ashwamedh yajna* with the *rishi*s from the clan of Bhrigu at that time.

After the gods completed their worship, Lord Vaman marched towards Bali's place of *yajna*. It seemed as if the earth was leaning under his weight. Bali's place of *yajna* was situated at the beautiful location of Bhrigukacch (the city of Bharauch in the present state of Gujarat).

Lord Vaman arrived at Bali's place of *yajna* in a moment. Exuding the divine radiance, he appeared as if he was real Sun (*Suryadev*). The radiance of all the *rishi*s of Bhrigu's clan present at the *yajna* diminished before his radiance. Then, coming forward, the king of demons, Bali, welcomed lord Vaman.

Bali offered seat to Lord Vaman and said in humble voice, "Son of Brahmin (*Brahminkumar*), it appears as if the emobodiment of the *tapasya* of *Brahmarshis* has come to my place of *yajna*. My forefathers have become satiated, my clan has become pious, and my *yajna* has become successful by your arrival. All of my sins have been destroyed by your visit to me. Hey *Brahminkumar*! Command me, what service may I offer you? Let whatever object of desire be in your mind – gold, money, grain, land – ask for it without hesitation. I will fulfil all of your wishes."

Listening the sweet words of Bali, Lord Vaman became pleased and said, "King! Whatever you have said is in accordance to the tradition of your family, full of religious feel, and grows your fame. In your ancestors, there has been no impatient and miserly man who would ever avoid donation to Brahmin or who would back out on his promise after making the promise. The coward has never born in your family who would turn away his face on the call of an alms-seeker or challenge of enemies during war. Several generous men have taken birth in your family. Your father Virochan was a great devotee of Brahmins. When his enemy gods asked donation of his life in the disguise of Brahmin, he gave it away though he was aware of their trick. You are following the same *dharma*. King of demons, you are capable of offering my desired object, hence I ask for three steps of land only. You are master of three *loks* and a kind soul but I do not want more than this."

The king of demons said laughingly, "*Brahminkumar!* Although your speak like a learned Brahmin, yet you have little intelligence, therefore you do not understand profit and loss. I, the ruler of three *loks*, am very happy with your speech and can offer you sufficient money and land in donation. Still, is it a matter of intelligence to ask for three steps of land? *Brahminkumar!* He who has come to my refuge should not need to ask anything from anybody ever. Therefore ask from me as much land as you need to carry on your livelihood."

Listening to his prideful talk, Lord Vaman said, "King! If man cannot control his senses, all the affluence of universe cannot fulfil his desires. He who cannot be contented with three steps of land will not be satisfied even if offered several vast pieces of land. The person lives happily who is contented with little while the dissatisfied person who cannot control his senses remains sad and discontented in spite of having three *lok*s. The dissatisfaction of money and pleasure is reason behind falling into the cycle of life and death. Therefore one should accumulate as much money as is needed. There is no doubt in it that you are the champion provider of desired objects, but I ask for three steps of land only. My job will be done with this much only."

"Alright, *Brahminkumar*! As you deem fit." Saying this Bali raised the water-pot to formalize the resolve for giving away three steps of land.

Hither, *guru* of demons, Shukracharya, had come to know the true face of Lord Vaman. Therefore, interrupting Bali, he said, "King! This is real Lord Vishnu in the appearance of Vaman who has incarnated from the womb of Aditi to accomplish the work of gods. He will snatch everything from you. Do not resolve to give him donation. This deed of yours will commit great injustice to demons. Vishnu, in the disguise

Message of the Purans

of Vaman, will take away your kingdom, affluence, money, brilliance, and fame and will handover you to your enemy Indra. What will be left for you and demons if you will give everything of yours to him? As large as the world, this Vishnu will measure the earth in one step and the paradise in the other step. Where will his third step go when his vast body will cover the sky? You will, however, suffer in horrible hell if you do not fulfil your resolve. Therefore king of demons, be careful! Leave this resolve."

Bali said with humility, "*Gurudev!* Your statement is absolutely correct, but I am the grandson of brilliant Prahlad and the son of king of demons, Virochan. After determining to donate once, I cannot turn away my face from it. I will not play trick with the *Brahminkumar* in the greed of kingdom. There is no greater sin (*adharma*) than being untruthful. I can bear everything but the pressure of falsehood is not acceptable to me. I do not dread horrible hell, poverty, grief, and death etc. as much as I dread to breach the words given to a Brahmin. After death money and other things are left behind, but what is good of it if one does not use it to satisfy Brahmins? Dadhich, Shivi and other *rishis* have benefited people by offering their lives.. *Gurudev!* Lord Vishnu who is prayed and worshipped by gods, *rishis*, *munis*, humans, etc. may have come in this form, but I will certainly donate the land according to his wish. Even if he will disillusion me by trick, I will not wish him unwell."

When Shukracharya saw that Bali was not paying heed to his advice and was violating his command, he became angry and said invoking curse on him, "Foolish Bali! Although you are an ignoramus, yet trying to prove yourself a great scholar of scriptures, you are disrespecting me by ignoring my advice. You have also violated my command, hence your affluence and wealth will vanish."

Shukracharya went away from there after pronouncing the curse. Bali remained determined on his resolve despite being cursed by *guru*. He methodically prayed and worshipped, Lord

Vaman. After that, taking water in his hand, he resolved to give away three steps of land to him.

As soon as Bali completed his resolve, a unique thing happened there. Lord Vaman made his body so huge that three *loks*, humans, gods, *rishis*, *munis*, animal, birds, the ten directions, etc. all submerged into him. All the *rishi-munis* and demons remained surprised seeing the vast appearance of God.

Covering the sky with his gigantic body and directions with arms, Lord Vaman measured up the entire earth in one step. His second step covered the *Satyalok* situated upwards. Washing the feet of Lord Vaman there with the water of Ganga in his *kamandalu*, Brahmaji along with Marichi and other *rishis* prayed him. Thus Lord Vaman measured the entire cosmos in his two steps only. Nothing owned by Bali was left to put his third step on.

Then Lord Vaman said, "King of demons! Fulfil your resolve. I have already measured the entire cosmos including three *loks*; now tell me, where should I put my third step? You had great pride on yourself. Now fulfil your promise right away, or be prepared to suffer in the hell for breaking your promise."

Bali said, "Abode of kindness! Although I have lost my kingdom, yet I will certainly fulfil the promise given to you. Kindly put your third step on my head. I have no regret for losing the kingdom or suffering in the hell. Neither am I afraid of being bound by some noose nor any punishment. You have always educated we the demons, therefore you are our supreme guru. When we become cruel by being blind in the false pride of superiority, power, and wealth, then you guide us taking those objects away from us. By worshipping you with devotion, *rishi*s find the place at your feet; the same is achieved by demons on being executed by you. The punishment offered by the supreme *guru* like you elevates fortune. I will accept it readily."

The supreme devotee of Lord Vishnu and his grandfather, Prahlad, arrived there while Bali was praying lord Vaman. Bowing to Lord Vaman, he said, "God! You had offered Bali

Message of the Purans

this grand position of Indra and you have now taken it away. You have done a great favour by doing so. In the ego of affluence and pleasure, even a learned man forgets his real self. Therefore it is great for man that he remain devoid of affluence and pleasure."

Then Brahmaji supplicated, "God! You have taken away all of Bali; now he does not deserve any punishment. He has surrendered his affluence, wealth, the three *loks*, and himself in your *Shri* (holy) feet. God! The man who remembers your holy feet with true heart and reverence after becoming free from materialistic pleasure, you provide him emancipation (*moksha*) being pleased on him. But the king of demons, Bali, has gladly donated his everything; how can he deserve punishment then? Therefore be pleased and forgive him."

Pleased Lord Vaman said to Bali, "Son! You have conquered the illusion (*maya*), which is very difficult to win. The *guru* of demons invoked curse on you, everything of yours has been taken away, kith and kin have deserted you; but you have observed your *dharma* and truthfulness with utmost diligence in spite of so much suffering. Therefore I offer you the position which is rarely available to great gods. Sitting on the position of Indra in *Savarni manvantar*, you will get the fortune to become my dear devotee. Until then you live in the *Patal lok* built by Vishwakarma. My blessing will remain on you even there."

That very moment Bali went away to the *Patal lok* with wife Vindhyawali and kith and kins. After that lord Vaman completed the *yajna* of Bali. After that he went to heaven with Brahma, Indra, and the councillors. Thus gods got back the paradise again by the blessing of Lord Vishnu.

•••

15

KOORM PURAN

Introduction

The holy '*Koorm Puran*' comes under the category of *Brahm varg*. The superior essence of all the four *Vedas* is available in this *Puran*. Lord Vishnu had taken *Koorm-avatar* on the prayer of gods to keep Mandarachal mountain stable during the churning of ocean. Thereafter, during his *Koormavatar*, he had provided the intriguing mysteries of knowledge, devotion, and *moksha* (emancipation) to king Indradyumn. His discourse, full of knowledge, has been compiled in this *Puran*. Therefore this *Puran* has been said to be *Koorm Puran*. Maharshi Vyas had given the knowledge of this *Puran* to his disciple Romharshan (Lomharshan) Sootji. After that Romharshan Sootji had narrated this *Puran* to Shaunak and other *rishi-munis* at the forest of *Naimish (Naimisharanya)*.

Although *Koorm Puran* is predominantly a *Vaishnav Puran*, yet the ideologies of *Shaiv* and *Shaakt* too have been discussed in it in detail. The five distinctions of *Puran – Sarg, Pratisarg, Vansh, Manvantar,* and *Vanshanucharit* – have been described in detail in this *Puran*.

Number of Verses and Sections (*Khand*)

There are narrated a total of eighteen thousand verses (*shlokas*) in the entire *Koorm Puran*. This *Puran* is divided into four *Samhitas* (*khand*) – *Brahmi, Bhagwati, Gauri,* and *Vaishnavi*. In the present time, however, *Brahmi Samhita* alone is available. The other three *Samhitas* have disappeared in time.

There are a total of six thousand verses (*shlokas*) in the *Brahmi Samhita*. This *Samhita* has been divided in two parts – pre-division and post-division. There are 51 chapters in the pre-division and 44 chapters in the post-division of the *Samhita*.

The Gist of *Koorm Puran*
1. Pre-Division (*Poorva Vibhag*)

This division begins with the birth of Maharshi Sootji and his popular name becoming Romharshan. Listening the joyful *Purans* from the revered mouth of Maharshi *Vyas*, every pore of Sootji had become exalted. His name became Romharshan Sootji due to this. Acknowledging him as the only deserving one to listen *Puran*, *Maharshi* Vyas had provided him the knowledge of *Purans*. Eighteen *Purans* and its *sub-Purans* have been listed in this chapter. After that, there are episodes of *Koorm-avatar* of Lord Vishnu and the emergence of Lakshmi. In this context, the birth of King Indradyumn in the *Brahmin yoni*, pleasing of Lord Vishnu through performing arduous *tapasya* by Indradyumn, and securing the knowledge of *Paratpara tatva* as boon have been elicited.

In the second chapter, emergence of Brahmaji, Shivji and Lakshmi from the fraction of Lord Vishnu, emergence of nine *manas putras* (sons), four *Vedas*, and four castes by Brahmaji, and establishment of the *varnashram dharma* on the basis of the knowledge of *Vedas* have been made.

In this *Puran*, Shri Vishnu has explained two distinctions of the four *ashrams*, namely *brahmcharya, grihastha, vaanprastha,* and *sanyas*. *Upkuvnik* and *Naishtik* are the two distinctions of *Brahmcharya* according to him. After acquiring the complete education of scriptures, the one who enters into *Grihastyashram* is called '*Upkuvnik brahmchari*' and the one who spends his whole life at the service of his *guru* is called '*Naishtik brahmchari*'.

Sadhak (peseverer) and *udasin* (neutral) are the distinctions of *grihasthashram*. The man who keeps busy in the sustenance of his family is called '*Sadhak grihastha*' and he who after becoming free from the debt of gods, debt of father, and debt of *rishi*s engages into the sustenance of his family is called '*Udasin grihastha*'.

The two distinctions of *Vaanprasthashram* are *tapas* and *sanyasik*. The perseverers who live in the forest and perform *yajna*, *hawan* and other religious rituals are called '*Tapas vaanprasthi*' and the perseverers who pray and worship God by arduous *tapa* are called '*Sanyasik vaanprasthi*'.

Paarmeshthik and *Yogi* are the distinctions of *Sanyasashram*. Keeping senses in control and thus desiring to get *moksha* (emancipation) through *Yog* are called '*Paarmeshthik sanyasi*' and they who view supreme soul in their soul are said to be the '*yogi sanyasi*'.

After that, *ashram dharma*, the steps to acquire *sanyas*, the signs of *brahm-arpan*, and the *karmyogi* have been explained in detail. The emergence of cosmos and the creation of universe have been narrated in detail in the fourth chapter. The different names of Lord Vishnu have been explained in this context.

Thereafter, there is description of four *yugs*, counting of period, salvation of earth by Lord Vishnu through *Varah-avatar*, creation of nine types of universe, birth of demon Madhu-Kaitabh, execution of Madhu-Kaitabh by Lord Vishnu, and different appearances and names of Lord Shiv.

Extremely intriguing description has been made of prayer and worship of *Shakti* (mother power) in the 11th chapter. There are episodes of the birth of Sati-Parwati, and Bhagwati showing Himalaya her vast appearance after narrating the glory of Bhagwati, and the prayer of the goddess by Himalaya with her 1008 names.

There are the stories of the birth of the daughters of Daksh, 49 fires, forefathers, and descend of Ganga in the 12th and 13th chapters. The story of King Prithu has been mentioned while describing the dynasty of self-styled Manu in the 13th chapter itself. After that, the episode related with Goddess Sati begins. But this episode is different in comparison to that described in the other *Purans*. There are narrations of Daksh organizing *yajna* at Kankhal, leaving of her life in Daksh's *yajna* by Sati, destruction of Daksh's *yajna* by Veerbhadra, and Lord Shiv appearing at Daksh's *yajna* and offering boon to Daksh.

First of all, in the 15th chapter, there is episode of the execution of demon named Hiranyakashipu by Lord Vishnu in the appearance of Nrisingh. After that, the execution of demon Hiranyaksh by Lord Vishnu's incarnate Varah and the story of Prahlad are described. In the story of Prahlad, there are episodes of the devotee Prahlad rising to fight against Lord Vishnu to avenge his father's death due to a curse of Brahmin and then taking refuge in Lord Vishnu and obtaining his supreme position.

Thereafter, there are stories of invoking curse on the envious Brahmins by *Maharshi* Gautam, Andhakasur launching an attack on Kailash after being attracted to the beauty of Bhagwati Parwati, battle between Shiv and Andhak, the defeated Andhak instituting prayer of Lord Mahadev, offerance of the position of Gana to Andhak, and accepting him as son by Shiv-Shiva. At the end of this chapter, there are the description of eating of the world by *Matrikaa*s produced by Lord Vishnu and *Matrikaa*s going to the refuge of Lord Shiv on being preached for doing so by Lord Vishnu.

The defeat of gods by the king of demons, Bali, Lord Vishnu incarnating as *Vaman-avatar* and asking Bali to donate three steps of land, and Bali proceeding to Patal are the stories which are narrated in the 16th and 17th chapters. The story of the birth of Ravan and Kumbhkaran, and the geneses of the families of Maharshi Vashishtha and Vyasji have been described in the 18th chapter. The sun dynasty in the 19th chapter and describing the Ikshvaku dynasty in the 20th chapter, an introduction has been made of Sagar, Asmanjas, Dilip, Bhagirath, Harishchandra, Shri Ram, Lav, Kush, and King Shratayu.

Describing the Moon dynasty in the 21st chapter, there is mention of Budh, Pururava, Nahush, Yayati, and other kings. The hierarchy of Yadu, the son of king Yayati, has also been described in this chapter.

The hierarchy of King Jaydhwaj and the character of King Durjay have been described in the 22nd chapter. In this context, there is the episode of the departure of King Durjay to Varanasi on the advice of Maharshi Kanva and becoming free of sins by praying and worshipping the *Vishveeshwar Jyotirling* situated there.

The detailed description of the kings of Kroshtu dynasty, Saatvat dynasty, and Krishna dynasty has been given in the 23rd chapter. The histrionics of Lord Shri Krishna has been described from the 24th to 26th chapters. Therein the stories are described about prayer of Lord Mahadev by Shri Krishna at Upmanyu's *ashram*, boon of a son to Shri Krishna by Shivji, Shri Krishna returning to Dwarka after visiting Kailash and preaching Markandeya muni about *Ling-tatva* and explaining the importance of the worship of *Ling*, birth of Samb from the womb of Shri Krishna's wife Jambvati as a result of the boon of Lord Shiv, execution of Kans and arrival of Shri Krishna at *Golok*.

From the 28th to 33rd chapters, outline of *Kaliyug-dharma*, the dialogues related with religion between Maharshi Vyas and Jaimini muni, and the glory of Kashi have been analysed. In this chapter, there is episode of the execution of Gajasur by Lord Mahadev and donning his skin as cloth and hence being called as Kritivasishwar. After that, introducing different pilgrim spots in Kashi, the glory of *Omkarishwar ling, Kapardishwar ling, Pishachmochan kund, Madhymishwar Mahadev* etc., their method of worship and related mythological stories have been described.

The *Poorva Vibhag* (Pre-division) concludes with the mythological geography of the earth that is Jumbu etc. seven islands, seven oceans, solar system and *nakshatra mandal* (system), glory of sun, *avatars* to be taken by Lord Shiv in *Kaliyug*, and the description of the seven *manvantars* of future.

Message of the Purans

2. *Upari Vibhag* (Post-Division)

The Post-Division of *Koorm Puran* begins with the dialogues between Lord Shiv and *rishi*s. This discussion has been known as *Ishwar Gita*. Extremely philosophical and spiritual analysis has been made of *Ishwar Gita* in this *Puran*.

Mentioning about *Atmatatva*, Lord Mahadev says in the *Ishwar Gita*, "Soul is only clean, free from vices, holy, and *tamoguni*. It is timeless according to *Vedas*. Soul is one only, but it acquires several bodies due to being engaged with illusory bonds. Like light and darkness, sunshine and shadow, there is no relation between supreme soul and illusion. They are totally different. But being inflicted with illusion, soul takes several births after which it does not attain freedom. Although knowledgeable and learned men consider soul to be free from vices and irrespective of nature, yet some men consider soul as consumer due to ignorance. Ignorance begets *avivek* (opposite to wisdom). Man engages in good and bad – all kinds of deeds – due to *avivek*, and becomes victim of sin and winner of *punya* according to deeds. Man takes birth to suffer for these deeds. Opposite to this, the soul is clear and free of vices. It illuminates in its own light. When scholars witness soul in this form, they realize Brahm."

In the context of *yog*, it is said that *yog* actually is the gist of *Vedant*. *Yog* means concentration of mind. *Yog* and knowledge are complement to each other. There is nothing unattainable in the world for the person who imbibes *yog* and knowledge.

Establishing the form of Pashupati, Lord Shiv says, "All the living beings of the universe are called animals if looked by the vision of soul, and for being their master, I am famous by the name of Pashupati (master of animal). *Jeev*s are bound in the noose of illusion due to my creation. I salvage them. There is no one else to free the people of the world except me. It is my radiance that spreads in the entire universe."

In this division (*vibhag*), following *Ishwar Gita*, the deep mysteries of different rituals and procedures of *Vyas Gita* have been described after establishing its extremely philosophical and precise meaning. *Vyas Gita* begins with *varnashram-dharma* and the description of good conduct. Regarding *Brahmcharya dharma*, Maharshi Vedvyas says that a *Brahmchari* (the man who is unmarried and observes celibacy) should be humble and obedient towards elder folks. He who provides worldly and *Vedic* knowledge should be treated like *guru*. Even elder relatives should be honoured like *guru* by mind, words, and body. *Brahmchari* should neither sit by the side of *guru* nor should engage in debate with him. The mother who gives birth, the nurse who fosters, scholarly woman who preaches knowledge, wife of elder brother, and wife of *guru* should be respected as *guru*. They who wish their well-being should not disrespect these five even by mistake.

Describing the *grihasth-dharma*, Maharshi Vyas says, "man should marry with decent, beautiful, virtuous, good mannered, well-behaved, and free-of-vice girl and should copulate with her during *ritukaal* (period when chances of conception are maximum). Bedding with woman is totally prohibited on sixth, eighth, twelfth, and fourteenth days of a month. Householders should keep away from such vices as killing of *jeev*, untruthful speech, and theft." Besides Vyasji has analysed *Gayatri mantra*, *Eikadashi vrat*, *shraadh* (post-funeral rites), and donation etc.

In the context of *Vanprastha-dharma*, it is said that man can enter into *Vanprastha-ashram* with his wife, but, leaving wife in the care of sons, the lonely *Vanprastha* is quite superior. Man should perform *tapa* and *sadhana* (steady meditation) in the forest. He should feed on fruits. Making a disciplined habit for meal, he should observe it stringently. *Vanprasthi* should take his meals everyday after offering food to God and guests. *Vanprasthi* should grow hair, feed on alms, keep control on his voice, and continuously engage into learning by himself.

Regarding *Sanyas-dharma*, Vyasji says that man should spend a fourth of his life into *sanyasashram*. Keeping quiet during this *ashram*, man should excel into *yog* and the knowledge of *Brahm* (*brahm-vidya*). Not staying at one place, he should keep wandering. His mind should be detached from all the worldy objects. *Sanyasi* (saint) should don clothes of bright red colour.

After *Vyas Gita*, the stories related with *Prayag teerth*, *Prabhas teerth*, *Kubjashram teerth*, *Saaraswat teerth*, *Pushkar teerth*, *Rudrakoti teerth*, *Devalaya teerth*, *Badrivan teerth*, etc. and their glory have been established.

At last, this *Puran* has been concluded with the prayer of Lord Vishnu and Vyasji and the glory of reading, listening, and reminiscing of *Koorm Puran*.

Story from *Koorm Puran* : Curse by Gautam *Rishi*

It is a tale of old time: Indra held rain for fifteen years to punish people for their sins. A severe famine followed resulting from no rain for so many years. Thousands of people began to die everyday. Huge piles of corpses became visible everywhere. In this situation, some *rishi-muni*s gathered to think that Gautam is a brilliant *rishi*. Only he can solve this sad situation. He regularly performs prayer and worship of Goddess Gayatri. Due to the boon of the Goddess, the harm of the famine has not reached at the *ashram* of Maharshi Gautam. Hence we should go to his refuge. Having thought this, all of those *rishi-muni*s along with their family went to the *ashram* of Gautamji.

Maharshi Gautam welcomed them with open heart. Then he asked the reason of their arrival. *Muni*s narrated their sorrow. Listening to this Gautam consoled them and said humbly, "Sirs! This *ashram* is actually meant for you people. I am only a servant of yours. You should not worry as long as I am there. You live here happily without worry."

Thus after providing shelter to all the *rishi-muni*s,

Maharshi Gautam started praying Bhagwati Gayatri with divine *stotra*s.

Pleased with the prayer and worship of Maharshi Gautam, Bhagwati Gayatri appeared before him and said affectionately, "Son Gautam! I am very pleased with your prayer. Tell me, what is your wish that I should fulfil?"

Gautam said in humble words, "Godmother (*Mateshwari*)! The earth is reeling under severe famine. There is great scarecity of grain and water everywhere. Thousands of people are dying everyday. Lakhs of people have taken shelter in my *ashram*. Mother, I am worried on the issue of feeding and nourishing them."

Then Bhagwati Gayatri offered him a *kamandalu* and said, "Son! This divine *kamandalu* will fulfil all your wishes. You will never be short of grain until it is with you." Bhagwati Gayatri disappeared after saying this.

Maharshi Gautam bowed to the *kamandalu* reverentially. Then expressing his desire, *kamandalu* produced huge piles of different kinds of delicacies, divine ornaments, the material for *yajna*, and grain etc. Gautam happily offered all the *muni*s money, wealth, clothes, and ornaments.

Maharshi Gautam's *ashram* had turned into a large refugee ground. All the objects visible in the *ashram* were produced through the divine *kamandalu* by the boon of Goddess Gayatri. There was neither fear of disease nor demons in the *ashram* by the blessing of Bhagwati Gayatri. Thus Gautam muni continued sustenance of all the *muni*s for twelve years.

Once, singing praise for the goddess, Devarshi Narad arrived at the *ashram*. He was seated in a gathering of *muni*s. Hailing Maharshi Gautam, he said, "Hey great among *muni*s! Your praise is being sung in the three *lok*s. Gods, *gandharva*s, *yaksh*s (demi-gods), *naag*s (snakes) – all bow their heads before your generosity and adherence to duty (*dharmanishtha*). Although you are sustaining so many people, yet you do not display even an iota of ego. King of gods, Indra, himself praises you highly in the paradise. I have visited you after listening your praise from his mouth.

There were some *rishi-munis* who envied Maharshi Gautam. Their envy grew even more when they heard Maharshi Gautam's praise from the mouth of *Devarshi Narad*. They decided to spoil the honour of Maharshi Gautam and started waiting for the right opportunity.

Some days later, by the kindness of Lord Vishnu, the rain started on the earth. Famine came to an end. Then the *rishi-munis* who were envious to Maharshi Gautam gathered and decided to invoke curse on Gautam. They created an illusory cow. It was mere skeleton of bone. When Maharshi Gautam was performing *hawan* at his place of *yajna*, the cow arrived there. Maharshi Gautam, out of compassion, thought to keep the cow in his cowshed. But it died as soon as he touched her.

As the cow died, those ungrateful *rishi-munis* arrived there speaking unkind words and alleging him responsible for the killing the cow and refused to accept his grain.

Seeing that the cow died merely by touching, Maharshi Gautam started pondering over it. Then, to know the reason of the cow's death, he closed his eyes and went into deep meditation.

Soon he came to know about the evil plot of the envious *munis*. Then he was filled with wrath like the annihilating Rudra, and, invoking curse on those ungrateful *rishi-munis*, said, "Wretched men! You will become incapable of praying and worshipping Vedmata Gayatri and Lord Shiv from today onwards. The men and women taking birth in your families would also be inflicted with this curse. You will live in the ponds of hell by the fury of mother Gayatri."

The *Gayatri mantra* became unapproachable for those ungrateful *munis* due to the curse of Maharshi Gautam. They forgot all the *mantras* of *Ved*. Then, filled with remorse, they went to Maharshi Gautam and falling on his feet begged forgiveness for their misdeed.

Their aggrieved entreaty melted Maharshi Gautam's heart. He said, "Sirs! My curse cannot forego. Therefore you worship Lord Shiv incessantly to reduce its influence. He is extremely kind and capable to end one's sufferings. He who goes to his shelter never returns disappointed. He fufils the wishes of everyone."

Aggrieved with the curse, the *rishi-munis* started praying Lord Shiv on the advice of Maharshi Gautam. Pleased with their prayer, Shivji consulted Lord Vishnu about the way of their salvation.

Then Lord Vishnu said, "God! Conduct against *Vedas*, and being unfaithful to the host erode one's all *punya* (holy reward) and one suffers the torture of hell for several *kalps*. However, since these *rishi-munis* have accepted their mistake by true heart, the only way for their salvation is that they pray and worship me after taking birth again in the human *yoni*." Thus, inflicted with the curse of Maharshi Gautam, the *rishi-munis* took birth again in the human *yoni* and prayed and worshipped Lord Vishnu. As a result, their salavation became possible.

•••

16

MATSYA PURAN

Introduction

'*Matsya Puran*' is mainly related with the Vaishnav ideology. Lord Vishnu, having incarnated as *Matsya-avatar*, had saved the lives of Vaivaswat Manu and *Saptrishis* during the annihilation. The extremely beneficial discourse that Lord Vishnu had given to Vaivaswat Manu and *Saptrishis* while sailing in the boat on the water has been analysed in detail in this *Puran*. Therefore this *Puran* has been named as *Matsya Puran*.

Number of Verses (*Shloka*s) and Sections

There are fourteen thousand (14,000) verses in the *Matsya Puran*. Two hundred and ninety one (291) chapters are there in this *Puran*. It has been presented in a series without being divided into section or *skandh*.

The Gist of *Matsya Puran*

This *Puran* begins with the mythological story of *Matsya-avatar* of Lord Vishnu. There are episodes of Vaivaswat Manu, the son of sun, securing boon from Brahmaji to protect moveable and immoveable world through performing arduous *tapa*, alerting about annihilation to Vaivaswat Manu by the fish (*matsya*) incarnate of Lord Vishnu, and protection of Manu and *Saptrishis* by Shri Vishnu. In this, there are inquiries by Vaivaswat Manu from Lord *Matsya* regarding universe. After that, in the context of the creation of universe it is said that Lord Narayan, having wish to create universe, created water at first and then sowed seed in it. A radiant egg emerged from that seed. Then Lord Narayan emerged from the egg in the form of Vishnu who produced Bbrahmaji from his lotus navel. After securing the *tatvagyan*, Brahmaji started the work of creation of universe.

Turning Kaamdev to ash and again his resurrection by Brahmaji and the emergence of four *varna*s from the different parts of Kaamdev have been described in this *Puran*. Thereafter, describing about Vairaj, Agnishwat, Bahirshad and other dynasties, different kinds of *shraadh* (post-funeral rites) have been identified.

After glorifying *shraadh*, introduction of the moon dynasty, extraordinary characters of brilliant kings namely Budh, Pururava, Raji, Nahush, Yayati etc. have been described. In the related discourse, the episodes are described of the birth of Budh from the fraction of moon, the marriage of Budh and Ila, birth of Pururava, the son of Budh, Pururava getting boon of beauty from Lord Vishnu, marriage of Pururva and Urvashi, Devraj Indra accepting to become the son of King Raji, King Yayati marrying Devyani, the daughter of Shukracharya, marriage of Yayati and Sharmishtha, Shukracharya invoking curse on King Yayati to turn old, and donation of his youth by Puru, the son of Yayati to his father.

After that, describing the character of kings from Andhak, Vrishni, Yadu, Kroshtu and Puru dynasties, the hierarchical record of Lord Shri Krishna has been presented. After that the glory of different *vrat*s and the stories related with its observance method have been described in detail from the 55th to 102nd chapters. These *vrat*s are – *Nakshatra vrat, Adityashayan vrat, Chandrarohini Shayan vrat, Subhagya Shayan vrat, Saptlok Aadhipatya Prapti vrat, Adityavar vrat, Akshaya Tritiya vrat, Shashthi vrat, Vibhuti Dwadashi vrat, Shiv Chaturdashi vrat* etc.

Message of the Purans

After describing the glory of *vrat*s, the appearance of the nine planets namely Sun, Moon, Mars, Mercury, Jupiter, Venus, Saturn, Pluto, and Neptune, their *mantras* of well-being, and the method of worship according to the scriptures have been described. The mythologically suggested geographical situation of the earth has been introduced along with the description of Jumbu and seven islands in this *Puran* too like other *Purans*.

Outlining the description of four *yugs*, namely *Satyug*, *Tretayug*, *Dwaparyug*, and *Kaliyug*, the situation of religion and justice, human nature, the religious rituals and its virtues and vices in these *yugs* have been discussed.

The battle of Tripurasur, execution of Jambhasur, birth of Parvati, firing of Madan, wedding of Shiv and Parvati, birth of Kartikeya, execution of Aadi, execution of Tarkasur, character of Nrisingh, the sighting of Balmukund by Markandeya and the stories of Lord Shiv accepting demon Andhakasur in the form of his son, emergence of *Maatrika*s – these famous mythological episodes have been described in detail in this *Puran*.

After that, the glory of Varanasi and Narmada has been made. In this context, the episode of arduous *tapa* performed at Varanasi by the son of *yaksh* (demigod) named Poornabhadra and pleased Lord Shiv offering him the designation of Ganeshwar has been described. After that, there are episodes of demon Banasur troubling gods, punishment to Banasur by Lord Shiv to help gods, prayer of Shiv by demon Banasur and installation of *Jwaleshwar ling* by him. In this *Puran*, there is episode of the birth of a daughter named Savitri in the house of King Ashwapati as a result of the boon of Goddess Savitri (Gayatri), marriage of Satyavan and Savitri, death of Satyavan, and resurrection of Satyavan by Yamaraj (the god of death) after falling helpless before the *pativrat-dharma* of Savitri.

The conduct of kings, glory of Prayag and good and bad omen, a thought on dream and signals have been established in detail.

After that the glory of Vaman and Varah *avatars* of Lord Vishnu has been described through the story of departure of king of demons, Bali, to *Patal*, and execution of Hiranayaksh. In this context, the stories of churning of ocean, emergence of nectar, and Lord Vishnu incarnating in Mohini-*avatar* and offering the nectar to gods have been mentioned.

Finally glorifying the reading, listening, and reminiscing of *Matsya Puran*, it is said that, having complete knowledge, the *Matsya Puran* is the most superior among all the scriptures and, destroying all the sins, provides *dharma, arth, kaam*, and *moksha*. Devotees' age, fame, progeny, power, fortune and wealth grow by reading and listening it reverentially.

Story from *Matsya Puran*: Puru's Devotion for Father

This is a story of old time. Demon named Vrishparva ruled over *Patal*. He had a beautiful daughter whose name was Sharmishtha. Devyani, the daughter of demons' *guru*, Shukracharya, was her dear friend.

One day, wandering on the earth with Devyani and other friends, Sharmishtha arrived at a garden. There was a nice pond. The lotuses blooming in the water were augmenting the beauty of the pond. Attracted to it, she started playing in the pond with her friends. Thus the whole day went by playing like this.

Coming out of the pond in the evening, they started changing their clothes. Sharmishtha, by mistake, wore the clothes of Devyani. Seeing this, she spoke angrily, "Wretched girl! How did you dare to put on my clothes? The Brahmins who have given the knowledge to this world through their *tapobal*, who always keep remembering *parbrahm* in their heart, who are prayed by even Indra and other gods, who are revered among all the living beings – we are the most superior among those Brahmins. Your father Vrishparva is our disciple. Then how did you, being the daughter of disciple, dare put on the clothes of the daughter of *guru*?"

Enraged by the bitter words, Sharmishtha said, "Devyani! Do not do proud on yourself so much. If we do not sustain you, your entire knowledge would go waste. And the clothes, you are mentioning about have actually been donated by us. I will certainly punish you for your misdemeanour of insulting me." Saying this, Sharmishtha pushed the clothless Devyani into the pond and returned to the palace with her friends.

After Sharmishtha went away, King Yayati of moon dynasty happened to come there while hunting. He was very thirsty. Pleased by seeing the clean water of the pond, he descended from the horse and came up to the bank. Suddenly his sight fell on the clothless Devyani. Devyani was a very beautiful maid who surpassed even the shine of moon. Yayati was attracted to her beauty. Covering Devyani with his shawl, he pulled her out of water. After that, he proposed her for marriage.

Devyani said coyly, "Hey King! Our meeting is the gift of the God's blessing. Earlier when I wanted to choose *Devguru* Brihaspati's son Katch as my spouse, he had refused to accept me. Then I had invoked curse on him that he would forget the knowledge of *Sanjeevani* learnt from my father. He also had cursed me that my marriage would not happen with a Brahmin. Hence our relation is in accordance with the wish of God." Saying this Devyani accepted Yayati's marriage proposal.

Returning to the *ashram*, Devyani told the entire episode to her father Shukracharya. Coming to know about the daring of princess Sharmishtha, Shukracharya's mind became upset and deciding to leave *Patal*, he walked out with her daughter.

When the king of demons, Vrishparva, came to know that *guru* of demons, Shukracharya, and Devyani have left *Patal* and were going elsewhere, he started thinking, "Shukracharya is supremely knowledgeable, brilliant, and our well-wisher. We have continuously defeated gods by his blessings. Even Lokpals fear to come before him. No one would save us if he will leave us wrathfully. Gods are always prepared for an opportunity to come and finish us when the *guru* goes away from us. Hence we must stop him. He is very kind. He will certainly forgive the misdeed of Sharmishtha."

Thinking this he ran to the *guru* and bowed his head at his feet and said, "Great *Muni*! What misadventure are you going to commit? Can a man live without soul? The world knows that you are supremely kind – why then are you being so harsh on an orphan like me? God, did I commit some mistake in your honour that you have decided to leave from here without giving a thought to demons? Although Sharmishtha, filled in false pride, has certainly insulted Devyani, yet do not give such a grave punishment for that. God! Kindly do not leave us."

The anger of Shukracharya was momentary. He said to Vrishparva in relaxed voice, "King! I will forgive you, but Devyani will not do so. I will have no hesitation to return if you succeed to please her by fulfilling her one wish."

Then Vrishparva asked Devyani about her wish. She said, "King! Sharmishtha has insulted me by calling me beggar and servant. She nurtures a large ego for being a princess; hence I desire that Sharmishtha along with her friends serve me like a servant wherever I go. My father will return with you if you will fulfil my wish."

Vrishparva told this condition to Sharmishtha. Sharmishtha accepted Devyani's condition for the well being of the race of demons. She along with her one thousand friends started to serve Devyani like a servant. Shukracharya married Devyani with Yayati.

After some time, Devyani gave birth to two sons named Yadu and Turvasu. Seeing Devyani's son, Sharmishtha also married clandestinely with King Yayati and gave birth to three sons named Druhyu, Anu, and Puru.

When Devyani came to know that the father of Sharmishtha's children was Yayati, she became infuriated and went to her father's house. King Yayati arrived there after her to placate her. Shukracharya was already hurt with the grief of his daughter, hence when he saw Yayati before him, he said invoking curse on him, "Shameless! You are very dimwit, untruthful, and carry a filthy perception for other women. You had promised to keep one wife only throughout your life, but the beauty of Sharmishtha illusioned you. Without giving a thought to the punishment, you have committed such an inferior deed which even demons fear to do. Go, I invoke curse on you that your youth should go away. Such an old age should set upon you which makes man extremely ugly."

Yayati immediately turned into an old man due to the curse of Shukracharya. His handsome body became very ugly. His back bent forward due to old age. His power waned excessively.

He became very sad to see his bad condition and said, begging forgiveness from Shukracharya, "*Munivar*! I had acted understanding that the desire of Sharmishtha was according to *dharma*; I was not influenced by lust at all. Do not give me such a severe punishment of this lapse. Great among *muni*s! Devyani and I are not satiated from materialistic pleasures so far. This curse will be harmful for your daughter as well along with me. Hence be kind to salvage me."

Listening to this Shukracharya said, "Go, exchange your old age with a man who donates his youth to you happily."

After returning to his capital with Devyani, Yayati narrated everything to his sons and asked them for their youth. But none of the sons was ready to donate his youth.

At last, his younger son Puru said, "Father! In fact, this body is given by you only. No son can ever repay the generosity of his father ever, hence he always remains indebted to his father. I am also indebted to you and happily offer my youth to you." Saying this Puru gave away his handsome youth to his father Yayati and accepted his old age in exchange. After that, angry with his remaining sons for being disobedient, Yayati cursed them to keep away from the throne of kingship and started enjoying the affluence like before with Devyani.

Time passed by. One day, feeling of detachment (*vairagya*) appeared in the mind of Yayati. Thinking that he is using Puru's youth while he was suffering from his old age, he felt ashamed. That very moment he returned Puru's youth to him and accepted his oldness. Then he went to forest to perform arduous *tapa*. There, remembering Lord Vishnu, he realized his supreme position.

•••

17

GARUD PURAN

Introduction

The king of birds and son of Maharshi Kashyap, Garud is said to be the vehicle of Lord Vishnu. Once Garud asked several deep and intriguing questions from Lord Vishnu regarding status of person after death, the journey of *jeev* to *Yamlok*, different hells met through different deeds, *yonis* and the bad condition of sinners. The knowledgeable discourse which Lord Vishnu had given to quench the curiosity of Garud has been analysed in detail in this *Puran*.

The supremely sacrosanct words related with the post-death status had appeared from the revered mouth of Lord Vishnu through Garud; hence this *Puran* is called '*Garud Puran*'. Established by Shri Vishnu, this *Puran* is mainly *Vaishnav Puran*. This *Puran* is also called as *Mukhya Garudi Vidya* (education).

First of all, Brahmaji had provided the knowledge of this *Puran* to Maharshi Ved Vyas. Thereafter Vyasji gave it to his disciple Sootji and Sootji gave it to Shaunak and other *rishi-munis* in the forest of *Naimish* known as *Naimisharanya*.

In the *Sanatan Hindu dharma*, there is provision of listening *Garud Puran* after death. There is description of '*Pretkalp*' in the *Uttar khand* of this *Puran*. It is said that it provides good position after death (*sadgati*). Besides, there is detailed description of *shraadh tarpan* (a post-funeral ritual), ways of emancipation, and the status of *jeev* after death in this *Puran*.

Number of Verses (*Shlokas*) and *Khand* (Sections)

The entire *Garud Puran* is the gist of nineteen thousand verses (*shlokas*). However, at present only seven thousand (7,000) verses are available. *Garud Puran* has been divided into two parts – *Poorva khand* and *Uttar khand*. There are 221 chapters in the *Poorva khand* and 35 chapters in the *Uttar khand*.

The Gist of *Garud Puran*

Garud Puran begins with a brief description of the twenty-four incarnations of Lord Vishnu. After that, there is detailed analysis of the essence of ethics, Ayurved, glory of the pilgrim spot of Gaya, the procedure for *shraadh* (post-funeral rites) in accordance to scriptures, and the histrionics of the ten *avatars* of Lord Vishnu.

After that, characters of several brilliant kings of moon dynasty and sun dynasty also have been elaborated in this *Puran* like other *Purans*. Besides, there is description of some other important dynasties as well.

The emergence of the universe from Manu, character of Dhruv, the story of twelve *Adityas*, Vishnu armour *stotra*, *Garudi Vidya*, *mantras* of sun and nine planets, *mantra* of Shiv-Shiva, *mantra* of Indra and other deities, Saraswati *mantra*, description of her nine forces, the method of Vishnu *deeksha*, method of praying and worshipping of nine mazes, thousand names of Vishnu and the *mantra* goddess Tripura have been mentioned in this *Puran*.

Analyzing the text of *Ratnasar* in the *Garud Puran*, there is the narration of the story of the defeat of gods by demon named Bal and emergence of the stores of gems facilitated by demon Bal on the request of gods. In this context, signs of different gems and stones have been elaborated in detail.

Astrology, *Saamudrik shashtra*, the science of ethics as told by Brihaspati, *Dharma shashtra* (theology), *Swarodaya shashtra* (science of speech), genesis of snakes, propitiation for Vinayak, *Varnashram dharma*, various *vrat*s and fasts, *ashtang yog*, Ayurved, glory of faithfulness (*pativrat dharma*), and chanting, *tap*, hymning, and method of worship have been described in detail and this is the important distinction of *Garud Puran*.

All the 35 chapters of *Uttar khand* are included in the *Pretkalp* of *Garud Puran*. In it, narrating the *jeev*'s journey to *yamlok*, the sufferings on the way due to different sins, and the torture instituted by *yamdoot*s (messenger of Yam, the god of death) have been illustrated. In this context, describing the appearance of Yampuri, the responsibilities of Dharmadhwaj who tells about good and bad deeds, Chitragupta, and Yamraj and the different hells assigned on the basis of sinful deeds have been illustrated.

There are eighty-four lakhs of hells in the *Yamlok* according to *Garud Puran* where the persons suffer through great torture according to their respective misdeeds. Different sins commited by men and resutant hells have been clarified in this *Puran* as follows :

Hell	Sin
Tamisra	He, who takes away other's money, woman, and son, suffers the ordeal of the hell named *Tamisra*. *Yamdoods* punish him here in many ways.
Andhtamisra	He, who deceives someone to coupulate with his wife, suffers severely in the hell named *Andhtamisra*. He becomes blind in this hell.
Raurav	They who engage in violence against someone, they become a dreadful animal named *Rur* and receive severe pain by falling in the hell named

	Raurav. It is said that the animal named *Rur* happens to be more dreadful than snake
Maharaurav	The carnivorous *Rur* animals make the *jeev* suffer in the hell named *Maharaurav*.
Kumbhipak	The man, who kills animals and birds and cooks them, falls into the hell named *Kumbhipak*. *Yamdoots* boil him here in the hot oil.
Kaalsootra	The person who antagonizes with father and Brahmin finds place in the hell named *Kaalsootra*. He is roasted in this hell in the severe temperature of sun and fire.
Asipatra	The man, who digresses from the path of *Vedas* and takes to quackery, is poked with double-edged sword after being whipped in the hell named *Asipatra*.
Shukarmukh	The man, who leads unreligious/atheistical life or inflicts physical pain upon others, falls in the hell named *Shukarmukh* and is crushed like cane in a crusher.
Andhkoop	In spite of being aware of the grief of the other person, he who makes him suffer falls in the hell named *Andhkoop*. Snake and other poisonous and dreadful animals drink his blood here.
Krimibhojan	The person, who, after preparing food, eat it all by himself fall into the hell named *Krimibhojan* and become a worm and suffer great pain.
Sandesh	The person, who steals or snatches money, falls in the hell named *Sandesh*. There he is scorched with burning mass of iron.
Taptsurmi	He, who rapes a woman, is beaten with whip and and is forced to embrace burning pillars of iron in the hell named *Taptsurmi*.
Shaalmali	The sinner who mates with animals etc. falls

Message of the Purans

	into the hell named *Shaalmali* where he suffers for his deeds by being grounded between the needles of iron.
Vaitarni	The person who does not follow *dharma* is thrown in the hell named *Vaitarni* in the river of blood, bones, nails, fat, flesh etc. and such unholy objects.
Puyod	The person, who, flouting the rules of good conduct, acts like animal, has to live in the hell named *Puyod* where he is fed on feces, urine, mucus, blood etc. and such horrible things.
Pranrodh	People who hunt the dumb animals are pierced with sharp arrows in the hell named *Pranrodh*.
Vishsan	The men who slaughter animal in the name of *yajna* are flogged in the hell named *Vishsan*.
Lalabhaksh	The sinner who, under the influence of lust, copulates with the woman of same *gotra* (family), has to drink seminal fluid while living in the hell named *Lalabhaksh*.
Sarmeyadan	The person, who robs or destroys other's property, falls into the hell named *Sarmeyadan* where an unusual animal named *Sarmeya* eats him by cutting into pieces.
Avichi	The person, who, despite being witness, gives false statement before court in the matter of donation or monetary transaction, is thrown from the top of the mountain on rocky field and is pierced with stones in the hell named *Avichi*.
Ayahpaan	The man, who drinks alcohol, is thrown into the hell named *Ayahpaan* where his mouth is pierced with the burning iron rods.

Ksharkardam	The person, who does not pay respect to men who are superior to him, suffers with numerous ordeals in the hell named *Ksharkardam*.
Shoolprote	Men, who entertain themselves by tying animals and birds and poke thorn into them, are pierced with thorn in the hell named *Shoolprote*. Crow and *Bater* make hole in their bodies with their beak.
Dandshook	The men, who are cruel by nature and do harm to others, are thrown among the snakes with five or seven hoods in the hell named *Dandshook*. These snake bite them day and night.
Avatnirodhan	The man who captures someone and keeps him at a dark place is placed in the hell named *Avatnirodhan* where he is made to suffer with the poisonous smoke of fire.
Paryavartan	The person, who looks upon the guests at home with the evil sight, is thrown into the hell named *Paryavartan* where cruel birds like crow, vulture, kite, etc. pull out his eyes with their sharp beaks.'
Suchimukh	The man, who always keeps busy in accumulating wealth and feels envious by growth of others, is sewn like cloth with needle by *yamdoot* in the hell named *Suchimukh*.

Further to this, there is detailed description of *pretyoni*, and method to avoid it, and securing *sadgati* (good position after death) without rituals. The glory of donation of *pind*, *Shraadh-karma* (post-funeral rites), and donation have been illustrated in it.

Finally, this *Puran* has been concluded with the glory of devotion of Lord Vishnu, prayer by Maharshi Markandeya, description of *Sankhya*, *Vedant-yog*, and establishing of the essence of *Gita*.

Story from *Garud Puran*: Story of Kashyap Brahmin

It is a story of ancient time. Abhimanyu's son, Parikshit, was a great religious king. He ruled Hastinapur righteously for sixty years.

Once upon a time, King Parikshit was in the forest for hunting. He became very tired chasing a deer. He was thirsty too. At that time his sight fell on Shamik muni, who was lost in meditation (*samadhi*). Parikshit, under emergency, asked water from him. But the *muni* remained quiet. He did not give any reply. Then, suffering from acute thirst, King Parikshit raised a dead snake lying nearby and put it around the neck of the *muni* and returned to his capital jeering at him.

Shamik muni had an extremely brilliant son named Shringi. When he came to know that King Parikshit had dishonoured his father, he invoked curse wrathfully, "the snake named Takshak would bite Parikshit on the seventh night from today."

Hither, when King Parikshit came to know about the curse given by Shringi, he moved to a safe palace after handing over the responsibilities of governance to his able ministers.

He appointed such scholars for his safety who were masters in the knowledge of gems and *mantras*. Further, several young soldiers were appointed to guard the gate of the palace. Their job was to prevent any from entering the palace. The arrangement was so foolproof that even a whiff of air could not enter without permission.

A learned Brahmin named Kashyap lived in a village of that kingdom. The Brahmin was a complete scholar of the subject of *mantras*. He was interested in money because he was poor. When he came to know the news of curse invoked on Parikshit, he began to think, "If I could save King Parikshit from Takshak snake, he will fill my purse with gold and silver." With this thought, Kashyap marched towards the palace.

On the other side, to fulfil the curse of Shringi muni, Takshak snake made disguise of an old Brahmin and set out from his house to bite King Parikshit.

Takshak saw Kashyap Brahmin on the way, who was pacing fast towards the kingdom. Then Takshak, in the disguise of old man, stopped Kashyap Brahmin and asked out of curiosity, "son of Brahmin! Where are you going in such a hurry? Kindly care to tell me."

Holding his steps, Kashyap said, "Brahmin *dev*! Takshak snake will bite King Parikshit after a few days due to a curse invoked by the *rishi* and the king would die of it. Being a scholar of the subject of *mantra*, I am well aquainted with the art of countering the effect of poison. I am going to King Parikshit with the purpose to save him. Should Lord Vishnu be kind, I will resurrect King Parikshit by antidoting the poison of Takshak snake with the influence of my *mantras*."

Listening to Kashyap, Takshak uttered laughing, "Brahmin dev! I am the Takshak snake whose bite will send King Parikshit to the mouth of death. My poison is very strong like *Halahal*. It cannot be antidoted by any *mantra* or medicine. It would be appropriate that you go back; otherwise you will be ridiculed.

Kashyap Brahmin spoke calmly, "hey king of snake! You are correct, but I have such an art by which I can destroy even the effect of the poison of Sheshnaag. I am confident that I will antidote your bite and will resurrect King Parikshit."

Then, in order to test the power of Kashyap's *mantra*, Takshak turned a tree into ash with the fire of his poison. But, in a matter of a few moments, Kashyap Brahmin revived the ash into a green tree with the influence of the power of his *mantra*.

Impressed by Kashyap's power of *mantra*, Takshak turned

into his actual appearance and said, "*Brahmin kumar*! You are a great holy soul. Kindly do not obstruct my mission. God has fixed King Parikshit's death by me. Hence you go back. I am ready to offer you your desired objects for this."

Kashyap Brahmin became pensive. He was going to get his desired objects. Then he meditated. Realizing that time in the life of King Parikshit was over, he happily accepted Takshak's proposal and returned back with the expected wealth. Thus Takshak snake had bitten King Parikshit to prove the words of Shringi *muni* true. In the context of this story of *Garud Puran*, it is said that Kashyap Brahmin had realized the divine art by listening to *Garud Puran*.

•••

18

BRAHMAND PURAN

Introduction

Brahmand Puran is placed on the eighteenth position in the series of eighteen *Purans* written by Maharshi Vyas. This *Puran* is called '*Brahmand Puran*' due to detailed geographical description of cosmos in it. *Brahmand Puran* has been said to be at the top in the texts of science and poetry due to detailed analysis of cosmic and astronomical position.

The first orator of this *Puran* is said to be Brahmaji and the first listener was Maharshi Vashishtha. After receiving the knowledge of this *Puran* from Brahmaji, Vashishtha muni gave it to his grandson Parashar, Parashar gave it to Jatukarnya muni, Jatukarnya muni gave it to Vyasji, Vyasji gave it to his disciple Lomharshan Sootji, and Sootji gave the knowledge of this *Puran* to Shaunak and other *rishi-munis*.

A detailed description of India is available in the *Brahmand Puran* in comparison to the other *Purans*. In fact, this *Puran* is extraordinary confluence of *dharma*, good conduct, and sience and knowledge.

It is said in the context of this *Puran* that when Indian *rishi-munis* went to the island of Java (Indonesia at present), they had taken with them the knowledge of this *Puran*. The presence of this *Puran* in the Indonesian language proves this statement.

Number of Verses (*Shloka*s) and Sections *(Khand)*

A total of twelve thousand (12,000) verses (*shlokas*) are described in the *Brahmand Puran*. The entire *Puran* is divided into three parts – Poorva (First), *Madhya* (Middle), *Uttar* (Last). There are two sections namely *Prakria* and *Anushang* in the *Poorva bhag*, one section namely *Upodghat* in the *Madhya bhag*, and one section namely *Upsanhar* in the *Uttar bhag* in this *Puran*. This *Puran* comprises 156 chapters.

Gist of *Brahmand Puran*
1. Poorva Bhag (First Part)

The *Poorva bhag* begins with the discourse of the forest of *Naimish (Naimisharanya)*. After that advent of the *Hiranyagarbha*, emergence of universe, *kalp, manvantar*s, the duration of Satyug etc., *Rudrasarg, Rishisarg,* and *Agnisarg* have been described in detail. The mythological episode of invoking curse on each other by Lord Shiv and Daksh Prajapati is also described in this *Puran*. After that an introduction of the ancestors of Manu's son Priyavrat has been made.

Description of *Bhuvankosh*, descent of Ganga, description of astronomy (sun and other planets, *nakshatra*, stars and several celetial objects have been discussed in it. Churning of ocean, episode of the creation of ling by Lord Vishnu, description of different distinctions of *mantras*, elaboration of the branches of *Vedas*, and discourse on *manvantar* are the main distinctions of the *Poorva bhag*.

2. *Madhya Bhag* (Middle Part)

In the context of religious rituals, *shraadh* (post-funeral rites), and donation of *pind* have been elicited with scriptural procedure in the *Madhya Bhag* of *Brahmand Puran*. Thereafter, under the extraordinary character of Parashuram, the entire story related with him is narrated in this part. After that presenting the episode related with King Sagar, his ancestral history has been introduced. In this context, bringing Ganga on the earth by Bhagirath has been narrated. The description of the episodes related with history of the kings of sun and moon dynasty is another importance of this part.

3. *Uttar Bhag* (Last Part)

All the seven *manvantar*s to come in the future have been discussed in the Uttar bhag. The famous mythological '*Lalitopakhyan*', in which Bhagwati Lalita (Tripur Sundari) executes demon Bhandasur and his entire family for the benefit of gods and the elimination of demons, has been described in it through the dialogue between Lord Vishnu in the form of Hayagreev and Maharshi Agastya. In the context of the story of demon Bhandasur, there are episode of Kaamdev being turned into ash due to Lord Shiv's fire of fury, making of an idol of a man from that ash by Chitravarma, its resurrection by Lord Shiv, and that becoming famous by the name of demon Bhandasur. At the end, describing the glory of this *Puran*, it is said that it destroys the sins of devotees and augurs longevity, power, fame, and prosperity.

Story from *Brahmand Puran*: Advent of Parashuram

There was a famous king named Kartveerya in the Hehaya dynasty. He was extremely brilliant and *tapasvi*. After pleasing the fraction-incarnate of Lord Narayan, Dattatreyji, with his services, he had earned one thousand arms. He became famous by the name of Sahsrarjun due to having thousand arms. But gradually he became egotist. He started thinking himself absolutely powerful.

One day, Sahsrarjun went to the forest for hunting. Hunting lions there, he arrived at the *ashram* of Maharshi Jamdagni. Jamdagni muni hosted him with fruits, and various edible food products. Sahsrarjun was surpised at his affluence. He inquired about the secret.

Then Jamdagni muni said, "King! This affluence is due to the blessing of Kamdhenu. She is mother of entire world.

It is she who takes care of my sustenance as well as that of my guests. We face no scarecity due to her blessings."

After listening about Kamdhenu, Sahsrarjun said, "*Munivar*! The affluence of paradise appears dim against your affluence. However, you are a *tapasvi* who lives in the forest and engages himself in the devotion to God, repudiating all the materialistic pleasure. What is the significance of the affluence and materialistic pleasure for you then? Therefore I will take Kamdhenu with me."

Saying this, without seeking the permission of Maharshi Jamdagni, Sahsrarjun commanded his soldiers to carry Kamdhenu with him. Jamdagni muni tried to hold him, but he failed to stop him and Sahsrarjun succeeded to take Kamdhenu with him to his capital Mahismatipuri.

Later when Parashuram returned to the *ashram*, he came to know about the misadventure of Sahsrarjun. Shaking with anger, he picked up his *farsa* (axe), bow, quiver, and armour and rushed after him to execute him.

Sahsrarjun was about to enter his city when he saw Parashuram coming after him. He came to a halt there and ordered his army to fight with him. Getting the hint of command the army charged at Parashuram. But Parashuram was fractional incarnate of Lord Shri Vishnu. How could those soldiers stand before him then? Soon he eliminated Sahsrarjun's army. Then Sahsrarjun came to fight himself. Soon, Parashuram ripped all his arms and beheaded him.

Soon he died, his ten thousand sons ran away from there out of fear. Parashuram returned to his *ashram* with Kamdhenu and explained everything to Jamdagni in detail on being asked.

Listening about the news of the death of Sahsrarjun, Jamdagni said in grief, "Son! What an undesired act have you done? Although you are a supreme warrior, yet you have executed King Sahsrarjun in vain. Son! We Brahmins are respectable in the world for our virtue of forgiveness. Grandfather Bramhaji has earned his position of Brahm due his ability to forgive. Brahmins' radiance lights up like sun because of forgiveness. Son! Assassination of king is more sinful than that of a Brahmin. Therefore you wash away your sin by taking to pilgrimage, reminiscing God." Accepting father's command, Parashuram went on pilgrimage.

The ten thousand sons of Sahsrarjun, who had run away for the fear of Parashuram, could not forget the execution of his father. When they came to know that Parashuram had gone on pilgrimage, they attacked the *ashram* of Jamdagni muni, realizing that it was the right opportunity. Sitting at that time in his *agnishala* (place where *hawan* is performed), the *muni* was in deep meditation of Lord Vishnu. He had no awareness of the outer world. Those sinners proceeded to kill him in that state.

Parashuram's mother, Renuka, tried to stop them by preaching *dharma* but those evil-doers beheaded Jamdagni muni by one swing of sword and went away with the head. Screaming with grief and sorrow, Renuka called Parashuram... Parashuram.

Listening the grief-striken call of his mother, Parashuram arrived at the *ashram* soon. He saw the headless body of his father at the *ashram*. He became aware of the entire incident using the knowledge of *yog*. His fury had no bound. His eyes statrted raining fireballs. Taking his favourite weapon, *Farsa* (axe) in his hand, he resolved to wipe the earth of *kshatriyas* for twenty-one times, and arrived at Mahishmatipuri making lion's roar.

Sky, *Patal*, and the earth – all the three *loks* began shaking from his horrific roar. It appeared as if the time for annihilation had arrived. Lions retreated in their dens out of fear. The pride of wild elephants broke down and they took shelter in the forest. After arriving in Mahishmatipuri, Lord Parashuram began execution of Sahasrarjun's sons.

In a very short period, a huge moutain of human skulls was built in the middle of the city. Their blood took shape of

Message of the Purans

a large river, which sent shivers of dread in the hearts of all the *kshatriyas*. Thus, devoiding the earth of *kshatriyas* for twenty-one times, Lord Parashuram created five lakes of blood in the region of Samantpanchak of Kurukshetra. Parashuramji resurrected his father with the power of his *mantra* by placing his head on the body. After that Jamdagni muni was designated as the seventh *rishi* in the group of *Saptrishi*. After that, returning to a calm disposition, Parashuram went on mountain Mahendra and started worshipping Lord Vishnu by engaging himself in arduous *tapa*.

Appearing in *Satyug*, Parashuram is in deep meditation on Mahendra mountain even today. He had appeared in the court of Janak at the event of breaking of Shiv's bow by Shri Ram. After that he had given weapon training to Devvrat (Bhism Pitamah) and Kunti's son, Karna, during *Dwaparyug*.

•••

Khand III

1

DESCRIPTION OF INDIA (BHARATVARSH) IN PURANS

India *(Bharatvarsh)* has been said to be a part of the mythological island of Jumbu in the *Purans*. This part was named '*Bharat*' after the name of Bharat, the son of King Dushyant and Shakuntala, according to the text of *Mahabharat* written by Maharshi Vedvyas. However, according to some other texts, this part was named Bharat on the name of Bharat, the son of king Rishabhdev who was fraction incarnate of Lord Vishnu.

The history of India is very old. This is also called as the birthplace of gods. Bharat (India) has been described on the basis of the institution of Koorm in some *Purans* as *Shrimad Bhagwat Puran, Koorm Puran, Markandeya Puran, Matsya Puran, Vaman Puran,* and *Brahmand Puran*: Dividing Bharat in the nine divisions on the basis of the different body parts of *Koorm* (tortoise) *avatar* of Lord Vishnu. Opposite to this, the description of Bharat (India) is found on the basis of *Karmuk* (bow) in the other *Purans*.

The mythological form, importance and specialities of *Bharatvarsh* (India) described in *Purans* can be understood in the following manner:

Nine Divisions of *Bharatvarsh*

The old *Bharat* has been distributed in nine divisions in the *Purans*:

Division	Previous Name	Present Name
1.	Indra Dweep	Andman Dweep
2.	Naag Dweep	Nikobar Dweep
3.	Saumya Dweep	Sumatra
4.	Gandharva Dweep	Phillipines
5.	Varun Dweep	Bornio
6.	Kaseruman Dweep	Sulavesi
7.	Gabhastiman Dweep	Papua New Guinea
8.	Tamraparna Dweep	Shri Lanka
9.	Kumarika Dweep	Bharatvarsh

Importance of *Bharatvarsh*

Describing the importance of Bharat in *Purans*, it is said that Bharat is the lone *karmabhoomi* (land of action) on the earth. Very old, related with *Vedas*, and provider of pleasure and emancipation, it is the supreme place. Heaven and hell are received due to actions done there. Man certainly enjoys the good or bad result of the sinful or holy deed done in Bharat. People of Brahmin and other *varnas* live there patiently and achieve great accomplishments by observing their duties.

The pious man of Bharat earns all the four accomplishments – *dharma, arth, kaam,* and *moksha*. Indra and other gods have achieved their godliness by performing auspicious deeds in Bharat only. Further, several men who had mastered their senses have realized emancipation by leading detached and calm life. Gods wish to visit Bharat by taking birth here.

The superior result, which is obtained by observing the *dharma* of *vanprasth* and *sanyas*, digging well, developing gardens, performing *yajna* and *hawan*, is easy to obtain in Bharatvarsh alone. The most superior, destructor of all the sins, extremely holy, and improver of intelligence, this is the holy land.

Inhabitants of *Bharatvarsh*

It is said in the *Purans* that Kirat live in the east and Yavan in the west of Bharat. *Brahmins, kshatriyas, vaishyas,* and *shoodras* reside in the middle part. They purify themselves by good deeds which are respectively *yajna*, war, and business. The *punya* (holy reward) earned in India provides heaven if accomplished with attachment and *moksha* (emancipation), if accomplished with detachment. Similarly the sinful deeds provide their result.

Mountains of *Bharatvarsh*

Mahendra, Shuktiman, Rikshparvat, Vindhya, Malay, Pariyaatra and Malaya – these are the seven main mountains of Bharat. There are many other mountains in the vicinity. They all are vast, high, and pleasant.

Rivers of *Bharatvarsh*

Ganga, Saraswati, Sindhu, Chandrabhaga (Chinab), Yamuna, Shatdru (Satluj), Iravati (Raavi), Vipasha (Vyas), Vitasta (Jhelam), Dhootpapa, Bahuda, Devika, Gandaki, Mahanadi, Chakshu, Drishdwati, Venya, Chandana, Shone (Sone), Avanti, Vedvati, Mandakini, Kuhu (Gomti), Mahi, Charmavati (Chambal), Vidisha, Kshipra, Sadaneera, Devsmriti, Suratha, Reva (Narmada), Devvati, Chitrakuta, Vetravati (Betwa), Shaktimati, Kamorda, Chitra, Tungbhadra, Tapi, Bhimrathi, Krishnavena, Gautami (Godavari), Kriya, and Taamravarni, etc. are the holy rivers which make the country of Bharat a holy land.

Districts of *Bharatvarsh*

Kuntal, Shamak, Kashi, Andhrak, Kaling, Kaushal, Matsya, Kekal, Kuru, Panchal, Vrik, Aatreya, Shoorsen, Shaalva, Maali, Pulind, Baudh, Shak, Bang, Ang, Videh, Vahik, Vidarbh, Malaj, Magadh, Mall, Sudeshna, Pankal, Surashtra, Vijay, Maalav, Chedi, Jaangal, Mallrashtra, Mahish, and Mukutkulya etc. have been said to be the districts of the country of Bharat.

•••

2

THE GEOGRAPHICAL DESCRIPTION OF EARTH

Although the mythological episodes, discourses, incidents, facts, and the stories related with different kings find minor or major differences in the eighteen *Purans*, yet the description, which is found in *Purans* in the context of the oldest geographical situation of the earth, is almost similar and logical.

How the seven islands and seven seas appeared on the earth? The answer of this interesting question has been presented beautifully by means of a story of a *Up-Puran* named *Shrimad Devi Bhagwat*. The story is like this:

The name of Swayambhoo Manu's elder son was Priyavrat. He was very brave, strong, and *tapasvi*. Once upon a time when sun went from one part to the other while revolving the earth, then deep darkness took over in the first part. Seeing this, a thought came up in the mind of Priyavrat, "there should be no darkness during my regime. I will solve this problem right away with the power of my *tapasya*." Taking this resolve, he seated in his divine chariot and started moving around the earth spreading light. Thus he revolved around the earth seven times. The depression on the earth surface created during his revolution by the wheels of the chariot eventually became seven seas. The land around which the revolution was made became seven islands.

Thus seven continents came into existence on the earth. The names of the islands of that time were, "Jumbu, Pluksh, Shalmali, Kush, Kraunch, Shaak, and Pushkar. The seven seas around it became famous by the names of Ksharod, Ikshursod, Surod, Ghritod, Kshirod, Dadhimandod, and Shudhod. King Priyavrat handed over the governance of Jumbu to his eldest son Aagneedhra, Pluksh to Idhmajisth, Shalmali to Yagyabahu, Kush to Hiranyareta, Kraunch to Dhritprishth, Shaak to Meghatithi, and Pushkar to Vitihotra.

Describing in detail the seven continents of the earth, namely Jumbu, Pluksh, Shalmali, Kush, Kraunch, Shaak, and Pushkar, its main mountains, oceans, rivers, districts, and different *varna*s living there have been written about in the *Purans*. A brief introduction of the seven islands is as follows:

Jumbu Island

Jumbu island (a portion of land of greater India at present) is situated at the middle of the earth. There is situated mount Sumeru in the middle, mount Himvan, Hemkut, and Nishadh in the south, and mount Neel, Shwet, and Shringwan in the north of this island. There are Mount Mandarachal in the east, mount Gandhmadan in the south, mount Vipul in the west, and mount Suparshav in the north of the mount Sumeru. There are the forests of Chaitrarath in the east, Gandhmadan in the south, Vaibhraj in the west, and Nandanvan in the north of mount Sumeru.

Likewise, there are four lakes namely Arunod, Mahabhadra, Asitod, and Manas in the different directions which are used by gods. A large town is situated on top of the mount Merigiri, which is called the court of Brahmaji. The towns of Indra and other *lokpal*s are around it. This town is called Brahmpuri. The holy Ganga that emerges from the lotus feet of Lord Vishnu falls around Brahmpuri. There, it is divided in the four parts namely Sita, Alaknanda, Chakshu, and

Bhadra. The island got its name Jumbu due to the presence of a large tree of blackberry (Jamun) there. This tree is situated on the mount Gandhmadan.

This island is spread in one lakh *yojan* (a unit of measurement of area). It has nine parts, each being of nine thousand *yojan*.

It is also called *Varsh*. The detail of nine *varsh* (part) of Jumbu island is as follows: (1) Bharat which is situated in the south of Himalaya. (2) Kimpurush, (3) Harivarsh, (4) The middle part of island, Ilavrat, in the east of which is (5) Bhadrashav and in the west (6) Ketumaal, (7) Uttar Kuru, (8) Ramyak, (9) Hiranyam.

Pluksh Island

The next is Pluksh island (Greece and Italy of present day), which is double of the Jumbu island. This island is situated around the Kshar ocean, which covers the Jumbu island. The Ikshuras island has covered this island. The seven sons of Medhatithi named Shiv, Shantbhaya, Sukhodaya, Shishir, Anand, Kshemak, and Dhruv became the kings of Pluksh island. This island has seven *varsh* (parts) in their names. The seven mountains, which are situated in this island, are – Gomed, Narad, Dundubhi, Chandra, Somak, Sumana, and Vaibhraj. Anutapta, Kramu, Shikhi, Viprasha, Tridiva, Amrita, and Sukrita – these are the seven rivers of this island. It is always like *Tretayug* there.

People of this island are divided in four *varna* namely Aryak, Kurar, Vidishay, and Bhavi which are respectively same as Brahmin, kshatriya, vaishya, and shoodra. All the people of this island pray and worship Lord Vishnu in the form of moon. A large fig tree (*pluksh* or *anjir*) is situated in the middle of this island. On that tree, the name of the island has been kept as Pluksh island.

Shalmali Island

Shalmali Island (the eastern part of Africa and Medagaskar at present) is situated around the Ikshuras ocean. King Vapushman has been said to be the ruler of this island. There are seven *varsh* (parts) in the names of his seven sons namely Shwet, Harit, Jeemoot, Rohit, Vaidyut, Manas, and Suprabh. There are seven mountains namely Kumud, Unnat, Nahish, Kank, Valahak, Drone, and Kakudyan and the seven rivers namely Shroni, Toya, Chandra, Vimochini, Shukra, Vitrishna, and Nivritti on this island.

Shalmali Island inhabits people of Kapil, Arun, Peet, and Krishna varna, who are respectively considered as Brahmin, kshatriya, vaishya, and shoodra. They pray Lord Vishnu's *vayu* (air) form. A tree of Shalmali (*Semal*) is situated there which is the reason behind the name of this island.

Kush Island

Kush Island (west Asia and north east Africa) is twice the size Shalmali island. Ghrit ocean has covered it from all sides. Its king was Jyotishman. Seven *varsh* (parts) are famous there on the name of his seven sons named Udbhid, Venuman, Randhan, Prabhakar, Dhriti, Surath, and Kapil. Along with humans, gods, demons, giants, *gandharva*, *naag* (snake), and *yaksh* (demigod) etc. also live there. The *varna* on the island are – Dami, Shushmi, Sneh, and Mandeh. They are said to be respectively of the same category as Brahmin, kshatriya, vaishya, and shoodra. They pray Lord Vishnu in his Brahma form. Vidrum, Hemshail, Dyutiman, Pustiman, Kushesheya, Hari, and Mandarachal are the seven mountains and Pavitra, Sammati, Vidyut, Shiva, Dhootpapa, Mahi, and Ambhas are the seven rivers of this island. It was called Kush island due to presence of a large forest of Kush (grass) there.

Kraunch Island

The ruler of Kraunch Island, (the Black Sea and the region around it at present) covered with Kshir ocean from all sides, is said to be King Dyutiman. There are seven *varsh* (parts) in the name of his seven sons named Kushag, Mandag, Ushna, Peevar, Andhkarak, Muni, and Dundubhi. Kraunch, Andhkarak, Dharma, Vaman, Devvrat, Pundareekvan, and Dundubhi are the seven mountains here, where live gods and *gandharva*. There are four *varna*s namely Pushkal, Pushkar, Dhanya, and Khyat in Kraunch island who are considered equivalent to Brahmin, kshatriya, vaishya, and shoodra respectively. All of them worship Rudra form of Lord Narayan by *dhyanyog*. The seven important rivers of the region are – Kumudwati, Khyati, Sandhya, Gauri, Ratri, Manojva, and Pundarika.

Shaak Island

Around Kshir ocean, there is expanse of Shaak island (the land of south east Asia at present), which is double in the size of Kraunch island. This island is covered from all sides by Dadhimand Sea. The ruler of this island is said to be King Bhavya (or Havya). He had seven sons named Jalad, Kumar, Sukumar, Manirak, Kusumod, Godaki, and Mahadrum. There are seven *varsh* (parts) by their names. There are seven mountains named Udaigiri, Jaldhar, Ambhogiri, Raivtak, Aastikeya, Shyam, and Kesari and seven rivers named Kumari, Sukumari, Nalini, Renuka, Ikshu, Dhenuka, and Gabhasti. Magadh, Manas, Mag, and Mandag – these are the four *varna* of the people, who, keeping control on their mind and senses, pray and worship the sun form of Lord Vishnu. There is a large tree of *Shaak* (teak) which became the reason for the name of the island as Shaak island.

Pushkar Island

Pushkar island (Japan, Manchurian, and southeast Siberia) is spread in twice the area of Shaak island. That island is covered with the ocean of sweet water. King Shravan was its ruler. He had two sons named Mahavir and Dhatik.

There are two *varsh* (parts) in the Pushkar island. There is only one mountain which is famous by the name of Mansittar. This mountain is situated in the middle of the island, which divides the island in two parts. There is no issue of caste and creed. All the people are immune to sorrow, disease, envy, greed, anger, and fear, etc. There is neither mountain nor river in the either part of the island. There men look as divine as gods. There is a Banyan tree on this island where Brahmaji lives.

•••

3

OTHER SPECIALITIES OF THE PURANS

Description of *Shraadh Kalp*

Regarding *Shraadh Kalp*, it is said in the *Purans* that Brahmin, Kshatriya, and Vaishya should accomplish the event of *shraadh* according to their *varna* by chanting *mantra* following the method prescribed in *Vedas*. Women and Shoodra should accomplish *shraadh* (post-funeral rites) in the due procedure without chanting *mantras* according to the direction of Brahmin. *Hawan* etc. are prohibited for them. Pushkar and other pilgrim spots, holy temples, mountain peaks, holy lands, holy rivers, lakes, seas, own house, under the divine trees, and the *yajna* pyre – are said to be auspicious places. Man can perform *shraadh* in any of these places. *Amavasya* (moonless) and *Poornima* (full moon) of every month are suitable for *shraadh* according to *Vedas* and scriptures.

Nitya, Naimittik, and Kamya – these are the three types of *shraadh*. It should be organized every year. When sun comes on the Pisces sign, then *Shraadh* should be performed methodically for fifteen days. Money comes by doing *shraadh* on *Pratipada* (first day of month). *Dwitiya* (second day of month) blesses with progeny. *Tritiya* (third day of month) blesses with a son. *Chaturthi* (fourth day of month) eliminates enemies. Man realizes Lakshmi by going for *shraadh* on

Panchami (fifth day of month). Man earns respect by performing *shraadh* on *Khashthi* (sixth day of month). Man becomes ruler of *ganas* by performing *shraadh* on *saptami* (seventh day of month), superior intelligence on *ashtami* (eighth day of month), female on *navmi* (ninth day of month), fulfilment of wish on *dashmi* (tenth day of month), and the knowledge of *Vedas* is earned by observing *shraadh* on *eikadashi* (eleventh day of month). Men who perform *shraadh* on *dwadashi* (twelfth day of month) benefit by victory, and they who perform *shraadh* on *trayodashi* (thirteenth day of month) are blessed with more children, cattle, intelligence, independence, long life, and affluence. Those whose forefathers die in young age, or are killed by some weapon, should perform *shraadh* on *Chaturdashi* (fourteenth day of month) to satiate them. They, who perform *shraadh* on *Amavasya* (the day of moonless night), realize permanent place in heaven and all of their wishes are met.

The donation of those is of permanent value who donate grains mixed with jaggery, sesame, and honey or grains mixed with honey during *shraadh*. *Eikodishta shraadh* should be performed every year on the same day whem mother-father have died. *Eikodishta shraadh* should be performed every year on the day of death of father's or your own brother who dies without progeny.

Satiate your forefathers with barley, paddy, sesame, wheat, green lentil (*moong*), mustard oil, rice, and such things. *Bel*, mango, pomegranate, *amla*, cucumber, coconut, orange, grapes, dates, *parwal*, *chiraunji*, Indian berry – these fruits must be used in the shraadh *karma*. Further jaggery, sugar, cow's milk, sesame oil, salt, ghee, curd, sandalwood, *Tulsi* leaves, and saffron should also be offered to forefathers. The use of onion, *ajwain*, garlic, asafoetida, mustard seed, lemon, turnip, spinach, carrot, chilli, dry ginger, and such things are prohibited in *shraadh*. The man, who follows the rules related with *shraadh*, enjoys all the affluence with long life, power, wealth, and progenies. Forefathers for three *yug*s eat the grain offered by him.

Of *Kaliyug*

In the context of *Kaliyug*, it is said in the *Purans* that marriage will not be considered an act of *dharma* in this *yug*. Disciples will not obey *gurus*. Sons will turn their backs to duty and *dharma*. Performing of rituals according to one's choice and fasting, hard work, expenditure of money will be looked upon as observance of *dharma*. Clothes and ornaments will be means to show off ego. Cow will command love and respect until she will give milk. But man can earn *punya* (holy reward) in *Kaliyug* by miniscule effort, hence *Kaliyug* has been said to be better than the other *yug*s. The reward of arduous *tapasya* will be obtained by mere remembrance of God.

Sankhya Yog

According to *Purans*, control of senses, mind, and intellect from all sides and integrating it with the omnipresent soul is said to be the *Yog*. *Yogi* should be equipped with *sham-dam*. He should follow the science of spirituality, should be affectionate to soul, and should perform good acts with detachment. Equipped with these means, *yogi* can obtain superior knowledge. *Kaam* (lust), *krodh* (anger), *lobh* (greed), *bhaya* (fear), and *swapna* (dream) – these are the five vices for *yog*. Therefore, a *yogi* person should leave these vices. Sitting at some reclusive place facing eastward, is said to be the superior way to perform *yog*.

Lord inhabits every *jeev* in the form of soul. The learned man who, repudiating all the pleasures, implicitly envisages *Parbrahm Parmatma* (supreme soul) in this body, realizes *Brahmbhav* (the wisdom of Brahm) after his death. The *jeevatma* (soul), which sees all beings in it and vice versa, attains emancipation after death. Man's body is like a city with nine gates where the swan-like soul resides. *Jeevatma* (soul) has been established by the name of swan, which is indestructible. Thus the learned man, who knows about indestructible soul, becomes free from the bond of life and death.

Domestic Conduct

Domestic conduct has been analysed in detail in the *Purans*. The domestic man should perform his duties with concentration through *dharma*, *arth*, and *kaam* according to *Purans*. He should provide sustenance to his family through the money earned by noble deeds. Further, he should always perform religious rituals for purging sins, and spiritual upliftment. He should get up with dawn everyday, and should contemplate on *dharma* and *arth*. Except emergency, he should never skip the routine of prayer and worship. False speech, lie, and bitter speaking, service of evil people, and following atheism are the reason of fall for the domestic man, therefore these practices should be stopped. Domestic man should always respect *guru*, mother, father, relatives, guests and Brahmins. He should take his meals after offering it to guest and his family. People who follow these household rules earn worldly pleasures and emancipation (*moksha*). *Yajna*, donation, *hawan*, and *tapasya* do not benefit those who break the good conduct. The man, who conducts badly, never gets power, potency, long life, and money; therefore domestic man should observe his *dharma* dutifully.

Thus we see that the detailed description from beginning to end of cosmos has been presented in *Purans*. *Purans* can be said to be the mirror of man's past, future and present. Man can see the face of each *yug* in this mirror. He can impove upon his present by seeing his past. What happened in the past, what is happening at present, what will happen in future – *Purans* say it all.

•••

DIAMOND POCKET BOOKS
Presents
Osho's illuminating and enlightening discourses

SUFI, THE PEOPLE OF THE PATH
- ☐ *Singing Silence 150.00
- ☐ *A Lotus of Emptiness 150.00
- ☐ *Glory of Freedom 150.00
- ☐ *The Royal Way 150.00

PHILOSOPHY & UPNISHAD
- ☐ * I am the Gate 150.00
- ☐ * The Great Challenge 150.00
- ☐ *A Cup of Tea 150.00
- ☐ The Mystery Beyond Mind 50.00
- ☐ Towards The Unknown 50.00
- ☐ A Taste of the Divine 50.00
- ☐ The Alchemy of Enlightenment 50.00
- ☐ Be Silent & Know 50.00
- ☐ A Song Without Words 50.00
- ☐ Inner Harmony 50.00
- ☐ Sing, Dance, Rejoice 50.00
- ☐ Secret of Disciplehood 50.00
- ☐ The Centre of the Cyclone 50.00
- ☐ The Greatest Gamble 50.00

MEDITATION
- ☐ *Meditation-The Art of Ecstasy ... 150.00
- ☐ Love & Meditation 50.00
- ☐ Meditation- The Ultimate Adventurer 50.00
- ☐ *The Psychology of the Esoteric .. 150.00

PATANJALI YOGA SUTRA
- ☐ *Yoga - The Alpha and The Omega-I (The Birth of Being) 150.00
- ☐ *Yoga - The Alpha and The Omega-II (The Ever Present Flower) 150.00
- ☐ *Yoga - The Alpha and The Omega-III (Moving to the Centre) 150.00

JESUS AND CHRISTIAN MYSTICS
- ☐ * I say unto You - I & II ..... Each 150.00

ZEN & ZEN MASTERS
- ☐ *Zen and the Art of Living 150.00
- ☐ *Zen and the Art of Enlightenment 150.00
- ☐ *Zen : Take it Easy 150.00
- ☐ *Zen and The Art of Meditation 150.00

OSHO ON KABIR
- ☐ *The Divine Melody 150.00
- ☐ Ecstasy : The Language of Existence 50.00

BAUL MYSTICS
- ☐ Bauls : The Dancing, Mystics 50.00
- ☐ Bauls : The Seeker of the Path ... 50.00
- ☐ Bauls : The Mystics of Celebration 50.00
- ☐ Bauls : The Singing Mystics 50.00

TANTRA
- ☐ Tantra Vision : The Secret of the Inner Experience 50.00
- ☐ Tantra Vision : The Door to Nirvana 50.00
- ☐ Tantra Vision : Beyond the Barriers of Wisdom 50.00
- ☐ Tantra Vision : An Invitation to Silence 50.00

VEDANTA
- ☐ Vedanta : The Ultimae Truth 50.00
- ☐ Vedanta : The First Star in the Evening 50.00
- ☐ Vedanta : An Art of Dying 50.00
- ☐ Vedanta : The Supreme Know 50.00

OSHO'S VISION FOR THE WORLD
- ☐ *And the Flowers Showered 150.00
- ☐ Be Oceanic 50.00
- ☐ One Earth One Humanity 50.00
- ☐ Freedom form the Mind 50.00
- ☐ Life, A Song, A Dance 50.00
- ☐ Meeting the Ultimate 50.00
- ☐ The Master is a Mirror 50.00
- ☐ From Ignorance to Innocence 50.00
- ☐ Eternal Celebration 50.00
- ☐ Laughter is My Message 50.00

BOOKS ABOUT OSHO
Dr. Vasant Joshi, Ma Chetan Unmani
- ☐ *New Vision for the New Millennium 100.00

Swami Chaitanya Keerti
- ☐ *Allah To Zen 150.00

Swami Arvinda Chaithnya
- ☐ Our Beloved Osho 195.00

Ma Dharm Jyoti
- ☐ One Hundred Tales for Ten Thousand Buddha 95.00

Order books by V.P.P. Postage Rs. 20/- per book extra.
Postage free on order of three or more books, Send Rs. 20/--in advance.

DIAMOND POCKET BOOKS (P) LTD.
X-30, Okhla Industrial Area, Phase-II, New Delhi-110020,
Phones : 51611861 - 65, Fax : (0091) -011-51611866, 26386124

HEALTHS Books

David Servan Schreiber (Guerir)
- The Instinct to Heal — 195.00
  (Curing stress, anxiety and depression without drugs and without talk therapy)

M. Subramaniam
- Unveiling the Secrets of Reiki — 195.00
- Brilliant Light — 195.00
  (Reiki Grand Master Manual)
- At the Feet of the Master (Manal Reiki) — 195.00

Sukhdeepak Malvai
- Natural Healing with Reiki — 100.00

Pt. Rajnikant Upadhayay
- Reiki (For Healthy, Happy & Comfortable Life) — 95.00
- Mudra Vigyan (For Health & Happiness) — 60.00

Sankalpo
- Neo Reiki — 150.00

Dr. Shiv Kumar
- Aroma Therapy — 95.00
- Causes, Cure & Prevention of Nervous Diseases — 75.00
- Diseases of Digestive System — 75.00
- Asthma-Allergies (Causes & Cure) — 75.00
- Eye-Care (Including Better Eye Sight) Without Glassess — 75.00
- Stress (How to Relieve from Stress A Psychological Study) — 75.00

Dr. Satish Goel
- Causes & Cure of Blood Pressure — 75.00
- Causes & Cure of Diabetes — 60.00
- Causes & Cure of Heart Ailments — 75.00
- Pregnancy & Child Care — 95.00
- Ladie's Slimming Course — 95.00
- Acupuncture Guide — 50.00
- Acupressure Guide — 50.00
- Acupuncture & Acupressure Guide — 95.00
- Walking for Better Health — 95.00
- Nature Cure for Health & Happiness — 95.00
- A Beacon of Hope for the Childless Couples — 60.00
- Sex for All — 75.00

Dr. Kanta Gupta
- Be Your Own Doctor — 60.00
  (a Book about Herbs & Their Use)

Dr. B.R. Kishore
- Vatsyana Kamasutra — 95.00
- The Manual of Sex & Tantra — 95.00

Dr. M.K. Gupta
- Causes, Cure & Prevention of High Blood Cholesterol — 60.00

Acharya Bhagwan Dev
- Yoga for Better Health — 95.00
- Pranayam, Kundalini aur Hathyoga — 60.00

Dr. S.K. Sharma
- Add Inches — 60.00
- Shed Weight Add Life — 60.00
- Alternate Therapies — 95.00
- Miracles of Urine Therapy — 60.00
- Meditation & Dhyan Yoga (for Spiritual Discipline) — 95.00

- A Complete Guide to Homeopathic Remedies — 120.00
- A Complete Guide to Biochemic Remedies — 60.00
- Common Diseases of Urinary System — 95.00
- Allopathic Guide for Common Disorders — 125.00
- E.N.T. & Dental Guide (in Press) — 95.00
- Wonders of Magnetotherapy — 95.00
- Family Homeopathic Guide — 95.00
- Health in Your Hands — 95.00
- Food for Good Health — 95.00
- Juice Therapy — 75.00
- Tips on Sex — 75.00

Dr. Renu Gupta
- Hair Care (Prevention of Dandruff & Baldness) — 75.00
- Skin Care — 75.00
- Complete Beautician Course (Start a Beauty Parlour at Home) — 95.00
- Common Diseases of Women — 95.00

Dr. Rajiv Sharma
- First Aid (in Press) — 95.00
- Causes, Cure and Prevention of Children's Diseases — 75.00

Dr. R.N. Gupta
- Joys of Parenthood — 40.00

M. Kumaria
- How to Keep Fit — 20.00

Dr. Pushpa Khurana
- Be Young and Healthy for 100 Years — 60.00
- The Awesome Challenge of AIDS — 40.00

Acharya Satyanand
- Surya Chikitsa — 95.00

Dr. Nishtha
- Diseases of Respiratory Tract (Nose, Throat, Chest & Lungs) — 95.00
- Backache (Spondylitis, Cervical Arthritis, Rheumatism) — 95.00
- Ladies Health Guide (With Make-up Guide) — 95.00

L.R. Chowdhary
- Rajuvenate with Kundalini Mantra Yoga — 95.00

Manoj Kumar
- Diamond Body Building Course — 95.00

Koulacharya Jagdish Sharma
- Body Language — 125.00

G.C. Goyal
- Vitamins for Natural Healing — 95.00

Dr. Vishnu Jain
- Heart to Heart (with Heart Specialist) — 95.00

Asha Pran
- Beauty Guide (With Make-up Guide) — 75.00

Acharya Vipul Rao
- Ayurvedic Treatment for Common Diseases — 95.00
- Herbal Treatment for Common Diseases — 95.00

Dr. Sajiv Adlakha
- Stuttering & Your Child (Question-Answer) — 60.00

Books can be requisitioned by V.P.P. Postage charges will be Rs. 20/- per book.
For orders of three books the postage will be free.

◉ DIAMOND POCKET BOOKS

X-30, Okhla Industrial Area, Phase-II, New Delhi-110020, Phone : 011-51611861, Fax : 011-51611866
E-mail : sales@diamondpublication.com, Website : www.fusionbooks.com

DIAMOND BOOKS PRESENTS

Srikantha Arunachalam
- Treatise on Ayurveda 295.00

David Servan Schreiber 'Gurier'
- The Instinct to Heal 195.00
  (Curing stress, anxiety and depression. without drugs and without talk therapy)

Swati Lodha
- Why Women Are What They Are . 195.00

Osho
- Nirvana : The Last Nightmare 195.00
- Yoga - The Alchemy of Yoga. 150.00

Dr. Bimal Chhajer
- Zero Oil Thali 150.00
- 201 Tips for Diabites Patients 150.00
- 201 Diet Tips for Heart Patients 150.00
- 201 Tips for Losing Weight 150.00

Joginder Singh
- For a Better Tomorrow 150.00
- Jokes of Joginder singh (I, II) 95.00

Pandit Atre
- Soul @ Universe.Com 75.00

M.G. Devasahayam
- India's IInd Freedom an Untold Saga 195.00

Vandana Verma
- Lovely Names for Babies (Male & Female childs) 95.00

BOOKS ON HINDU MYTHOLOGY

Prafull Goradia
- The Saffron Book 150.00
- Anti Hindus 150.00
- Muslim League's Unfinished Agenda 150.00
- Hindu Masjids 195.00

Dr. Brij Raj Kishore
- Essence of Vedas 195.00

S. N. Mathur
- Gautam Budha 295.00
- The Diamond Books of Hindu Gods and Goddesses (4 Colour) 295.00

B.K. Chaturvedi
- Shiva Purana 95.00
- Vishnu Purana 95.00
- Markandeya Purana 75.00
- Bhsvishya Purana 75.00
- Narad Purana 75.00
- Kalki Purana 75.00
- Linga Purana 75.00
- Devibhagwat Purana 75.00

Dr. Kiran Bedi Presents'
- Shadow in Cases 225.00
- Rest in Piece 95.00

LITERATURE

Rabindranath Tagore
- Boat Accident (Translation of नौका डूबी) 95.00
- Inside Outside (Translation of घरे बाइरे) 95.00

Iqbal Ramoowalia
- The Death Of A Passport 150.00

Ed. Rajendra Awasthy
- Selected Gujrati Short Stories 95.00
- Selected Hindi Short Stories 125.00
- Selected Tamil Short Stories 95.00
- Selected Malayalam Short Stories 95.00
- Selected Punjabi Short Stories 95.00

GREAT PERSONALITIES (BIOGRAPHY)

Meena Agarwal
- Indira Gandhi 95.00
- Rajiv Gandhi 95.00

Anuradha Ray
- The Making of Mahatma 95.00

Prof. Gurpreet Singh
- Ten Masters (Sikh Gurus) 60.00
- The Soul of Sikhism 95.00

B.K. Chaturvedi
- Messiah of Poor Mother Teresa 60.00
- Chanakya 95.00
- Goddess Durga 95.00

S.P. Bansal
- Lord Rama 95.00
- Gajanan 75.00

Dr. Brij Raj Kishore
- Ram Krishna Paramhans 95.00

Purnima Majumdaar
- Yogiraj Arvind 75.00
- Neel Kanth (Lord Shiva) 95.00

Dr. Bhwan Singh Rana
- Swami Vivekanand 95.00
- Chhatrapati Shivaji 95.00
- Bhagat Singh 95.00
- Maharana Pratap 95.00

Mahesh Sharma
- Dr. A.P.J. Abdul Kalam 95.00
- Sonia Gandhi 95.00
- Atal Bihari Vajpayee 95.00
- Lal Krishna Advani 95.00

Books can be requisitioned by V.P.P. Postage charges will be Rs. 20/- per book. For orders of three books the postage will be free.

◎ DIAMOND POCKET BOOKS

X-30, Okhla Industrial Area, Phase-II, New Delhi-110020, Phone : 011-51611861, Fax : 011-51611866
E-mail : sales@diamondpublication.com, Website : www.fusionbooks.com